Philosophy
of
Democratic Government

Philosophy
of
Democratic Government

YVES R. SIMON

PHOENIX BOOKS

THE UNIVERSITY OF CHICAGO PRESS

CHICAGO & LONDON

CHARLES R. WALGREEN FOUNDATION LECTURES

THE UNIVERSITY OF CHICAGO PRESS, CHICAGO & LONDON
The University of Toronto Press, Toronto 5, Canada

TO

James and Suzanne Corbett

IN GRATEFUL AFFECTION

FOREWORD

✦

TWICE during the first half of the twentieth century, totalitarian systems have challenged the concept of democracy. These systems have put forward complete philosophies of man and the state, philosophies strong enough to inspire their followers with a crusading spirit.

Democracy has been on the defensive; it has been defended more and more often with the pragmatic argument. But this argument has proved no match for the competing systems. Democracy works, it is true—but so did fascism, until it was destroyed from outside. The need for a philosophy that shows democracy to be grounded firmly on rational principles—this need is apparent.

These considerations have prompted the Walgreen Foundation to issue a series of volumes setting forth the basic principles on which democracy rests. These books, it is hoped, will help people everywhere to understand the foundations of democracy and to realize that this system stands on those principles that are necessary to maintain human dignity.

The present volume is the second in the series.

JEROME G. KERWIN
*Chairman, Charles R. Walgreen Foundation
for the Study of American Institutions*

TABLE OF CONTENTS

✣

CHAPTER I

GENERAL THEORY OF GOVERNMENT

❋

COMMUNISM and national socialism have come to resemble each other in so many respects that their historical diversity and their lasting opposition arouse wonder. In spite of common features that are profound and increasingly obvious, they prove altogether repugnant to effecting any kind of merger. The task of fighting them would be greatly eased if followers, actual and potential, were led to believe that one system, i.e., the one which appeals to them, is substantially identical with the other, i.e., the one which they hate; but such identification never was very successful as a polemical instrument. Conservatives in the 1930's were given a fair chance to understand that naziism was but brown bolshevism;[1] yet many of them helped the Nazis. Today it seems that it should be easy for all concerned to recognize in communism the very features that they hated most in naziism; but not all do.

The persistent conflict of these two systems is traceable in part to their opposite stands on the class struggle and to the operation of class allegiances. But in the minds of many followers the decisive influence is exercised by representations of the ultimate future. For with regard to the future and more particularly to the remote portions of the future, where the assertion of an ideal cannot be hampered by any experience or fact, the two totalitarian systems differ widely. In fascism or naziism the totalitarian state is exalted as the highest product of life and history.[2] In spite of the evolutionistic language in

1. See Waldemar Gurian, *The Future of Bolshevism*, trans. E. I. Watkin (New York: Sheed & Ward, 1936).

2. Mussolini, *Fascism: Doctrine and Institutions* (Rome: "Ardita" Publishers, 1935),

1

which such things are spoken of, it plainly enjoys the character of a terminal accomplishment. Is it going to endure forever? At any rate, not a word is said about how it might come
to an end and what might come after it. Communism, on the
other hand, promises the withering-away of the state.[3]

At an early stage of its history, socialism was characterized
as pessimistic with regard to accomplished facts and optimistic with regard to facts to be accomplished.[4] Communism, in
our time, remains optimistic about facts to be accomplished
ultimately. Its gruesome view of the non-Communist society
and the ruthlessness of its revolutionary means are associated
with a picture as radiant as anything ever produced by the
spirit of utopia. The rational organization of economic relations will bring to an end the division of society into classes,
the exploitation of man by man, the war of man against man.
But the state is born of this division, this exploitation, this

p. 10: "Anti-individualistic, the Fascist conception of life stresses the importance of
the State and accepts the individual only in so far as his interests coincide with those
of the State, which stands for the conscience and the universal will of man as a historic
entity. It is opposed to classical liberalism which arose as a reaction to absolutism
and exhausted its historical function when the State became the expression of the conscience and will of the people. Liberalism denied the State in the name of the individual,
Fascism reasserts the rights of the State as expressing the real essence of the individual.
And if liberty is to be the attribute of living men and not of abstract dummies invented
by individualistic liberalism, then Fascism stands for liberty, and for the only liberty
worth having, the liberty of the State and of the individual within the State. The Fascist conception of the State is all-embracing; outside of it no human or spiritual values
can exist, much less have value. Thus understood, fascism is totalitarian, and the Fascist
State—a synthesis and a unit inclusive of all values—interprets, develops, and potenti-
ates the whole life of a people."

3. Gurian, *op. cit.*, p. 61: "The Bolshevik leaders Lenin and Stalin profess their
ideal, the ultimate supersession of all state authority, rendered superfluous by a perfect society. It is on the contrary the aim of Hitler's party to establish it on a firmer
basis and stabilise it by a genuine union with the will of the people embodied, so it is
claimed, in the Fuehrer [this statement of the National Socialist ideal had been taken
from the Nazi jurist, Huber-Kiel]."

4. P.-J. Proudhon, *Système des contradictions économiques*, ed. C. Bouglé and H. Moys-
set (Paris: Rivière, 1923), I, 69.

war. The classless society will be a stateless society. The totalitarian increase of the powers of the state is a temporary measure necessary to bring about a social structure that will render the state unnecessary and establish forever the brotherhood of men.

In Marxian communism the philosophy of evil is characterized by a sort of monism which proves very handy when there is a question of stirring men to action; for, if all particular injustices ultimately merge into one absolute injustice, it should be possible to do away with injustice, once and for all, in a Napoleonic victory.[5] Social visions, in the tradition of liberal

5. A Napoleonic victory is one which but a short time after the opening of hostilities puts an end to the fighting power of the enemy. It presupposes a heavy concentration of enemy forces. A Napoleonic victory was possible on December 2, 1805, as the allied emperors had decided to gamble their armies, but not in the Russian campaign.

The myth of a revolutionary victory which would constitute an all-embracing redemption of mankind and a basic solution to the problem of evil took hold of the mind of Marx at an early stage of his development; it impressed upon his revolutionary plans features in striking contrast with the principles then commonly received among Socialists. A good description of this contrast is given by Daniel Halévy (*La Vie de Proudhon* [Paris: Stock, 1948], pp. 362 ff.). In the fall of 1844, Marx arrived in Paris; he was in charge of founding a periodical designed to promote the collaboration of French and German radicals, the *Deutsch-französische Jahrbücher*. "He ran into the opposition of the French leaders and became acutely aware of the necessity of supplementing his doctrine in order to meet their objections. . . . They all were anxious to forestall the growth, in France, of a class similar to the proletariat that existed in England. For the young Marx, such concern was childish and silly. He realized keenly the inevitability of the industrial revolution and of its consequences, one of which is the rise of the proletariat; further he considered that the duty of the revolutionist is not to 'emancipate' the proletarians (a rather ill-defined undertaking) but to gather them up, such as they are, and to organize them for a fight.

"Far from wishing that the proletarian masses should be prevented from increasing in number and that their sufferings should be prevented from getting worse, Marx, a tough and smart young fellow, wants these masses to be allowed to grow, and he wants their sufferings to be allowed to get worse. The greatest evil would give birth to the greatest good; according to the Hegelian dialectic, this is how history proceeds. This dialectic holds in the order of concrete action. Consequently, the practical revolutionist of 1840 must encourage the constitution of an extreme class. . . ." Follows a partial quotation of this striking passage of "Criticism of Hegel's Philosophy of Law," a contribution of Marx to the first issue of the *Deutsch-französische Jahrbücher* (Paris,

democracy, lack such tragic and appealing simplicity; yet the basic theory that evil alone makes the state organization necessary appeared first in liberal democracy. Recall the celebrated propositions of Tom Paine: "Society is produced by our wants and government by our wickedness; the former promotes our happiness positively by uniting our affections, the latter negatively by restraining our vices . . . the first is a patron, the last a punisher."[6] Strikingly, a theory worked out by men whose great concern was to limit the powers of the state was not rejected, but rather transfigured, by the planners and by the founders of the first modern totalitarian state.

The theory that government is rendered necessary not by nature but by deficiencies—let it be called, from now on, "The deficiency theory of government"—should not be confused with the theory describing government as a necessary evil. A Fascist would never grant that the state is an evil; on the contrary, he proudly asserts that it is the highest value. Yet, if he

---

1844), p. 84: "Under such circumstances, where does the *positive* possibility of German emancipation lie?—*Answer:* In the formation of a class suffering from *radical enslavement* [*mit radicallen Ketten*], of a class existing in the bourgeois society without belonging in it, of a social condition [*Stand*] characterized by its being the dissolution of all social conditions, of a sphere rendered universal by the universality of its wretchedness, dedicated to no particular right because the injustice inflicted upon it is not a particular injustice but the absolute injustice, of a sphere whose titles are no longer historical but only human, whose opposition is not limited, and concerned with consequences, but all-embracing, and concerned with the very premises of the German state; a sphere, finally, which cannot emancipate itself without emancipating itself from all the other spheres of society and, thereby, emancipating all the other spheres of society; which, in one word, is the *complete loss* of man and consequently cannot save itself without effecting the complete *redemption of man*. Such dissolution of society, erected into a social condition, is the *proletariat*."

On the theory of the state in Marxism see F. Engels, *The Origin of the Family, Private Property, and the State* (New York: International Publishers, 1942); V. I. Lenin, *The State and Revolution*, in *Selected Works* (New York: International Publishers, 1935–38), Vol. VII; F. Gerlich, *Der Kommunismus als Lehre vom Tausendjährigen Reich* (Munich: H. Bruckmann, 1920); Sherman H. M. Chang, *The Marxian Theory of the State* (Philadelphia, 1931).

6. *Common Sense* in *The Writings of Thomas Paine* (New York: G. P. Putnam's Sons, 1894), I, 69.

undertakes to set forth the reasons why the state is thought to
be such a noble thing, he is likely to indulge in a pessimistic
description of human societies and to declare that an overwhelming force is everlastingly needed to crush ever recurrent
evil.[7] In so far as the Fascist exaltation of the state is linked
to such pessimism, the deficiency theory is not foreign to
fascism itself. Contrary to a belief current in classical democracy, this theory does not constitute a guaranty against
overgovernment. In fact, systematic determination to prevent
the government from doing more than a very small amount of
governing did not originate in the deficiency theory. It originated in the belief that the greatest good of the greatest number is most safely brought about by the operation of individual
initiatives. Even the needed convergence of multiple endeavors
was reputed to be best achieved without any human management; for it was assumed—explicitly or implicitly and always confusedly—that there exists, inside the spontaneous
course of events, a highly dependable person who inconspicu-
ously directs chance occurrences toward a definite goal. According to times and circumstances, this person was called
"nature," "Providence," or "evolution."

The naturalistic optimism on which early liberalism thrived
is a thing of the past. We are aware of the shortcomings of human management, but dire experience has made it impossible
for us to intrust the destiny of men and the survival of nations
to the hazards of universal competition. We have come to
recognize the jungle character of the wilderness which our
fathers mistook for a land of harmony. The case is so plain as

7. This consideration supplies a partial explanation for the help that totalitarianism was given by conservatives in quite a few instances of decisive importance. There is
something paradoxical about a conservative supporting a system headed by plebeians-
in-chief and determined to crush many traditional privileges. But a conservative generally has a low idea of human kind. He enjoys imagining the great number of men as
weak and rather vicious creatures. He can, under the proper circumstances, come to
terms with a totalitarian regime which promises that there will always be a powerfully
armed state to maintain order.

to be reflected in the meaning of words. In the golden age of liberalism the word "liberal" designated a supporter of the laissez faire system, and one was reputed to be a liberal in so far as he was known to oppose state intervention, the organization of the workers, etc. The most radical among liberals were hardly distinguishable from individualistic anarchists. Today, a systematic adversary of economic planning, price control, labor laws, etc., is what everybody calls a "reactionary" and nobody is considered a liberal unless he is willing to support heavy programs of state intervention. The liberals of our time confess that a huge amount of government has become a condition for the preservation and normal growth of all the goods that society stands for. In terms of the deficiency theory, this is a bewildering situation. If evil alone makes government necessary, a demand for increased government activity means either increased evil or better awareness of evil or both. True, we feel that some things have become worse, and we have developed an ability to see many shortcomings that used to pass almost unnoticed, but there are not a few circumstances in which the call for more government activity seems to result from unqualified progress. It then becomes supremely important that the boundaries of the domain conceded to the state should never be left uncertain. If it is granted that progress itself, in a certain way, demands the growth of the state, it is more necessary than ever that disorderly expansion of the state machinery—a frequent accident under all circumstances—be held in check by the power of clearly defined principles.

This chapter will present a reconsideration of the deficiency theory. Since the difficulties that stand at the opening of the question pertain to the concept of government or authority in general, the first sections of our inquiry will be concerned not with any problem peculiar to civil society but to the general problems of authority.

THE PATERNAL FUNCTION OF AUTHORITY

The issue of authority, just as much as the related issue of freedom, is one plagued by the kind of confusion that intractable emotions cause and entertain. A common mistake is to identify authority with coercion, which is but the most conspicuous of its *instruments*. It is important, also, not to postulate a necessary connection between the essence of authority and any of the particular *forms* in which this essence is embodied; yet many hold it axiomatic that authority means absolutism and exploitation. Finally, few, if any, bother about distinguishing, within authority itself, a diversity of *functions;* yet this diversity is so fundamental that, if it is not expressed, we hardly know what we are talking about when we speak of authority. Clouded by such confusions, an unfruitful dialogue goes on between those who feel inclined toward authority and those who, on principle, put all the emphasis on liberty. Platitudes about the difficult task of maintaining the proper balance between the two are nearly all that can be expected.

Our present purpose is to describe the diverse functions of authority and to show that authority, according to the diversity of its functions, calls for diverse interpretations in terms of foundation, duration, relation to progress, and relation to freedom. Instruments and forms will be discussed in later parts of this book.

By way of mental experiment, let us assume a radical negation of authority and watch the unfolding of its implications. This puts a heavy strain on our imagination. Let us boldly picture towns without town meetings, cities without aldermen and mayors, workshops without foremen, committees without chairmen, rescue parties without leaders, universities without chancellors, and republics without presidents. The hardest is to imagine a home where little children would not be subjected to any sort of authority. It is desirable that children, even very young ones, should be trained in self-government; but, unless children, even big ones, are governed to some extent by persons possessed with more mature intellects, stronger wills, and wider experience, they cannot survive. These words describe completely the *paternal* function of authority. Let us formulate its characteristics.

First, in this function, authority aims at the *proper* good of the governed. A child needs direction because he is not able to take care of *himself*, i.e., to direct himself toward his own preservation and perfection. Thus, apart from all consideration of social good or common good, authority is needed for the survival and development of the immature person.

Secondly, authority here is made necessary by a deficiency. Parents take care of the child, inasmuch and in so far as the child is *unable* to take care of himself. The father substitutes his mature judgment and will for the judgment and will of the child, which are still immature. The paternal function of authority is not essential but *substitutional*.

At this point it seems necessary to elaborate briefly on the concept of "deficiency." This concept admits of degrees. Deficiency always signifies the lack of a perfection that a subject should possess in order to satisfy fully the demands of its nature. Yet a deficiency is not necessarily an evil, since a nature subject to growth normally goes through a period of inachievement.[8] A child is an incompletely developed person, and there is nothing wrong about a child's having only a child's powers; but there is something wrong about an adult person whose mental age is seven. Thus, among the deficiencies that make paternal authority necessary, some have the character of evil, and some do not. Some are normal, and some are not. There would be no room for paternal authority in a society free from deficiencies, but there would be plenty of room for it in a human society free from evil, since the mem-

8. See Aristotle *Met.* 5. 22 (on privation).

bers of human societies are bound to be children before they
are men.

Thirdly, paternal authority is *pedagogical* and consequently
aims at its own disappearance. This follows from its substitutional character. It is wholly good for a child to be guided
by a mature person, but the main purpose of this guidance consists in the attainment of the ability to exercise self-government. If paternal authority remains necessary past the earliest
possible date for its disappearance, it has failed to a degree; if
it intends its own maintenance and manages things in such a
way as not to have to disappear, it is guilty of abominable
abuse.

Authority as engaged in this substitutional and pedagogical
function we call "paternal," following the good usage that
extends to the whole genus the name of the most familiar
species. Besides the father-to-son relationship, there are many
situations in which authority of the paternal type is exercised.
Let us briefly discuss some of these situations.

1. Controversies about the freedom of women supply a perfect example of the confusion which spoils ethical issues
when a stand is taken for or against authority without any attention being paid to the diversity of its functions. At the time
when the feminist movement took shape, it was still a common belief that women, with rare exceptions, were imperfectly able to take care of themselves and to manage their own
affairs. Accordingly, legal systems kept many self-regarding
actions of the adult woman subjected to control by some male
person—father, husband, or guardian. The feminist movement asserted the ability of the woman to govern herself and
fought all legislation enforcing the postulate of her lasting
minority. In short, it wanted the adult woman to enjoy
freedom from paternal authority. The cry for the "emancipation of woman" might have meant nothing else. But for many
it meant much more. Most societies, then, granted the woman

but incomplete citizenship and barred her from many occupations and from many phases of public life. Such restrictions might have expressed nothing else than the belief that law, war, politics, surgery, etc., are masculine concerns. Actually, tradition connected these exclusions with the theory of woman's permanent minority. In most phases of feminism, argumentation designed to refute this theory was supposed to destroy also the foundation of the traditional restrictions. In good logic the ability of the adult woman to govern herself does not entail the desirability of her going into such occupations as law, surgery, etc. The contention that all offices and careers should be open to women has to be vindicated in terms of calling and in relation to the proper division of tasks between man and woman. Feminism suffered from a much more serious lack of logic, as the refutation of the permanent minority theory was understood to imply also the end of structural inequality in the couple. Confusedly the movement for the emancipation of the woman asserted (1) a claim for the complete legal majority of the adult woman, (2) a claim for the lifting of traditional restrictions with regard to trades and public office, and (3) a claim for the abolition of man's authority in the man and wife community. The notion that authority has essential functions, i.e., functions determined not by any deficiency but by the nature of community, was ignored. This was very much in harmony with the anarchistic and liberal views then in fashion. Notice, however, that J. S. Mill, in his celebrated book on the subjection of women, hints at the need for a leader in common action. But he does not see why leadership in the couple should always belong to the same person. Most of all, he does not see why the leader should be designated by law.[9]

2. Let it be observed that the *proper* good with which paternal authority is concerned is not necessarily individual:

9. J. S. Mill, *The Subjection of Women*, in *On Liberty and Other Essays* (New York: Macmillan Co., 1926), pp. 236 ff.

the common good of a city has the character of a proper good for any unit in which the city is contained and for other cities as well. Just as an individual may need to be directed in the pursuit of his individual good, so a community may be unable to attain its own common good without guidance. Thus, if certain duties relative to the welfare of a city and normally discharged by it are taken over by the state on account of the city's inability to discharge them satisfactorily, the authority so exercised by the state is of the paternal type: it is not concerned (at least directly) with the common good of the state but with the proper good of the city; it is substitutional, since it does things that the governed should be able to do for themselves; and it aims at its own disappearance or becomes abusive. As in the case of individuals, the deficiencies calling for the exercise of paternal authority over communities may either be abnormal and have the character of evil or consist in conditions of immaturity normal for societies as well as for individuals during early phases of growth. The status of territory, as opposed to statehood, is the legal expression of a condition of immaturity, of incomplete development on account of which a community is supposed not to be able to exercise all the prerogatives of self-government and consequently remains, with regard to its own affairs, subjected to guidance by a more perfect community, viz., the Union. The legal concept of "territory" does not imply any pejorative connotation; aside from any accident or mischief, the newly settled wilderness does not admit of the completeness required for the full exercise of self-government. The status of territory is a condition of minority. But a time comes when subjection to paternal authority can no longer be maintained without there being something wrong, either on the side of the subordinate society by way of failure to accomplish normal development or on the side of the controlling society through abusive maintenance of power.

What holds in the case of territories is supposed to hold also in the case of colonies. The extreme frequency of abuse gives an appearance of falsehood and dishonesty to any interpretation of the concept of colonial rule in terms of ethics. Yet this concept is intelligible and the conditions under which it finds application are by no means fictitious, though they may not have been realized very often in the history of colonization. When European nations, for example, subjected to colonial rule the tribes of Equatorial Africa, their action was rendered suspicious from the beginning by the fact that these tribes were not, prior to the establishment of power by conquest, contained in these nations. Plainly, there is no ground for the paternal authority of one community over another unless the latter is contained in the former as a child in his family. The colonization of African tribes by European nations had an ethical title if, and only if, the colonizers acted as agents of the human community, then entirely unorganized. With such attempts at the organization of the human community as the League of Nations and the United Nations, things became definitely clearer; the character of colonial rule as paternal authority was proclaimed and to some extent sanctioned. The very substitution of the words "mandate" and "trusteeship" for the word "colony" signified that the justification for the rule over primitive peoples resided in duties of paternal authority to be discharged by mankind toward immature societies.

3. There are many instances of a colonial rule being exercised at home by an upper group over a lower one. Particularly clear examples are supplied by societies sharply divided into a so-called "superior" race and a reputedly "inferior" one: North Africa, the southern states, the Union of South Africa, etc. In order to understand the practices prevalent in such societies, it is necessary to consider, beyond an extremely high amount of falsehood and iniquity, the system of relations which justify those practices (or some of them) if they are

justifiable at all. The so-called "inferior" race is considered as a distinct society, contained in the bigger unit of which the upper race is the main part, but not merged with the upper race into an integrated community. It is generally assumed that in the lower race most individuals never attain complete majority; accordingly, their personal happiness depends upon helpful guidance by the master-race. Too immature to share in self-government by way of merger, the lower race is also too immature to found a self-governing community of its own by way of secession. Further, secession is, in almost all cases, ruled out by the physical circumstances. Thus a compromise is effected. There is but one state, one political community. The upper race identifies itself with this community. The lower race is contained within the community as a sort of collective and permanent guest and is subjected to the paternal authority of the upper race. Such colonial rule at home has been operating silently, if not harmoniously, in many countries and over centuries. In our time it does not work either harmoniously or silently.

Colonial rule at home helps to understand the situation of the *common people* in the conservative theory. A conservative of the usual description postulates, most of the time confusedly and not quite consciously, that every society, according to the statement of Alexander Hamilton,[10] divides itself into the few and the many. The few are men of property, of education, of quiet judgment; their economic position, together with their experience and knowledge, enables them to resist the whims of the moment and to conceive and perseveringly to carry out long-range policies. They identify themselves with the nation, just as the whites of Georgia, in the theory of white supremacy, are the State of Georgia. The many are like an inferior race; there may be among them men of great ability, who will

10. Alexander Hamilton, *Speeches in the Federal Convention*, in *Works*, ed. Henry Cabot Lodge (New York and London: G. P. Putnam's Sons, 1904), I, 401.

inevitably find a place sooner or later among the distinguished few; on the whole, they are juvenile, immature, im-
pulsive, subject to irrationality, easily duped by flatterers, ignorant, incapable of foresight. The few have a group consciousness of their own, and so do the many. The many make
up a distinct community inside the state which is properly the
concern of the few. They are the guests of the distinguished
few, and perfectly welcome ones so long as they behave. Thus,
in conservative philosophy or at least in its extreme forms, the
domain of paternal authority comprises, over and above children, feeble-minded, habitual felons, criminals, communities
in the early stage of development, primitive tribes, decadent
societies, etc., the multitude of the common people.[11] Let it be
noticed that the feeling of paternal responsibility toward the
common man, in conservative circles, is not always insincere.
Great historical movements were dominated by the conviction that most men are permanently incapable of autonomy
and that the best that can be done for them is to turn out,
from within the world of the distinguished few, an elite of
leaders trained and educated by men of rare knowledge and superior virtue. There is nothing particularly mysterious or
perverse about such an ideal, but it is not a democratic one.

Let us, to conclude, consider whether democracy has a stand
of its own on the subject of paternal authority. This function

11. There is a striking resemblance between the conservative theory of paternal
government by an enlightened elite and the concept of revolutionary leadership generally received among Marxists. See Édouard Berth, *Du "Capital" aux "Réflexions sur la
violence"* (Paris: Rivière, 1932), p. 111: "According to the conventional interpretation
of Marxism, the proletariat is not yet a mature person; it is still a kind of *passive instrument* in the hands of a general staff of 'revolutionary thinkers,' an army whose role
it is to take by storm the capitalistic stronghold and to establish in it these possessors
of the definitive social truth in whom we recognize, accordingly, mere successors to the
ancient utopists: the latter expected that a millionaire, an emperor, a king, or a prince
would give them the power of realizing their utopias; our 'revolutionary thinkers,' our
'Marxist leaders,' expect the same service of the proletariat, considered as an *arm* of
which they are the *head:* that is all the difference."

of authority, as repeatedly mentioned, is animated with a dynamism of autonomy. Its substitutional character entails its being pedagogical, so that its very essence necessitates that it aim at its own disappearance. It is impossible to posit the principle of paternal authority without positing simultaneously a principle of autonomy. With regard to the proper good either of the individual or of the group, the possibility of self-government makes it obligatory for authority to disappear; and the possibility of progress toward self-government makes it obligatory for authority to follow the ways of such progress. The undue postponement of self-rule can never find an excuse in the principle of paternal authority, which contains a demand for the production of autonomy. In so far as government exercises paternal authority, it is plainly true that the best government is that which governs least. It was said that an ideally successful government can afford to disappear; this proposition certainly holds for the paternal function of authority, both in civil government and in any kind of government. Whether it holds for the other functions of authority remains to be seen.

The dynamism of autonomy, contained in the essence of paternal authority, is very congenial to the democratic mind. Yet it does not by any means pertain to the distinctive features of democratic government; it rather pertains to the common features of just government, whether democratic or not. A democratic rule that proceeds according to justice would not exercise any paternal authority without also practicing thorough dedication to the production of autonomy. But a nondemocratic rule, if it is just, would not act differently. The annihilation of paternal authority into autonomy, whenever possible, is an affair of justice, not an affair of democracy.

The distinct stand of democracy with regard to paternal authority concerns primarily the relations between those whom Hamilton calls "the few" and those whom he calls "the many." Any theory which maintains that the many need to be governed by the few in paternalistic and quasi-colonial fashion is undemocratic. There is no question of denying that in certain times and places a quasi-colonial government of the many by the few may be the best arrangement or even the only conceivable one. Under these circumstances democratic government is not possible, and there is no more to be said. But the philosophical conservative maintains that such circumstances are not particular to a time and to a place. He believes that, so long as men are what they have always been, nothing will be better for the many than paternal domination by the few. Democratic doctrine has nothing to say about the relation actually existing between the many and the few under particular circumstances; such relation is no more than a matter of fact. But the theory that paternal rule of the few over the many is necessarily and always a desirable state of affairs is in plain conflict with democratic doctrine. If this theory were true, democracy would not admit of any application: this theory is refuted by any successful operation of democracy.

Against a fanciful interpretation of what is confusedly called "democratic faith," let it be said that it is not up to democratic doctrine or to any doctrine, frame of mind, vision of life, or spirit to determine judgments concerned with factual reality. There are circumstances in which paternalistic government alone can remove both anarchy and tyranny; such seems to be the case, inevitably, wherever ignorance is so prevalent as to render election by universal suffrage nonsensical. An act of "democratic faith" which would proclaim the wisdom of the many when the circumstances are such that the many cannot possibly know what it is all about would be obnoxious absurdity.

Besides its willingness and anxiousness to declare that there are cases, whether frequent or not, in which the many do not need to be ruled paternalistically, the democratic spirit is characterized by a certain sort of audacity highly uncongenial to conservatives. Consider that the ability of the grown subject to achieve self-government is never perfectly ascertained until it is confirmed by practice. In a number of cases events have demonstrated that it had been overrated; the disappearance of paternal authority produced disorder and revolt rather than autonomy. In order to give the subject a chance to be autonomous, society has to accept a risk. So far as the common man is concerned, democracy demands that such risks be accepted. It also favors early granting of autonomy in all domains of paternal authority. Under the general influence of the democratic spirit the adult woman obtained a status of complete majority, and the domain of authority conceded to young people by laws and mores was considerably increased. In our time the same spirit urges the end of almost all colonial rule, regardless, as it were, of the risks.

All too often the hard exigencies of democratic action were concealed by the association of democratic rhetoric with hedonistic philosophy. Politicians and theorists, all hungry for cheap popularity, spread the belief that democracy exacts little, welcomes soft characters, keeps men away from heroic enterprises, lessens pain and exertion, shuns dreams of grandeur, and prefers the easy way. This picture became so accredited that one method used by Fascist parties to win over the youth was emphasis on the beauty of the dangerous life. The success of hedonistic expediency in the democratic movement shows how an institution may incidentally lend itself to interpretations in sharp opposition to the requirements of its essence. In order to understand that democracy increases enormously the demand for heroism, it suffices to consider the risks that the abolition of paternal rule, in no matter what domain, inevitably involves. Again, paternal authority commits abuse whenever it outlives its necessity. Yet, after it has ceased to be strictly needed, it may prove very handy in forestalling evil, and the granting of autonomy, even when altogether desirable, may release forces whose control requires additional fortitude. Few persons would, in our time, object to the emancipation of women in so far as it means the end of paternal rule over adults. But it cannot be doubted that the end of paternal authority in the relation of man to woman is partly responsible for the unprecedented trials to which the family institution is subjected today. This remark does not mean that women should have been kept in a status of minority; it means that the emancipation of women demanded as its proper counterpart new forms of discipline calculated to guarantee the stability of the home against the threats resulting from newly won liberty. Instead of which, the feminist movement, in the vast majority of its expressions, promoted soft emotions, identified freedom with the whims of desire, and exalted pleasure. Similarly, increased independence conceded to young people often caused sheer disorder.

Many conservatives, considering that the end of the quasi-colonial rule of the few over the many opened an era of uncertainty, feel confirmed in their paternalistic philosophy. Yet the conclusion suggested by the restlessness of the emancipated is not that the many should have been kept under quasi-colonial rule; it is rather that the end of traditional paternalism called for new and costly forms of heroism. Feats of organization accomplished, in the last decades, among industrial laborers give an idea of the kind of creative struggle which ought to follow upon the end of paternalism in order that genuine autonomy may be produced. The general evolution of modern societies suggests that the regrets of conservatives are all in vain; whenever there are fair evidences that self-government is possible, paternalistic rule is actually forced to go. The operation is known to be risky, but modern societies seem to be necessitated by the weight of their history to accept the risk. Under such circumstances, the promise of an easy life is but seduction into decadence.

AUTHORITY AS CAUSE OF UNITED ACTION

Throughout the preceding exposition we emphasized the substitutional character of paternal authority. We now must consider whether authority has essential functions. That it has no essential function at all is a proposition current among liberal writers.

Let us bear in mind the picture of a society made exclusively of clever and virtuous persons. If such a picture was necessarily utopian, it might still satisfy the conditions of a mental experiment. In fact, it is not unreal; e.g., a man and his wife make up a society; both of them may be virtuous and enlightened. There exist societies whose members are all perfectly good; but these societies are very small. We want to know whether such societies need authority. If they do, authority is not devoid of essential function.

Even in the smallest and most closely united community, unity of action cannot be taken for granted; it has to be caused, and, if it is to be steady, it has to be assured by a steady cause. Here are a man and his wife—both are good and clever, but one thinks that the summer vacation should be spent on the seashore, and the other would rather spend it in the hills. If they remain divided, one goes to the seashore, the other to the hills, and common life ceases temporarily. It would come to an end if a similar divergence concerned an issue of lasting significance.

Now unity of action depends upon unity of judgment, and unity of judgment can be procured either by way of unanimity or by way of authority; no third possibility is conceivable. Either we all think that we should act in a certain way, or it is understood among us that, no matter how diverse our preferences, we shall all assent to one judgment and follow the

line of action that it prescribes. Whether this judgment is
uttered by a leading person or by the majority or by a majority within a leading minority makes, at this point, little difference. But to submit myself to a judgment which does not,
or at least may not, express my own view of what should be
done is to obey authority. Thus authority is needed to assure
unity of action if, and only if, unanimity is uncertain. The
question is whether unanimity can be established in better
than casual fashion among the perfectly clever and well-
intentioned members of a society which is, by hypothesis,
free from deficiencies.

In science, lack of unanimity always has the character of an
accident, and there is something scandalous about it; people
spontaneously trace it to failure, for science is supposed to
proceed by way of demonstration and demonstration is held
to communicate knowledge with necessity. What is taught
and learned in our courses and treatises under the name of science contains a large amount of opinions and beliefs; but it
also contains an inconspicuous, though all-important, nucleus
of propositions possessing certainty, universality, and clarity, which satisfy all requirements for steady communicability. *De jure*, it is always possible to necessitate unanimous assent to a scientific proposition; unfolding the demonstration
is all that needs to be done. Let it be said that a genuinely
scientific proposition is, *de jure*, communicable without limits.
Yet, when a proposition fails to win assent beyond the
boundaries of a group of kindred minds, one should not infer,
from this sheer fact, that it is devoid of scientific character. A
proposition may be, *de jure*, communicable without any limit,
though its *de facto* communicability proves narrowly limited.
That a discrepancy should take place between *de jure* and *de
facto* possibilities is a common occurrence in this world of
contingency. The propositions of positive science are incomparably more communicable, in fact, than those of philos-

ophy; yet some philosophic propositions are fully demonstrated and consequently possess the objective foundation of unlimited communicability; their relative incommunicability is purely factual. It is by accident that only a few people can understand the terms out of which they are made, know what the question is all about, master the prerequisites to the demonstration, and follow the demonstration itself.

Thus, in the field of scientific thought, unanimity is guaranteed, *de jure*, by a process of rational communication whose possibility results necessarily from the nature of scientific objects. Faultless scientific minds, no matter how many, would be unanimous with regard to scientific truth. The problem with which we are now concerned is whether what holds for scientific propositions holds also for those practical propositions which rule the action of a multitude: Do they possess the power of commanding unanimous assent, at least when conditions are entirely normal?

The theory of practical certainty and of practical truth, worked out by Aristotelianism, is a first step toward an answer. The very exacting definition of science in the *Posterior Analytics* seems to make hopeless the case of certainty in practical matters. If the certainty of science demands that the scientific object should possess the kind and degree of necessity that is found in universal essences alone, it seems that practical knowledge admits of no certainty, for human practice takes place in the universe of the things that can be otherwise than they are.[12] Events constantly give the lie to our prudence. After careful deliberation we conclude that this course of action is the right one, yet what it brings about is a catastrophe. The head of a family, for instance, decides, after having conscientiously weighed advantages and disadvantages,

12. On the theory of prudence see Aristotle *Ethics* 6; Thomas Aquinas *Sum. theol.* i–ii. 57. 4, 5, 6; 58. 4, 5; 65. 2; ii–ii. 47–56; John of St. Thomas *Cursus theologicus* i–ii, disp. 16, a. 4, 5 ([Paris: Vivès, 1885], VI, 466 ff.); disp. 17, a. 2 (VI, 534 ff.).

that a certain trip would be a good thing for his family. A train wreck occurs. A child is killed. Yet this honest man had a right to believe in the course of action that he had selected.

Such a simple example is all we need to perceive the twofold meaning of a practical proposition. "This trip is going to be a good thing"—this proposition is given the lie by the train wreck; it is found at variance with facts; between it and the real, there turns out to be no relation of conformity; it happens to be false, it never was certain. However, and no matter what happens, it will remain everlastingly true that the proposition "this trip is going to be a good thing" was the right conclusion of a properly conducted deliberation. No one could do better. Our calculations are not supposed to be infallible. This proposition was what it was supposed to be. It was what good will and loving devotion wanted it to be. Its agreement with the real was but probable, for the operation of a railroad line is subject to accidents; but its agreement with the demands of a good will was certain. Such agreement is a kind of truth, and the train wreck is no ground for charging the man with lack of judgment. He judged well, inasmuch as his judgment was what it was supposed to be. The conformity of a practical proposition with the real cannot be perfectly established; but such conformity is absolute truth, theoretical truth; it is not the truth that belongs to the practical proposition qua practical. Practical truth is a relation of conformity between a judgment or a proposition and the requirements of an honest will.[13] When a decision is what honesty demands

13. On practical truth see Aristotle *Ethics* 6. 2. 1139a21, trans. W. D. Ross: "What affirmation and negation are in thinking, pursuit and avoidance are in desire; so that since moral virtue is a state of character [*habitus*] concerned with choice, and choice is deliberate desire, therefore both the reasoning must be true and the desire right, if the choice is to be good, and the latter must pursue just what the former asserts. Now this kind of truth is practical; of the intellect which is contemplative, not practical nor productive, the good and the bad state are truth and falsity respectively (for this is the work of everything intellectual); while of the part which is practical and intellectual the good state is truth in agreement with right desire." Also: *Com. of St. Thomas*, les. 2;

that it should be, this decision is true in a practical sense, and its practical truth is certain and unqualified. The uncertainty of our calculations entails painful consequences, but it does not affect the possession of practical truth, which retains its firmness amid ruins.

So far as its cause is concerned, the judgment possessed with practical certainty must be described as a particularly clear and familiar case of *affective* knowledge.[14] In rational knowledge, a judgment which is not self-justified owes its justification to antecedent cognitions and finally to self-justified or obvious cognitions. The dispositions of the will and the heart have nothing to do with the determination of knowledge; they concern only its exercise. It is not by being docile

---

Sum. theol. i–ii. 57. 5 ad 3, trans. A. C. Pegis: "As is stated in Ethics VI, truth is not the same for the practical as for the speculative intellect. For the truth of the speculative intellect depends on the conformity of the intellect to the thing. And since the intellect cannot be infallibly in conformity with things in contingent matters, but only in necessary matters, therefore, no speculative habit [*habitus*] about contingent things is an intellectual virtue, but only such as is about necessary things.—On the other hand, the truth of the practical intellect depends on conformity with right appetite. This conformity has no place in necessary matters, which are not effected by the human will, but only in contingent matters which can be effected by us, whether they be matters of interior action or the products of external work. Hence it is only about contingent matters that an intellectual virtue is assigned to the practical intellect, viz., *art*, as regards things to be made, and *prudence*, as regards things to be done." [I wish to express my gratitude to Random House, Inc., New York, for permmission to quote extensively from *The Basic Writings of Saint Thomas*, trans. A.C. Pegis.] Cajetan's commentary on this text is very enlightening.

14. On knowledge through affective connaturality see Thomas Aquinas *Sum. theol.* i. 1. 6 ad 3, trans. A. C. Pegis: "Since judgment pertains to wisdom, in accord with a twofold manner of judging there is a twofold wisdom. A man may judge in one way by inclination, as whoever has the habit [*habitus*] of virtue judges rightly of what is virtuous by his very inclination towards it. Hence it is the virtuous man, as we read [Aristotle *Ethics* 10. 5. 1176a17] who is the measure and rule of human acts. In another way, a man may judge by knowledge, just as a man learned in moral science might be able to judge rightly about virtuous acts, though he had not virtue." Also i–ii. 65. 1, 2; 95. 2 ad 4; ii–ii. 45. 2; John of St. Thomas *Cursus theologicus* i–ii, disp. 18, a. 4, ([Paris: Vivès, 1885], VI, 634 ff.); J. Maritain, *Réflexions sur l'intelligence* (Paris: Nouvelle librairie nationale, 1924) (later eds., Paris: Desclée De Brouwer), pp. 88 and 110 ff.

to the inclinations of our heart that we shall ever *establish* the true answer to a question of theoretical science. On the contrary, when I am concerned with the question "What do I have to do, here and now, in the midst of this unique, unprecedented and unrenewable congeries of circumstances, in order to make a good use of my freedom, in order to preserve the good of virtue?" I know that no deduction, no induction, no argumentation, can supply the final answer. The science of ethics, i.e., the rational knowledge of morality, would supply an initial answer but not the final one. Between the last rationally established conclusion and the entirely concrete rule that action demands, there is a gap that no argumentation can bridge. Doubt cripples action, or an uncertain rule is issued, unless the will and the heart are so dedicated to the good of virtue that their inclinations can be relied upon. The ethical man may be unable to explain why, ultimately, he comes to such and such a decision; he may have nothing to say, beyond mentioning an inclination to act in this way and an insuperable repugnance to act in the opposite way. That is all he needs to direct his action, but more would be needed to bring about conviction in the mind of his neighbor. Unlike scientific judgment, practical judgment, for the very reason that it is ultimately determined by the obscure forces of the appetite, does not admit of rational communication. It is, as it were, a secret.

Let these propositions be exemplified briefly. When a teacher of ethics shows that the right of private ownership is suspended in case of extreme necessity, so that a starving person may use things which under ordinary circumstances belong to his neighbor, some listener inevitably raises the following question (which constitutes, in the listener's mind, an unanswerable objection): "But who is going to decide whether or not I do find myself in the state of extreme necessity?" The only possible answer is calculated to discourage those who expect of the science of ethics things that no science can ever procure. Let the answer be that everyone has to make such decisions for himself and that the conditions to be satisfied, if such decisions are to be made safely, are extremely costly. In order to know for sure whether I find myself in the state of extreme necessity, I must possess the virtue of justice; by it I shall be inclined away from my neighbor's property and prevented from using goods that do not belong to me until my want is actually extreme. But unruly desires would interfere with the operation of justice; thus temperance also is required. And so is fortitude, for a coward would act too early, out of fear of a danger, or too late, out of fear of another danger. In short, practical wisdom or prudence, the virtue whose act is certain knowledge of practical truth, presupposes all moral virtues.

In an early writing on the subject of authority I stated that, on account of the incommunicability of the prudential judgment, unanimity in practical matters is always precarious or casual.[15] I wish to criticize this view, in which I now recognize a serious error.

15. *Nature and Functions of Authority* (Milwaukee: Marquette University Press, 1940). After having established the incommunicability of the prudential judgment, I wrote (pp. 28-29): ". . . it can never be shown evidently that this or that practical judgment, to be taken as a rule for our common action, is the best possible one. However conscientious the deliberation may be, since it cannot afford to prove its conclusions, anybody can, at any time, object that a better course of action could be conceived, and the unity of action which is supposed to be required by the pursuit of the common good will ceaselessly be jeopardized unless all members of the community agree to follow one prudential decision and only one—which is to submit themselves to some authority." I was assuming that rational communication alone can assure unity of judgment. For the correction of this error, as well as for countless greater blessings, I am indebted to Professor Maritain. In a discussion of my booklet (*Review of Politics* [Notre Dame, Ind.], III, No. 2 [April, 1941], 250-54) he sums up my exposition as follows: "Let us suppose . . . a community made up of *perfectly intelligent* and *perfectly virtuous* human beings. Even in this case, the necessity of a ruling authority is required by the nature of things; because in the order of prudential judgment no agreement is certainly and *de jure* to be expected even from perfectly intelligent, perfectly well-informed and perfectly virtuous men. "Professor Maritain goes on with these critical remarks: "Now this seems to be certainly true even of perfectly intelligent and perfectly well-informed

Consider a group of persons confronted with a duty of united action for the common good. We assume that they are all virtuous; by their virtues they are properly related to the common good as end. We assume also that they are all enlightened and that no ignorance or illusion interferes with their ability to determine the proper means. Unanimity cannot be brought about by demonstration, for the proposition that such and such a course of action ought to be followed is not demonstrable. Attempts at its rational establishment, no matter how sound and helpful, will fall short of necessitating the assent of the minds. Let an example be that of a nation threatened in its freedom and existence by an ambitious competitor. A time comes when survival demands war-readiness, and a time comes when fighting alone can preserve the common good. Yet it is never possible to demonstrate that whoever loves the common good must support a policy of war and that whoever opposes such a policy is wrong. Who knows? Decisive factors often are extremely unobvious. A policy of abstention may not bring about the calamities whose unfolding is considered evident by some. And war is a risky enterprise. The dialogue goes on, though the situation imperatively demands that all should contribute full measure of devotion, with all their minds and hearts, to a uniquely determined

---

men. But if they are at the same time *perfectly virtuous*, what must we say? Prudence as such is infallible; therefore, if we suppose two men perfectly intelligent, well-informed *and virtuous*, placed in the same circumstances, will not the prudential judgment of these two men necessarily be the same, since in both of them it is taken in conformity with an appetite that perfect virtues cause to be right toward the end? If such is the case, we should say that in a community made up of perfectly intelligent, well-informed *and virtuous* human beings, there will surely be agreement among them in the prudential judgments concerning the good of this community,—an agreement which is not due to any demonstration, but to the common rightness of their appetite for the end." The problem of the plurality of the means is not considered here. Plainly, "the common rightness of their appetite for the end," which causes unity with regard to the end and the necessary means, does not cause unity with regard to a particular means in no necessary connection with the end.

policy. The question is whether such disagreement can take place among citizens that are both good and enlightened.

One thing is plain: if unanimity can be achieved in non-fortuitous fashion, it is not by way of necessitating argumentation and rational communication. But the analysis of practical judgment, which rules out rational communication as a steady cause of unanimity in these matters, shows also that a steady cause of unanimity is found in the inclination of the appetite, whenever the means to the common good is uniquely determined. If there is only one means to the common good, only one proposition—viz., the proposition expressive of this means the only one that admits of practical truth. It is the only one that conforms to the requirements of a properly disposed appetite, and a properly disposed appetite cannot make any other proposition win assent. The community of the end and the unique determination of the means bring about a situation distinguished by happy simplicity.

The proper mystery of practical wisdom (prudence) has been so commonly ignored by philosophers that its rediscovery is not unlikely to cause some sort of intoxication. In sharp contrast to the youthful ideal of a science-like knowledge of action, the theory of prudence describes a universe of normally and necessarily different judgments, each of which, on close examination, turns out to bear a mark of secrecy. Two brothers, for instance, would govern their families in strikingly different ways, and each of them may be unable to understand why the other one uses what seems to him queer and irrational methods. Unless they answer similar problems in similar fashions, should it not be said that one of them is wrong, or both? But the situations of two individuals are really dissimilar whenever the unique implications of individual history play a part in the statement of the problem. A feeling for the mysterious operation of individual history in the regulation of individual conduct is a most important element of practical wisdom. When such a feeling has just awakened in our souls, we come to imagine the ethical destinies of individual men as a multitude of universes governed by so many unique and incommunicable rules of action. But all at once the spirit of rebellion endangers the universality of the law and the unity of common action. Indeed, diversities resulting from the uniqueness of individual situations never can supply a ground for dispensing with the law, for it is within the unity of the law that they take place. As to the necessary unity of common action, how could it be affected by the diversity of our individual histories? When there is a question of common action for the common good, such diversity no longer matters; the only history which matters is that of the community. In the case of two individuals who pursue individual goods belonging to the same genus, duality on the part of the good intended and duality on the part of the agent supply grounds for possible divergencies regarding the rule of action. In the case of a community in quest of its common good, the good intended is one and the intending agent is one; the only just ground for divergent opinion is the diversity of the means capable of leading the same collective agent to the same common good. Whenever there is only one means, there ought to be unanimity, and failure to achieve unanimous agreement is traceable to some deficiency.

Consider, again, the case of a nation whose salvation, in justice, demands that war be fought. What about dissenters? They may be ill-intentioned citizens, who do not love the common good but wish for the enemy's victory or who place above anything else the specific pleasures that attach to obstinacy. They may be well-intentioned citizens but lack intelligence; or they may have intelligence and good will but lack information and, by accident, be fooled into believing that they have all the information needed for the uttering of a fully determinate judgment as to what the country should do. From our present viewpoint, whether or not these erring citizens retain their respectability does not matter. What matters is that their error is definite and traceable to a deficiency, which may or may not involve guilt.

In the daily life of small communities—I refer principally to the couple and the family—unanimity plays a great part as a factor of unified action. When the means to the common good is uniquely determined—the only case in which there is a firm foundation for unanimity—it is not infrequently recognized and assented to in unanimous fashion. In large societies —state, nation—the astonishing thing is not that complete unanimity is never realized but rather that situations closely resembling unanimity, so far as most practical purposes are concerned, arise not rarely when the threat to the common good is dire. Notice that a situation resembling unanimity does not necessarily imply overwhelming majority; a substantial majority within the part of the nation—perhaps a minority—which is actively interested suffices. If no such situation is produced, in spite of the seriousness of the common predicament, salvation becomes uncertain, and a doubt appears whether there still is anything to be saved. For it can be wondered whether a multitude incapable of achieving some kind of unanimity in the hour of extreme peril retains the character of a community; it is feared that disintegration is too far advanced. The hopeless plight of a society that is no longer capable of achieving an approximation to unanimity bears witness to the absolutely normal character of unanimous assent to the uniquely determined means of common salvation.

To sum up: When the means to the common good is uniquely determined, affective community supplies an essential foundation for unanimous assent; unanimity is, then, the only normal situation, and, if everything is normal, authority is not needed to bring about unified action. Unity of action requires authority in so far as not everything is normal, in so far as wills are weak or perverse and intellects ignorant or blinded. The function of authority remains substitutional.

But when, on the other hand, there is more than one means of procuring the common good, there is no foundation whatsoever for unanimity. Anyone may disagree without there being anything wrong either with his intentions or with his judgment. It is only by chance that unanimity can be achieved, for it has no essential cause. Even in a very small society it will partake of the unsteadiness of the fortuitous and fail to assure unity of action; yet unity of action may be indispensable and all-important in spite of the plurality of the means leading to the common good. Shall we drive on the left side of the road, as in Great Britain, or on the right side, as in most countries? The common good, i.e., order and safety, admits of either method, and prior to the establishment of definite habits it seems that neither method enjoys any superiority. Here the rule of action is entirely optional. But it is all-important that one and the same rule should govern the behavior of all drivers; lack of unity of action, in such a simple case, would entail catastrophes. The common good does not demand that we should drive on the right side, and it does not demand that we should drive on the left side; but it does demand that all should drive on the same side. Of the two opposite judgments (drive right, drive left), it does not make either one mandatory, but it demands that one of them should become mandatory and be obeyed by all, regardless of their preference. In other words, the common good demands that a problem of united action which cannot be solved by way of unanimity should be solved by way of authority.

Considering, thus, the function that authority plays as an indispensable principle of united action when there are several means to the common good, let the question be asked whether this function is essential or substitutional. Since the need for authority here is properly caused by the plurality of the means, the real question is whether this plurality of means is itself caused by a deficiency or by the good nature of things; in the latter case alone will the function under consideration prove to be an essential one.

Without being stated in these very terms, this question was often examined and was given a definite answer by various schools of scientific anarchism. Ever since the awakening, early in the nineteenth century, of a rationalistic enthusiasm for the possibilities of social science, it has been a current belief that the indetermination of the means, which makes unification by way of authority necessary, is but an appearance due to our inability to identify the appropriate means. The situation could be described as follows: on the basis of our incomplete information, a, b, and c seem to be so many adequate means to the good that we are aiming at. United action, if needed, has to be procured by the decision of authority. But if we knew more about a, b, c, . . . , there would be no need for such decision; for we would realize that only one course of action is really appropriate and to this uniquely determined course of action honest and clever people would give unanimous assent. In other words, our ignorance opens a phase of indetermination that authority, in blind fashion, closes. Better knowledge would eliminate the phase of indetermination and its unenlightened ending. Authority substitutes for a determinate knowledge of a situation which is really determinate—its role remains substitutional.

In order to ascertain the real meaning of this argument, let us apply it to a simple example. Consider, again, the case of a family that is deliberating about the summer vacation: some would like to stay home, some would rather go to the hills, and some to the seashore. Let it be granted that these three are the only existent possibilities. According to the argument that we want to test, one of the three ways is right and the other two are wrong. But, as an effect of insuperable ignorance, these people, in spite of their good will, may remain divided, in which case unity will be brought about by authority.

Later developments, in fact, sometimes show that, out of several ways which all seemed proper, only one was really conducive to the good; we really had no choice, although we honestly believed that we had plenty of it. But the relevant question is this: Supposing that there is only one real means, what kind of factor causes it to be uniquely determined? and supposing that there is a plurality of genuine means, what kind of factor causes them to be several?

One obvious reason why a family should stay home during the summer is the high cost of a vacation in the hills or at the seashore. Thus poverty is a factor of unique determination. Wealth, on the contrary, makes for choice; this is what men of property know very well, and poor people still better. One obvious reason why a family should not stay home during the summer is the condition of the health of its members; if some of them, or all, are in such bad shape that, without the stimulation of a period of rest in the hills or at the seashore, they are likely to catch bad diseases next winter, then (all other things being equal) one possibility out of three is ruled out. If, on the contrary, all are in very good health, they can stand, without ill effect, a summer in town. Supposing that they leave home, one reason why they may have no choice between hills and seashore would be the restlessness of some or all, since restless people at the seashore tend to become sleepless and more restless than ever. It happens also that a family, in spite of financial strain, feels obliged to move to the country for a while, just because a young man is going through a period of moral uncertainty out of which he can be helped by a change in environment and by wholesome entertainment. If all the family, on the contrary, are robust characters, you can trust that they will fight their way through, regardless of whether they stay at home or go away. In short, wealth, health, and strength are factors that cause independence from particular courses of action, dominating indifference, mastery over several means, freedom. Destitution, ill health, uncertainty, weakness, are factors that cause dependence upon determinate means. Plenitude causes choice, poverty leaves no choice. Deficiency, such as lack of knowledge, may render the genuine means undistinguishable from the illusory one and thus make a plurality of means appear where there is really no more than one. But fulness, actuality, determination, achievement, accomplishment, power and greatness, knowledge and stability, produce or increase liberty in societies and individuals as well. A society enjoying a supremely high degree of enlightenment would, all other things being equal, enjoy much more choice than ignorant societies and have to choose among many more possibilities. It would not need authority to choose between two courses of action one of which is bound to lead to disaster, since, by hypothesis, knowledge would rule out illusory means. But it would need authority, *more than ever*, to procure united action, for, thanks to better lights, the plurality of the genuine means would have increased considerably. The function of authority with which we are concerned, i.e., that of procuring united action when the means to the common good are several, does not disappear but grows, as deficiencies are made up; it originates not in the defects of men and societies but in the nature of society. It is an essential function.[16]

16. In his *Theoretical Essay on Natural Law* Taparelli d'Azeglio emphasizes the function of authority as cause of united action. To my knowledge he fails to show that this function is merely substitutional when there is but one means to the common good; and he does not show clearly that, even when it is essential, it is not (as we shall see) the most essential function of authority (see Luigi Taparelli, *Saggio teoretico di dritto naturale* [Palermo: Antonio Muratori, 1840], II, 67-68): "Society consists in a union of intelligent beings which tend toward a common end; now whence comes to these essentially free intellects this common tendency? A common end is already a principle of social unity. However, in the present case, the end is not connected with any deter-

Doubts affecting this issue result from a general philosophic situation which confusedly tends to identify freedom and indetermination. In fact, freedom is indifference, and there are two sorts of indifference.[17] There is the passive indifference of the indeterminate subject which can receive any of several determinations precisely because it is indeterminate. The highest degree of such indifference is realized in prime matter, a pure "out of which" that is not of itself any determinate thing and therefore cannot exist by itself but can receive any essential determination and exist under it. Nothing is further removed from freedom than the indetermination of matter, for freedom is mastery and proceeds not from a lack of determination but from a particularly full and hard kind of determination. A free cause is a superdeterminate cause. The trouble comes from the fact that these two opposite realities—the indifference of indetermination, passivity, inachievement, and the indifference of superdetermination which is freedom—have in common the property of being distinct from sheer determinate causality. Further, there is in the human will a combination of active indifference and of passive indifference. The latter is an obstacle to freedom; yet it is not always easy to distinguish, in the

---

mined means in such a close way that all minds be bound, and spontaneously agree, to consider it as a necessary means; reason and experience show, on the contrary, that unanimity of opinions and sentiments is a thing rare and difficult to obtain. On the other hand, the good and the perfection of society pressingly require the conformity of tendencies, the co-ordination of internal and external means in relation to this end; since, for lack of such a co-ordination, the aim is not attained or is attained but in an imperfect way. . . . In short, being endowed with intellect and free-will, the members of a society must tend by several means toward a common end; they can choose between those means. Since diverse and opposite means would abolish social unity and destroy the essence of society, it is necessary to have an intelligent principle regulate the minds and impress the same tendencies on all the wills. Now we call authority this power which binds all members of society. Thus authority is an essential element of society."

17. On the all-important subject of the two indifferences found in the human will see Thomas Aquinas *Sum. contra gentes* i. 82; John of St. Thomas *Cursus philosophicus* iv, q. 12, a. 2 (Marietti, III, 387); *Cursus theologicus* i. disp. 24, a. 4 (Solesme, III, 89); i–ii, disp. 3, a. 2 (Vivès, V, 373).

twilight, the force which is supposed to be overcoming (i.e., active indifference, that is, freedom) and the force which is supposed to be overcome (i.e., passive indifference, indetermination, perplexity, irresolution) if the former is to assert itself. When psychologists do not altogether deny freedom of choice, they generally trace it to an imperfection or uncertainty of the will, to an element of looseness in its operation. Similarly, many social thinkers, when confronted by a seeming plurality of means, trace it to inadequate knowledge and fail to see that plurality of genuine means can be caused by excellence of knowledge and power. In both cases a misunderstanding concerning indifference results from an insufficiently elaborate notion of causality.[18]

18. Unity is needed in action toward the common good (order of means); it is needed, also, as a most important element of the common good itself (order of ends). In either case unanimity is unable to procure it except in precarious and casual fashion.

The consideration of unanimity supplies a fitting background to the theory of unity in government proclaimed by Aristotle, with the help of a Homeric line, at the climax of his *Metaphysics*: ". . . and they give us many governing principles; but the world refuses to be governed badly. The rule of the many is not good; one ruler let there be" (*Met.* 12. 10. 1076a3; trans. W. D. Ross). This is the answer of Thomas Aquinas to the question *Whether the world is governed by one?* ". . . since the end of the government of the world is that which is essentially good, which is the greatest good, the government of the world must be the best kind of government. Now the best government is government by one. The reason for this is that government is nothing but the directing of the things governed to the end; which consists in some good. But unity belongs to the notion of goodness, as Boethius proves from this, that, as all things desire good, so do they desire unity, without which they would cease to exist. For a thing so far exists as it is one. Whence we observe that things resist division, as far as they can, and that the dissolution of a thing arises from some defect in the thing. Therefore the intention of a ruler over a multitude is unity, or peace. Now the proper cause of unity is that which is one. For it is clear that several cannot be the cause of unity or concord, except so far as they are united. Furthermore what is one in itself is a more apt and a better cause of unity than several things united. Therefore a multitude is better governed by one than by several. From this it follows that the government of the world, being the best form of government, must be by one. This is expressed by the Philosopher . . . [above]" (*Sum. theol.* i. 103. 3; trans. A. C. Pegis). Commenting on this article, Cajetan writes: ". . . the essential cause (*per se causa*) of unity is what is essentially one (*per se unum*). This is manifested by the consideration that the many do not cause the one except insofar as they are in some way united. But a thing is more fittingly produced

THE VOLITION OF THE COMMON GOOD

The problem of united action is relative to means. Now it is perfectly evident that all operations concerning means are conditioned and sustained by more basic operations, i.e., the volition and intention of the end.[18a] Associates may unify their action by way of authority or have to content themselves with the risky procedures of unanimity; clearly, there would be no action to be unified if these men had not antecedently determined that a certain object should have for all of them the character of an end to be pursued through common action. Thus, beyond the problem of united action, we have to inquire into a more profound issue, i.e., that of the very intention of the common good. We know that authority is necessary,

---

by a proper cause than by an incidental cause. Therefore . . ." (from the Leonine ed. of the *Sum. theol.*).

If government by one is compared with government by unanimity, the contrast between proper cause and incidental cause plainly holds. An assembly subjected to the rule of unanimity is but incidental cause of unity. But what about an assembly proceeding by majority vote and so organized as to make a tie impossible? The many who make up this assembly are but the incidental cause of unity; it is not on account of what they are that they cause unity but on account of something superadded to their multiple entities, viz., the form which gathers them into an assembly subjected to a system of rules and bound to elicit definite conclusions by majority vote. Considered *with* its form, this assembly is no longer a merely incidental cause of unity. In so far as it is actually informed by its constitution, it has within itself a pattern of unity on account of which it produces unity in no incidental fashion. An assembly acting by unanimous vote lacks such pattern. Now, because regulations admit of loopholes and can be disregarded, an assembly may be unable to reach a decision; it may also endanger unity by frequent change in policies according as influence shifts from one component, person, or group to another. Thus an assembly subjected to a rule of majority is in imperfect fashion an essential cause of unity. A human monarch does not, either, cause unity in perfect and indefectible fashion. Just as conflict of groups may deadlock an assembly, so a person may be doomed to preplexity and inaction by conflicting inclinations, and he may change his policies according to changing whims. Between an assembly bound by the rule of unanimity and an assembly proceeding by majority vote, the distance is immensely greater than between the latter and a single ruler.

18a. Let it be recalled that *volition* is concerned with the end considered absolutely and *intention* with the end considered as term of a means or set of means.

under definite conditions, for the proper working of the means; the next question is whether the proper intention of the common good requires the operation of authority.

If we were concerned with a society including stupid or vicious members, the answer would be so plain as to make the statement of the question superfluous. People lacking good will or understanding obviously have to be directed toward the common good; they even have to be compelled not to harm the common good and to serve it positively. The relevant and difficult question concerns a society composed exclusively of good and enlightened people. At first glance, the answer may seem obvious: if all these people are well-intentioned, they *spontaneously* intend the common good and do not need to be directed toward it. By the very operation of their virtue they aim at the common good and want to subordinate to it their private advantages; without such basic volition and orderly subordination, they would be selfish people, bad citizens, or, at best, well-meaning people misled by illusions.[19] Thus all conceivable function of authority, with regard to the volition and intention of the common good, seems to be merely substitutional.

The question with which we are concerned here is one whose difficulty equals its profundity. It has rarely been considered in proper isolation. The preceding discussion removed the risk that it should be confused with the problem of united action, but there remains a risk of confusion with another neighboring issue. Briefly, most societies are divided into two groups of persons, i.e., those who govern and those who are governed. Now throughout the history of political literature there is a tendency to identify the two following questions:

19. Thomas Aquinas *Sum. theol.* i–ii. 19. 10, trans. A. C. Pegis: "But a man's will is not right in willing a particular good, unless he refers it to the common good as an end, since even the natural appetite of each part is ordained to the common good of the whole."

(*a*) whether society needs to be governed and (*b*) whether it needs to be governed by a distinct personnel. In fact, there are many instances of direct government of the multitude by itself; unless it is claimed, arbitrarily enough, that these constitute abnormalities, they should suffice to show that the essence of government is independent of these two peculiar modalities: embodiment in a distinct personnel, embodiment in the entire multitude. Citizens of a great nation, we obey laws made by a small body of elected legislators; but members of a New England community were no less *governed* by the regulations that the whole community issued in its town meetings. The constitution of a distinct governing personnel has to do with the modalities of authority, not with its functions and the grounds of its necessity. How the confusion takes place is easy to grasp. Wonder is aroused by the power that the few claim to have over the many and that the many acknowledge not too reluctantly. This power, if justifiable at all, should be justified by the requirements of the common welfare. It is realized or strongly suspected that the common welfare needs to be taken care of by a body of public persons. There are instances in which the entire people is such a body; but in most cases and in the most impressive and best-known cases the public persons in charge of the common good are, of necessity, specialized, as it were, in the pursuit of the good which is not special or private but common. Thus, in most cases and in the best known of them, the body of public persons called for by the common good is determinately a distinct governing personnel. The positing of government and the positing of a distinct governing personnel are empirically one conclusion, and experience does not direct attention to the difference of grounds. Further, the operation of a distinct governing personnel implies an element of paradox which will be most felicitously dealt with if, by letting it resolve into the more fundamental issue of government itself, we manage to ignore its specific difficulty.

In order that the problem of authority, with regard to the volition and intention of the common good, may be properly isolated, it is helpful to keep in mind, whenever possible, pictures of government without distinct governing personnel, as in the case of a New England town, a Swiss canton, or a nation deciding an issue by way of plebiscite. The entirely different problem of the necessity of a distinct governing personnel will be discussed in another part of this book.

That virtuous people, as a proper effect of their very virtue, love the common good and subordinate their choices to its requirements is an entirely unquestionable proposition. Thus, *in a certain way at least*, the volition and intention of the common good are guaranteed by virtue itself, independently of all authority. Of this *way* we do not know, as yet, anything, except that it is essential and basic; for it is not by accident or in any superficial fashion that the just love the common good and surrender for it their private interests. The problem, accordingly, is to determine whether the virtue of the private person regards the whole of the common good or merely some fundamental aspect of it. If, and only if, the latter is true, authority may have an essential part to play in the volition and intention of the common good. We are wondering, in other words, whether the *way* in which virtue guarantees adherence to the common good is an all-embracing one; should the guaranty supplied by virtue fail to cover some essential aspect of the common good, then direction by authority might be needed, in order that the adherence of society to all essential aspects of its good might be steadily assured. The examination of a few typical instances will provide an answer.

Let the first instance be that used by Thomas Aquinas in his inquiry into the general conditions of morality. The question is whether the human will, in order to be good, ought to agree with the divine will *in volito*, in other words, whether it must carry agreement with the divine will so far as to desire the very thing whose coming into existence is desired, or permitted, by the divine will[20] (e.g., if God let me know that he wants my father to die tomorrow at noon, would ethical perfection demand that I should refrain from any action calculated to prolong the life of my father beyond tomorrow noon?). Aquinas says that, when a thing is good in one respect and bad in another respect, there is nothing wrong about its

20. *Ibid.* 19. 10. The title of the article, as translated by A. C. Pegis, reads: *Whether it is necessary for the human will, in order to be good, to be conformed to the divine will as regards the thing willed?* It is fitting to quote in its entirety the body of this article, in which few seem to have recognized the most precise exposition ever made of the principles commanding the theory of government:

"As is evident from what has been said above, the will tends to its object according as it is proposed by the reason. Now a thing may be considered in various ways by the reason, so as to appear good from one point of view, and not good from another point of view. Therefore, if a man's will wills a thing to be according as it appears to be good, his will is good; and the will of another man, who wills that thing not to be, according as it appears evil, is also good. Thus a judge has a good will in willing a thief to be put to death, because this is just; while the will of another (e.g., the thief's wife or son) who wishes him not to be put to death, inasmuch as killing is a natural evil, is also good.

"Now since the will follows the apprehension of the reason or intellect, the more universal the nature of the apprehended good, the more universal the good to which the will tends. This is evident in the example given above, because the judge has care of the common good, which is justice, and therefore he wishes the thief's death, which has the nature of good in relation to the common welfare; whereas the thief's wife has to consider the private good of the family, and from this point of view she wishes her husband, the thief, not to be put to death. Now the good of the whole universe is that which is apprehended by God, Who is the Maker and Governor of all things. Hence, whatever He wills, He wills it under the nature of the common good; and this is His own goodness which is the good of the whole universe. On the other hand, the apprehension of a creature, according to its nature, is of some particular good, proportioned to that nature. Now a thing may happen to be good under a particular aspect, and yet not good under a universal aspect, or vice versa, as stated above. And therefore it happens that a certain will is good from willing something considered under a particular aspect, which yet God does not will under a universal aspect, and vice versa. And hence, too, it is that various wills of various men can be good in respect of opposite things, inasmuch as, under various aspects, they wish a particular thing to be or not to be.

"But a man's will is not right in willing a particular good, unless he refer it to the common good as an end, since even the natural appetite of each part is ordained to the common good of the whole. Now it is the end that supplies the formal reason, as it were, of willing whatever is directed to the end. Consequently, in order that a man will some particular good with a right will, he must will that particular good materially,

being desired by one, to whom it is related in its desirable aspect, and hated by another, who happens to occupy such a position as to regard the thing in its undesirable aspect. Thus the wife of a murderer hates the prospect of her husband's being put to death; she is normally and virtuously concerned with the good of her family, and, from the standpoint which is and ought to be hers, the death of the murderer is an evil. On the other side, the judge, who stands for society, sees in the death of the murderer elements of the common good: justice and determent from crime. The common good, of course, shall prevail, but, significantly, Aquinas considers altogether sound and honest the opposition made to the requirements of the common good by the person in charge of the particular good. The common good itself demands that wives should want their husbands to survive, even though the latter happen to be criminals. *That particular goods be properly defended by particular persons matters greatly for the common good itself.* The wife of the murderer, as she fights for the life of the man whom the common good wants put to death, does precisely what the

and the divine and universal good, formally. Therefore the human will is bound to be conformed to the divine will, as to that which is willed formally, for it is bound to will the divine and universal good; but not as to that which is willed materially, for the reason given above.

"At the same time in both these respects the human will is conformed to the divine will in a certain degree. For, inasmuch as it is conform to the divine will in the common nature of the thing willed, it is conformed thereto in the point of the last end. But inasmuch as it is not conformed to the divine will in the thing willed materially, it is conformed to that will considered as the efficient cause; for the proper inclination consequent upon nature, or upon the particular apprehension of some particular thing, comes to a thing from God as its efficient cause. Hence it is customary to say that, in this respect, a man's will is conform to the divine will, because it wills what God wills him to will.

"There is yet another kind of conformity in respect of the formal cause, consisting in man's willing something from charity, as God wills it. And this conformity is also reduced to the formal conformity, that is based on the relation to the last end, which is the proper object of charity."

These views are explained by John of St. Thomas with great thoroughness in *Cursus theologicus* i–ii, disp. 11, a. 4 (Vivès, VI, 41–55).

common good wants her to do. It is in a merely material fashion that she disagrees with the requirements of the common
good: by doing what the common good wants her to do, she
formally desires the common good. The common good formally understood is the concern of every genuine virtue, but it is
the proper concern of the public person to procure the common
good materially understood, which the private person may
virtuously oppose.

This analysis of human relations receives increased significance from the truth that it is calculated to manifest in the
relation between man and God. To the question whether the
human will, in order to be good, must conform to the will of
God *in volito*, Aquinas answers that the only conformity required is formal and that a formal conformity may well be
compatible with material disagreement or even demand such
disagreement. God, who takes care of the common good of the
universe, holds me responsible for some particular goods and
wants me to discharge my responsibility. God may want my
father to die tomorrow, but he certainly wants me to do all I
can to prolong the life of my father; and if I were told by
special revelation, under circumstances making for absolute
certainty, that the definite will of God is that my father
should die tomorrow at noon, it would still be the will of God
that I should struggle against the death of my father until it
has become a fact.[21]

Let a second instance be drawn from military life, where
hierarchical relations are defined with particular clarity. A
commanding officer is ordered to hold a certain position at all
costs. His orders do not mention any circumstances under
which he might retreat. We suppose that his will is entirely
good. As a good soldier and a good citizen, he wants and intends the common good of the army and of the whole nation
at war, viz., victory. It is in relation to the common good of

21. John of St. Thomas *op. cit.* p. 48*b*.

the army and nation that he aims at this particular good, viz., the holding of this position. Without such subordination of purposes he would not be a true soldier and a good citizen. A mercenary or an adventurer might pledge himself to hold a place without caring who wins the war, but not a soldier. Thus the particular good—holding the place—is willed because of the common good, on the ground of the common good, under a determination supplied by the common good. In other words, there is, as a proper effect of military and civic virtue, volition and intention of the common good formally understood.

It is assumed, of course, that the orders are not absurd and that the holding of this position, at all costs, is precisely what the common good requires. But this *material* issue concerns the high command or, according to the felicitous expression recently coined, the *over-all* strategy board, not this particular commanding officer. All are supposed to refer all their actions to victory, but, so far as material objects of intention are concerned, the good to be intended by this officer is the holding of this position and nothing else, until another task becomes his. He is not in charge of determining what operations over-all strategy demands; the high command is.

This is what becomes tragically clear when those in charge of the common good materially considered fail to fulfil their task. Anxiety fills the soul of particular persons as it becomes increasingly dubious that the objects assigned to their care are what the common good demands. Holding this position one more day will mean the annihilation of the defenders, with no advantage whatsoever; that is clear, but there is no news from the high command. Those whose job it is to care for the common good materially considered have vanished. By now the defender of a particular position has to do two things: (1) to defend this particular position or to counter-attack or to withdraw his unit safely and (2) to decide what is best for the final victory of the army and nation—defending the place to the last man? counterattacking? retreating? This duality of duties, viz., taking care of both the *particular* good materially considered (defending the position, counterattacking, organizing a safe withdrawal) and of the *common* good materially considered (deciding whether it is better to hold the position or to counterattack or to retreat) is known to induce a sentiment of helplessness that the strongest characters alone can overcome. When the private person has to emerge above his capacity and substitute for nonexistent public persons, an awe-inspiring solitude makes him realize that the structure of society has broken down.

Lest this example should suggest that the care of the common good necessarily belongs to distinct persons, consider, instead of an army, a group of pioneers in which there is no government except that of the majority. Suppose that, during an initial phase implying a great deal of scattered activity, the group gathers every second day to make decisions concerning common interests. A flood, a snowfall, or interference by a party of competitors may make it impossible for the group to convene over a long period. Then each individual will experience the unnatural situation which confronts an army unit when the high command remains silent in spite of the emergency. Private persons have to take care both of their own business and of the public business. Confusion comes to an end when the assembly convenes again and relieves private persons of cares which are not theirs. The same persons, in fact, labored in isolation yesterday and today act as one public character. But, in isolation, they are normally qualified for the pursuit of particular goods alone; in assembly they are the mind and will to which it pertains to understand and intend the common good; this difference of capacity is all that essentially matters.

An example of another type would be supplied by a school

comprising, say, a teacher of English, a teacher of philosophy, a teacher of Latin, a teacher of history, and a teacher of mathematics. The good pursued by each of these men is not particular in the way in which the field plowed by its owner is particular. The teacher of Latin has for his proper purpose the maintenance and promotion of Latin culture in the community; this pertains to the common good, but, inasmuch as it is only one aspect of the common good, the purpose of the Latin teacher remains particular.

Consider now that the frame of mind of a conscientious Latin teacher may conceivably be either of two. There are Latin scholars of whom one says that, if they had their own way, they would convert every youngster into a Latin scholar, regardless of how ignorant their pupils might be in mathematics, modern languages, and even Greek. Such ardent characters supply cartoons and comedies with congenial fun, but their social significance is well known to wise people. There is something absolute about their dedication, the urge of which they are possessed is as uncompromising as a categorical imperative, they are determined to crush obstacles; they show, in fact, little consideration for obstacles arising from their own person, and their devotion generally wears them out. They are good teachers of Latin, their better pupils are fairly good. But what is it that inspires them with such fierce determination? Is it just a passion, to be likened to that of the stamp-collector or of the mountain climber? Not necessarily. The toughest and roughest determinations are those derived from a sense for the *function* that one has to fulfil in society. This old scholar who so faithfully, unambitiously, taught Latin so well for so many years: do not believe that he overdoes the importance of classics and ignores that of mathematics. He may be fully aware of the modesty of his job; his occupational conscience may be pervaded with humility. But one day he realized that his unglamorous job, rather thankless, poorly paid, and not too highly considered, was needed for the common good and that a society in which a few men appreciate Vergil is, all other things being equal, better than a society in which Vergil is entirely unknown; and, because there is something divine about the common good, his vocation, from that day on, was animated with a sense of fervor whose expressions were rough and tough, like everything that is concerned with the absolute. Society is well served by such individuals.

There are, on the other hand, men of skill who feel that it is their duty to keep their own concern well within the proper limits of its real importance. If they happen to be Latin teachers, they will refrain from anything that might look like fanatical zeal for Latin; they will not recommend Latin studies except as part of a balanced program comprising also modern languages, mathematics, history; if they were consistent, they would not recommend any schooling except as a part of a balanced program of human activities, comprising the proper amount of sleep, sport, social life, etc. Although such fellows, for obvious reasons, never attract much attention, we know them by daily experience. They do not cause any complaints; they are occasionally congratulated on their wiselooking serenity; they do not accomplish great things; they pass for civilized and enjoy their reputation. Social observers, stirred by the greater accomplishments of barbarians, would wonder what is wrong and would come to understand that some fundamental error causes the dynamism of the particular skill to be extinguished by improper brainwork. What happens here is the fateful accident of *confusion*, which, understandably, blunts every instrument, stultifies every energy, rules out thoroughness, and causes forces to compromise before the elements of necessity in them have had a chance to work. No part of the land will be thoroughly tilled unless each laborer has a distinct field to plow. And no function will be exercised with thoroughness unless my function—say, that of teaching Latin—is distinct from any other function and thereby particularized. But if my function is a particular one, if, in other words, the good with which I am concerned is but a particular aspect of the common good, then it is necessary that there be, above me, a person or a group of persons properly concerned, not only formally but also materially, with the whole of the common good.

Again, let it be remarked that the positing of a distinct governing personnel does not necessarily follow. An assembly of specialists, acting as a body, may transcend the division of labor and have for its proper object the whole of the good whose diverse aspects constitute as many proper objects for its members, when the latter are not convened and do not act as a body. For instance, it is not impossible that the general policy of a school be adequately managed by a committee of teachers. When such a committee convenes, the teacher of Latin is no longer a person whose life is dedicated to the maintenance of Latin culture; he is, by now, a faculty member dedicated to the whole purpose of the school, understood and desired in its entirety, with all the relations of priority and subordination that the good of a society implies. Shifting from a particular function to an over-all concern is possible, but generally difficult; the mental habits of the specialists are hard to overcome. Hence the rule that the authority in charge of controlling experts should be made of nonexperts. It is understood that the latter are supposed to be expert in a pursuit known to involve special difficulties, viz., that of the good which is not, by any means, special.

The theory emerging from these and such examples and analyses can be summed up in the following propositions:

Under the assumption that the society with which we are concerned is aiming at a common good, it is stated:

1. That virtue implies love for the common good, willingness to sacrifice one's own advantage to its requirements.

2. That the common good may be intended formally without being intended materially.

3. That the virtue of the private person guarantees the intention of the common good formally considered, not the intention of the common good materially considered.

4. That society would be harmed if everyone intended the common good not only formally but also materially; that, in a material sense, particular persons and groups ought to intend particular goods.

5. That the intention of the common good, materially considered, is the business of a public reason and a public will.

6. That the intention of the common good by the public reason and will necessarily develops into a *direction* of society, by the public reason and will, toward the common good considered not only formally but also materially; which is the same as to say that the intention of the common good, materially considered, demands the operation of authority.

Let our exposition proceed, for a while, by way of a comment on these propositions.

The preliminary assumption specifies that the theory holds only for societies aiming at a common good. In fact, many theorists take it for granted that without a common good there is no society. Yet, according to universal and very ancient usage, the term "society" can be predicated of such a partnership as that of a handicraftsman and a moneylender. If a partnership of this sort were relative to a common good, the argumentation which derives the need for authority from the requirements of the common good would be invalidated, for the relation between handicraftsman and moneylender is purely contractual. They exchange promises, but from their promises it does not result that anyone should command and anyone obey. In the incidental case of broken pledges, authority would step in and see that contracts are lived up to; but it would be the authority of civil society, not any authority immanent in the society under consideration. True, it looks as if the moneylender and handicraftsman society was founded for the pursuit of a common good. The gentlemen speak loudly of their common interest. Suppose that in case of prosperity one of them gets 10 per cent of the invested capital and the other one 20 per cent; is it not clear that such prosperous returns constitute the purpose for which these men became associates, the common good of their association? The case is of great theoretical interest, because it supplies a perfectly pure example of *pseudo-common good*. One of these gentlemen proposes to get 10 per cent, and this is an entirely private good; the other proposes to get 20 per cent and this is a no less private good; as to the 30 per cent which constitutes the sum total of the coveted return, it is a sum of private goods which looks like a common good but is not. It lacks one of the defining features of the common good, viz., the intelligible aspect by which the common good calls for communion in desire and common action. In order that a good be common, it does not suffice that it should concern, in some way or other, several persons; it is necessary that it be of such nature as to cause, among those who pursue it and in so far as they pursue it, a common life of desire and action. Whenever the good interesting several persons or groups causes (or, more precisely, is of such nature as to cause) such common life, it is a genuine common good and renders authority necessary. If, on the other hand, a good interesting several does not call for a common life of desire and action, it does not call for authority either, and it admits of purely contractual relations. Rather than a common good, it is the sum of particular goods that happen to be related to one another. The moneylender is looking for his own income and the handicraftsman is looking for his own

income; but their two particular goods are parts of a sum—
hence the partnership and the appearance of a common good.

It was often remarked that the expressions "the greatest
good of the greatest number" and "the general interest,"
which prevailed throughout the golden age of individualism,
designated a sum of individual goods rather than a common
good. Strikingly, the same age and the same schools of
thought cherished, in varying degree of radicalism, a contractual interpretation of the state or the ideal of a purely contractual society into which the state would have resolved.
This is perfectly logical. Let us say, to sum up, that the
ground for the constitution of a society is either the attainment of a common good or that of interdependent private
goods; in the first case there is need for authority; in the
second, contract suffices. Conversely, if a society needs authority (for essential reasons), it has a common good for its
ground, and if a society can afford to be purely contractual, it
has no other ground than the interdependence of private
goods.

The difficulties involved in the first statement ("that virtue
implies love for the common good . . .") concern general
treatises, most properly the treatise on moral virtues. Let us
merely remark that the principle of the primacy of the common good, often misunderstood or denied by the theorists of
ethics, has, in fact, an extraordinarily powerful hold on the
consciences of men. People of debased conduct and skeptical
judgment still find it natural to die for their country or for
such substitute for a country as a gang. And during the golden
age of individualism the conscience of men, in spite of what
the theorists had to say, often recognized the common good
and served it with devotion under such improper names as
"general interest" or "greatest good of the greatest number."

The second statement ("that the common good may be intended formally without being intended materially") ex-

presses a sheer fact and needs merely to be illustrated by examples. This has been done. An army officer, wholly dedicated to victory and determined to hold a certain position according to his orders, may not be intending the common good materially considered; he may not be intending what is actually required by the common good, for new circumstances may require evacuation and withdrawal. And the son of a murderer, himself a good citizen, wants the life of his father to be preserved, even though the common good may demand capital punishment.

The third statement ("that the virtue of the private person guarantees [only] the intention of the common good formally considered") signifies that failure to intend the common good materially considered is not necessarily traceable to lack of moral excellence. If what victory demands is evacuation and withdrawal, it is up to the high command to issue new orders; and it is up to the courts to see that society is protected by adequate punishment of crime. Any particular difficulty raised by this statement resolves into the difficulties pertaining to statement No. 4 ("that, in a material sense, particular persons and groups ought to intend particular goods"), which is the keystone of the whole theory.

Seemingly, all would be best if each member of a community intended the common good both in formal and in material fashion. Because of the limitations of men, a continual and unfailing adherence of everyone to what is actually demanded by the common good cannot be realized. But why should it not be desirable, if it were realizable? Why should it not be posited in the construct of an ideal community? Why not promoted, in so far as it is realizable, in our imperfect societies? The statement seems to put a restriction on love for the common good, as if too much of it might harm.

It is, indeed, harmful to ignore the laws of the one and the many. These laws are independent of human deficiencies and

transcend human affairs; they are metaphysical. Goodness implies unity, but the notion of unity, as divided into "unity of
the individual" and "unity of the multitude," involves an
order of anteriority and posteriority. The unity of a properly
unified multitude is less of a unity than the unity of an individual. The degree of unity that a multitude admits of is the
same thing as the kind of unity that it calls for. Although
unity is an absolute perfection, there can be too much of it,
inasmuch as, beyond a certain measure, the inappropriate
kind forcibly displaces the proper one and destruction results.
Such is the meaning of Aristotle's celebrated objections to the
communism of Plato.[22]

22. Aristotle refers to *Rep*. iv. 423E; v. 457C and 462–64. Here is the latter passage
(trans. Jowett):

"Shall we try to find a common basis by asking of ourselves what ought to be the
chief aim of the legislator in making laws and in the organization of a State,—what is
the greatest good, and what is the greatest evil, and then consider whether our previous
description has the stamp of the good or of the evil?

"By all means.

"Can there be any greater evil than discord and distraction and plurality where
unity ought to reign? or any greater good than the bond of unity?

"There cannot.

"And there is unity where there is community of pleasures and pains—where all
the citizens are glad or grieved on the same occasions of joy and sorrow?

"No doubt.

"Yes; and where there is no common but only private feeling a State is disorganized
—when you have one half of the world triumphing and the other plunged in grief at
the same events happening to the city or the citizens?

"Certainly.

"Such differences commonly originate in a disagreement about the use of the terms
'mine' and 'not mine,' 'his' and 'not his.'

"Exactly so.

"And is not that the best-ordered State in which the greatest number of persons
apply the terms 'mine' and 'not mine' in the same way to the same thing?

"Quite true.

"Or that again which most nearly approaches to the condition of the individual—
as in the body, when but a finger of one of us is hurt, the whole frame, drawn towards
the soul as a center and forming one kingdom under the ruling power therein, feels the
hurt and sympathizes all together with the part affected, and we say that the man has
a pain in his finger; and the same expression is used about any other part of the body,

It is very easy to see how uniformity can do violence to the nature of multitude and cause waste. The systematic extinction of qualitative diversity impairs the very kind of plenitude that it is the metaphysical function of the many to achieve; and if the purpose is to effect the highest degree of unity, a multitude, no matter how subjected to uniformity, is bound to remain second to individuality, that is, one man would be nearer to the goal than any commonwealth, even though it be made of puppets all carved and dressed after the same pattern. At this point, the statement under discussion acquires a new clarity, for we come to recognize in it a particular case of a familiar, altogether congenial, and almost uncontroverted formula. Imagine a multitude in which all intend the common good, materially as well as formally, and refrain from intending any particular good, even though in merely material fashion; this multitude has accomplished thorough

which has a sensation of pain at suffering and of pleasure at the alleviation of suffering.

"Very true, he replied; and I agree with you that in the best-ordered State there is the nearest approach to this common feeling which you describe.

"Then when any one of the citizens experiences any good or evil, the whole State will make his case their own, and will either rejoice or sorrow with him?

"Yes, he said, that is what will happen in a well-ordered State. . . .

"But would any of our guardians think or speak of any other guardian as a stranger?

"Certainly he would not; for every one whom they meet will be regarded by them either as a brother or a sister, or father or mother, or son or daughter, or as the child or parent of those who are thus connected with him. . . ."

Here is the main part of Aristotle's discussion (*Pol.* 2. 2. 1261a10, trans. Jowett): "There are many difficulties in the community of women. And the principle on which Socrates rests the necessity of such an institution evidently is not established by his arguments. Further, as a means to the end which he ascribes to the state, the scheme, taken literally, is impracticable, and how we are to interpret it is nowhere precisely stated. I am speaking of the premiss from which the argument of Socrates proceeds, 'that the greater the unity of the State the better.' Is it not obvious that a state may at length attain such a degree of unity as to be no longer a state? since the nature of a state is to be a plurality, and in tending to greater unity, from being a state, it becomes a family, and from being a family, an individual; for the family may be said to be more one than the state, and the individual than the family. So that we ought not to attain this greatest unity even if we could, for it would be the destruction of the state."

uniformity. Its uniformity is the most radical of all and comprises virtually all kinds of uniformity. Behind the uniformity resulting from rationalized industry and mass production, qualitative diversity survives, so long as my heart is filled with love for persons of unique significance; but suppose that, through a skilful arrangement of society, no woman is more of a wife to me than any other woman, no old man is known to have the distinction of being my father, no man is known to be more of a brother to me than any other man, and no boy is known to be more of a son to me than any other boy; permanent grounds for the love of the particular are destroyed. A man may happen to have a special affection for a certain old man, but the common good has a monopoly on permanent grounds for love and devotion. In the order of final causality, the common alone stands; the particular no longer plays the part of a cause. Its causal power has disappeared into the causal power of the whole. But the end is the form of the will; in so far as the whole alone retains the character of an end, only one form is left for all wills.

The construct of a society in which the common good is intended materially by all results from an accident in the treatment of the subordination of causes. When the supremacy of a subordinating cause, its uniqueness, and the unutterable qualitative distance which separates it from the subordinated causes are keenly realized, the metaphysical intellect happens, not infrequently, to lose its balance. An exalted vision of the subordinating cause brings about, after the fashion of a by-product, the impairment and, as a limit, the annihilation of the subordinated causes. In not a few systems of metaphysics or theology, God alone is the genuinely efficient cause, and his sovereign power confronts a universe deprived of causality, of life, of liberty, and perhaps of reality. Contrasting with this picture of a waste land, the God of the living, who does not need to lay things waste in order to assert his power, is

powerful enough to cause every thing and every act and every
modality of every act in a world whose law is one of plenitude
and superabundance, in a world full of reality, of autonomy,
of activity, of life, and of liberty.

A society in which none intends, even materially, a particular good is like a dead world. Would such destructions serve
any purpose? Far from being genuinely exalted, the common
good has become a mere appearance. Common good cannot
exist unless it does exist as the good of a multitude; but there
is no good "of a multitude" unless particular goods are intended by particular appetites and taken care of by particular
agents. The laws of distinction inside the multiple were ignored; confusion ended in destruction.

The *Republic* of Plato supplies a clear pattern of institutions
designed to keep down to a minimum all interest in particular
goods. On the other hand, Plato perceives with unique keen-
ness the need for distinction in society. The meaning of this
contrast can be explained by considering that there are two
ways in which a good can be particular: (1) particular, as opposed to common, qualifies the good whose subject is but a
part of society; (2) particular, as opposed to "over-all" or
"whole" or "general"—we do not have very good words to
express these important concepts—qualifies the good which is
but a part or an aspect of the common good, although its subject is not a part but the whole of society. Referring to the examples described above, let it be said that the welfare of a
family, as distinct from the welfare of the state, has the character of a particular good in the first sense; that the objective
of an army unit (e.g., holding a strategic position), as distinct
from the objective of the whole army and of the nation at war
is likewise particular in the first sense; that the good pursued
by an ardent teacher of Latin is particular in the second sense
and—in case the latter example is not deemed clear enough—
that the objective of the director of public health is also partic-

ular in the second sense. Public health is obviously a good whose subject or beneficiary is the whole of society; but this good is not the whole of the common good, it is only an important part or aspect of it. In order to clarify our terminology, we shall, from now on, call "private" the good which is particular in the first sense, "special" the one particular in the second sense, and use the word "particular" itself only to express the likeness, the relative unity, of the "private" and the "special." A homestead owned by a farmer is particular as private; a function exercised by a public servant is particular as special: the terms "homestead" and "function" may be conveniently used as symbols of these two principles of distinction.

In order to remove confusion from their midst, most societies use both principles. Plato opposes the former, or at least opposes several important aspects of the former, and consequently is led to emphasize strongly the latter. That everyone should mind his own business is for him an intrinsic condition of justice; but, with regard to the way of establishing a clear distinction between the business of the one and the business of the other, he tends to rely exclusively upon the division of social labor into functions, as if the division of the land into homesteads should endanger the unity of the commonwealth.

If statement No. 4 is considered established, statements Nos. 5 ("that the intention of the common good, materially considered, is the business of a public reason and of a public will") and 6 ("that the intention of the common good, materially considered, demands the operation of authority") hardly call for elaboration. It is obvious that the common good has to be intended not only formally but also materially; if it is established that it should not be intended materially by particular persons, it follows that a nonparticular reason and will ought to be constituted; otherwise the common good, materially considered, would not be intended at all. But what relation will obtain between those in charge of the common good and those whose duty it is to intend, in a material sense, particular goods? Clearly, the very principle of the primacy of the common good demands that the intentions of the latter be subordinated to the intentions of the former. The primacy of the common good demands that those in charge of particular goods should obey those in charge of the common good. It is, in the last analysis, as simple as that. And let it be remarked, once more, that these propositions do not imply any definite stand concerning the creation of a distinct governing personnel. Those in charge of the common good and those in charge of particular goods may be distinct groups of persons—this is what happens in most cases; but the private persons who make up the multitude may all convene in a town meeting or Landgemeinschaft; they no longer are private persons, they are the public reason and will, endowed with the power to direct private persons toward the common good.

Throughout this inquiry into the intention of the common good, we have been referring both to the particularity of the homestead and to that of the function. Each kind of particularity suffices to make authority necessary. If the particularity of the homestead, i.e., particularity by way of privateness, were done away with—as in a thoroughly Communist society —the particularity of the function, i.e., particularity by way of specialty, would still, all by itself, render authority indispensable. Actually, experience does not suggest that the importance of authority declines when functional diversity stands as the only way to remove confusion from society. Authority is overwhelming in the *Republic* of Plato, and it is, to say the least, very strong in all communities which tend to do without the homestead as a factor of distinction. Considering, on the other hand, that diverse functions are, or may be, all relative to the common good, we come to understand that, with regard to the intention of the common good, authority is necessary on two grounds: (1) in order that there be intention of the common good materially considered and (2) in order that the common good materially considered be intended in its totality and according to all the relations of priority and posteriority, pre-eminence and subordination, that its integrality requires. Consider, for instance, the various great administrations which constitute the permanent structure of government in modern states: interior, treasury, foreign affairs, army, navy, agriculture, education. The men who make them up are adequately called "functionaries"; their tasks are directly related to the common good, none of them is supposed to labor for any private good, except in so far as he gets a recompense for services that are essentially public. If a cabinet is needed, on top of these administrations, it is not precisely in order that private agents should be directed toward the public welfare; the agents are already public, they are, by occupation, servants of society, and, in so far as they behave ethically, none of their activities during working hours is related to private purposes. In line with the hypothesis needed in this search for the essential, let us assume, comic though it may sound, that these functionaries are all perfectly competent and thoroughly disinterested. Under such an assumption it is not precisely in order that they be watched, stirred to action, kept from doing harm, encouraged, and punished that a cabinet is needed. Yet, although public administrations are, by essence, relative to the common good, as distinct from the private good, and even though we suppose the administrators to be free from private concern, the sheer fact that each administration has a *special* task to fulfil makes it necessary that there be, on top of all departments, a nondepartmental agent, a nonspecialized agent, or, if this expression is clearer, an agent specialized in having the point of view of the *entire* common good prevailing over any special angle.

Thus the proposition that authority is necessary to the intention of the common good has a double meaning. It means, first, that authority is necessary in order for private persons to be directed toward the common good; it means, second, that authority is necessary in order for functional processes, each of which regards some aspect of the common good, to be directed toward the whole of the common good.

Of the three functions of authority that we have surveyed, the first is substitutional, the second is essential, and the third deserves to be termed "most essential," since it concerns the most fundamental act of social life. In a society composed exclusively of clever, virtuous, and fully mature persons, authority would have no paternal duty to exercise; it would have to effect unity of action whenever the means to the common good is not uniquely determined; it would, above all and first of all, have to procure the intention of the common good. Considered in its essential functions, authority is neither a necessary evil nor a lesser good nor a lesser evil nor the consequence of any evil or deficiency—it is, like nature and society, unqualifiedly good.[23]

23. The essential functions of authority, as distinct from the functions made necessary by deficiencies, are referred to in the following texts:

In *Sum. theol.* i. 96. 4. Thomas Aquinas states the question *Whether in the state of innocence man would have been master over man?* Following a distinction made by Aristotle (*Pol.* 3. 6. 1278b33), he answers that the dominion of servitude, in which a man is governed for the private welfare of another man, would have been unknown in the state of innocence, but even that happy state would have known government for the sake of the governed and for the sake of the common good. "Mastership has a twofold meaning. First, it is opposed to slavery, in which sense a master means one to whom another is subject as a slave. In another sense, mastership is referred in a general way to any kind of subject; and in this sense even he who has the office of governing and directing free men can be called a master. In the state of innocence man could have been a master of men, not in the former, but in the latter sense. This distinction is founded on the reason that a slave differs from a free man in that the latter *has the disposal of himself* [*liber est causa sui*], as is stated in the beginning of the *Metaphysics*, whereas a slave is ordered to another. And so, that man is master of another as his slave when he assigns the one, whose master he is, to his own—namely, the master's use. And since every man's proper good is desirable to himself, and consequently it is a grievous matter to

It is now possible to gather up the elements of an answer to the question of the state of affairs that lies at the origin of civil government. According to Tom Paine and not a few others,

---

anyone to yield to another what ought to be one's own, therefore such dominion implies of necessity a pain inflicted on the subject; and consequently in the state of innocence such a mastership would not have existed between man and man.

"But a man is the master of a free subject by directing him either towards his proper welfare, or to the common good. Such a mastership would have existed in the state of innocence between man and man, for two reasons. First, because man is naturally a social being, and so in the state of innocence he would have led a social life. Now a social life cannot exist among a number of people unless under the governance of one to look after the common good; for many, as such, seek many things, whereas one attends only to one. Hence the Philosopher says, in the beginning of the *Politics* [1. 2. 1254a28], that wherever many things are directed to one, we shall always find one at the head directing them. Secondly, if one man surpassed another in knowledge and justice, this would not have been fitting unless these gifts conduced to the benefit of others." Children are left out of the picture. (They certainly need paternal guidance even in the state of innocence.) Considering a community of adults free from evil, Aquinas shows that government is needed (*a*) for the direction of the community toward its common good —this covers the two functions which we described as essential; (*b*) in order that men who are free from evil, in other words, already good, should benefit by the excellence of the best among them. This refers to a function of authority not included in our analysis, a function which is neither substitutional, since the governed is supposed to be free from evil and even from deficiency, nor essential, since the common good is taken care of by another function; let it be called the "perfective" function of authority. Assuming that a community is made of people fully capable of self-government in the pursuit of their personal good; assuming that their direction toward the common good and the unity of their common action are assured by proper authority, it is still expedient that those who are less gifted—less intelligent, less experienced, less strong-willed, less virtuous—be guided by those who possess a more excellent degree of reason, will power, and virtue. This guidance is not absolutely indispensable as is that exercised over the child; it is not so cogently needed as is the power which directs society toward its common good and unifies its common action. It is not indispensable to the *esse* of the personal good or to that of the common good, but it is necessary to their *bene esse*. In fact, the psychology of those who are intelligently submitted to intelligent leadership shows that the good leader is appreciated not only for his ability to direct common action but also for inspirations by which everyone is inclined toward nobler ways of life. When the members of a community love their leader and are proud of him, their predominant feeling is that under him everyone becomes better—occupationally, socially, morally, humanly. In the relation of man to woman, Aquinas sees, over and above the need for direction toward the common good of the family and independently of all deficiencies, a case of perfective authority; see *Sum. theol.* 1. 92. 1 ad 2um, on the

[Footnote 23 continued on p. 61]

"Society is produced by our wants and government by our wickedness." Our central purpose has been to determine whether government is produced by our wickedness (more

[Footnote 23 continued from p. 60]

condition of woman in the state of innocence (Pegis translation, slightly modified): "Subjection is twofold. One is servile, by virtue of which a superior makes use of a subject for his own benefit; and this kind of subjection began after sin. There is another kind of subjection, which is called economic or civil, whereby the superior makes use of his subjects for their own benefit and good; and this kind of subjection existed even before sin. For the good of order would have been wanting in the human multitude if some were not governed by other wiser than themselves. So by such a kind of subjection woman is naturally subject to man, because in man the discernment of reason predominates. Nor is inequality among men excluded by the state of innocence, as we shall prove." Thus the analysis of the functions of authority set forth in this chapter does not claim to be complete; a complete list would comprise (1) the substitutional function exercised by authority in the order of theoretical truth (*magisterium*, "teaching authority"); (2) the substitutional function exercised by authority in the guidance of immature and deficient persons or societies toward their proper good (paternal authority); (3) the substitutional function exercised by authority in the unification of action for the common good when the means to the common good is uniquely determined (so that there *should* be unanimity); (4) the essential function exercised by authority in the unification of action for the common good when the means to the common good *is not* uniquely determined (so that there is no ground for unanimity); (5) the most essential function exercised by authority in the volition of the common good, and of the whole of the common good materially considered; (6) the perfective function exercised by authority for the improvement of people who are already good. (In my essay *Nature and Functions of Authority*, the most essential function of authority is not distinguished from No. 4. I wish to express my regrets for this major failure.)

In the opening chapter of the treatise *On the Governance of Rulers*, Aquinas leaves aside all substitutional and perfective functions of authority and delivers a straight exposition of its essential functions, without, however, distinguishing, as we did, between the problem of unity in the pursuit of the common good and the problem of the volition of the common good materially considered. *On the Governance of Rulers*, trans. Gerald B. Phelan (London and New York: Sheed & Ward, 1938), pp. 33 ff.: "But the light of reason is placed by nature in every man, to guide him in his acts towards his end. Were man intended to live alone, as many animals do, he would require no other guide to his end. Then would each man be a king unto himself, under God, the highest King, inasmuch as he would direct himself in his acts by the light of reason given him from on high.

"However, it is natural for man to be a social and political animal, to live in a group, even more so than all other animals, as the very needs of his nature indicate. . . .

[Footnote 23 continued on p. 62]

generally, by our deficiencies) or by our wants (more generally, by the tendencies of our nature). It has been established that authority, considered in its essential functions, is as natural as the association of men for a common good. Thus civil government is as natural as civil society if, and only if, a common good is the object of civil association. The only way

---

[Footnote 23 continued from p. 61]

"If, therefore, it is natural for man to live in the society of many, it is necessary that there exist among men some means by which the group may be governed. For where there are many men together, and each one is looking after his own interest, the group would be broken up and scattered unless there were also someone to take care of what appertains to the common weal. . . . With this in mind Solomon says (*Prov.* XI, 14): 'Where there is no governor, the people shall fall' " (p. 35).

"Indeed it is reasonable that this happen, for what is proper and what is common are not identical. Things differ by what is proper to each: they are united by what they have in common. For diversity of effects is due to diversity of causes. Consequently, there must exist something which impels towards the common good of the many, over and above that which impels towards the private good of each individual."

This very argumentation is used by Leo XIII in *Immortale Dei* (1885): "Man's natural instinct moves him to live in civil society, for he cannot, if dwelling apart, provide himself with the necessary requirements of life, nor procure the means of developing his mental and moral faculties. Hence it is divinely ordained that he should lead his life—be it family, social or civil—with his fellow-men, amongst whom alone his several wants can be adequately supplied. But as no society can hold together unless some one be over all, directing all to strive earnestly for the common good; every civilized community must have a ruling authority, and this authority, no less than society itself, has its source in nature, and has, consequently, God for its author. For God alone is the true and supreme Lord of the world."

Let us quote, lastly, a page where A. de Tocqueville shows rather clearly (in spite of his inadequate terminology) how the essence of authority can still be honored where there is systematic determination to ignore paternal authority, perfective authority, and natural inequality (*Democracy in America*, Part I, chap. v; trans. Henry Reeve [New York: P. F. Collier & Son, 1900], I, 63–64): "In the nations by which the sovereignty of the people is recognized every individual possesses an equal share of power, and participates alike in the government of the State. Every individual is, therefore, supposed to be as well informed, as virtuous, and as strong as any of his fellow-citizens. He obeys the government, not because he is inferior to the authorities which conduct it, or that he is less capable than his neighbor of governing himself, but because he acknowledges the utility of an association with his fellow-men and because he knows that no such association can exist without a regulating force. If he be a subject in all that concerns the mutual relations of citizens, he is free and responsible to God alone for all that concerns himself."

to escape the conclusion that civil government is produced "by our wants"—in other words, by the nature of things—would be to show that civil society has no common good for its object. The question boils down to this: Is it possible to conceive civil society after the fashion of a mere partnership, involving no common existence, no common life, no common love, and no common action?[24]

As recalled above, there has been, in some phase or phases of the adventurous history of liberal individualism, a tendency to substitute a sum of particular goods for the common good of civil society. No doubt, such a tendency could appear only in an environment saturated with the theory that government is evil, but in such environment it was bound to appear, even though, most of the time, in uncertain or disguised form; for, if government is evil by essence, the problem of evil is not solved until government is entirely eliminated. But it is not easy to ignore the connection between government and common good and the logic which demands that society be without a common good if it is to be without a government.

Let us assume, for the sake of greater precision, that what is in question is not civil society as such but its being a society relative to a common good, and let us further define civil society as the society within which all the tendencies of man, so far as temporal life is concerned, can normally find satisfaction. In order to determine the nature of the good that such a society proposes to procure, viz., whether it is a common good or a sum of particular goods, let us disengage, from typical examples, the distinguishing features of a society rela-

24. That not every society is a community is hinted at by Aristotle in relation to animal societies (*History of Animals* 1. 1. 488a7–10): "Sociable animals are those which all together accomplish a work that is one and common to all: this is not always the case with animals living in herds. Such sociable animals are man, the bee, the wasp, the ant, the crane."

tive to a common good. Then we shall see whether these features are recognizable in civil society as defined above.

As typical examples of societies relative to a common good let the football team, the team of workers, and the army be singled out. Let the contrasting example of the handicrafts-man and moneylender association be borne in mind. And, in order to simplify our vocabulary, let us call "community" the society which is relative to a common good; "mere partnership" the society which is not.

1. That the football team, the team of workers, and the army are communities is evidenced, first of all and most strik-ingly, by the fact that some transitive actions are traceable not to any particular individual but to the team or to the army. Such operations do not necessarily involve the actual participation of all; an act exercised by some remains the act of the whole if those who are actually engaged in action act as the organ of the whole. This is plainly what happens in the case of an attacking army: the attack is traceable to the army as to the cause of which it is the action; yet members of the army, possibly many, are waiting, watching, resting, healing their wounds, not attacking. In mere partnership each action is traceable to some partner, e.g., all the work is traceable to the handicraftsman and all the financing to the money-lender, none is traceable to the partnership itself.

2. The transitive actions of a community are prepared and intrinsically conditioned by immanent actions of knowledge and desire in which members commune. The members of a football team or of an orchestra always know very well why they are gathered together and always desire very ardently the attainment of the common objective. Members of a working group do not always understand very clearly what they are doing together and do not always desire ardently the effect of their common action. Members of an army are often unaware of the cause for which they are fighting. Such failures con-

stitute a telling counterproof, for, in so far as there is lack of knowledge or love with regard to the object of common action, the community is poorly integrated, incompletely constituted, and its efficiency is uncertain. Let it be noticed, further, that communion in immanent actions does not consist in the sheer fact that several know the same object and wish it to be brought about. Prisoners toiling in isolation would contribute to the production of a certain effect, would all know what this effect is, and would all desire its coming into existence without there being any communion among them. Communion implies, in addition to immanent acts relative to the same object, my knowing that the others know and desire the same object and want it to be effected by the action of our community. Communions in immanent actions make up the most profound part of social reality; theirs is a world of peace where ennui is impossible and where death itself can be sweet—there alone the individual is freed from solitude and anxiety. Mere partnership, on the other hand, does not do anything to put an end to the solitude of the partners. They may be better off as a result of their contract, but their contract will not relieve their lonesomeness. There is not, between them, any communion in an immanent action. It may be that in our time mere partnership plays too great a role in the life of men at work; according to certain criticisms, this would be a major cause of the anxiety prevalent in our societies.

3. Communications, as such, are merely interindividual processes. They obviously play an essential part in mere partnership. But in communities they assume a new character, inasmuch as they are calculated to produce communions and to entertain them. In the teams and in the army as well there is a constant exchange of signs, not all of which are words, whose purpose it is to cause in souls certain cognitions and certain emotions and awareness that the objects of these cognitions and emotions of mine are also objects for the cogni-

tions and emotions of my companions, superiors, and subordinates. Presiding over these communion-causing communications is one of the major tasks of a leader and a very precise test of his ability. A good leader sends the appropriate
messages—words, gestures, examples, silences—at the proper
time, this may be the easiest part of the job. It is more difficult
to obtain a steady flow of appropriate messages from his subordinates, and the most difficult and finest accomplishment
would be to assure the regular operation of communion-causing communications among equals, at all levels of the hierarchy.

To sum up: collective causality, communion in immanent
actions, and communion-causing communications are the criteria of the community as distinct from the mere partnership.

But who can fail to recognize these criteria in anything that
deserves in any degree the name of civil society? Directing attention to a few obvious facts should suffice to bring our inquiry to a firm conclusion. Under the first heading, i.e., effects
traceable to the civil multitude as to its proper cause, let us
mention the following: security against enemies, both foreign and domestic; binding commitments with foreign societies; over-all status of expansion, both within existing boundaries and toward new boundaries; over-all status of ownership,
of education, of temporal life in its relation to the spiritual.
Under the second heading (communion), refer to any aspect of
the feelings known as patriotism, loyalty, or allegiance to one's
country, especially as expressed in ceremonies whose purpose
it is to give the individual comfort and the community more
abundant life, by bringing civil communions to a high pitch
of intensity, e.g., military parades, inaugurations, national
funerals, the daily raising of the flag in the schoolyards of the
United States. Third heading: these ceremonies themselves are
perfect examples of communion-causing communications
proper to the civil society and of such a nature as to demon-

strate its being a community. To show how easily countless other examples could be found, let us merely mention the teaching of civics at school and such risky procedures as government-inspired propaganda.

Two further remarks are needed: (1) Among the above-described features, some would make no sense in a society free from evil (e.g., effecting security against the enemies of peace); but most would make sense and would assume a more intense significance in a society made of ideally perfect people (e.g., over-all status of temporal life in its relation to the spiritual, civic friendship, ceremonies). It is not because of evil in men but in spite of all evil and deficiencies that civil societies have the character of communities. (2) The expression "civil society" ought to be understood here in a broad sense, as admitting of a great variety of forms and dimensions; it covers the city-state of ancient Greece and sharply defined and highly centralized nation-states, such as modern France or modern Italy; it covers federal organizations which are essentially ambiguous, since, in certain respects, the civil society of which one is a member is a larger unit (federal union), while, in other respects, it is a smaller unit contained in the larger (canton, state). The defining feature of the civil society, viz., sufficiency with regard to temporal needs, suggests that no particular city, state, empire, or federation has ever possessed the character of civil society in absolute and unqualified fashion. In order to be complete and entirely actual, a civil society would have to be such that it should never be necessary to go abroad or to call for help from abroad, in order that a temporal need be satisfied. No civil organization has ever satisfied such requirements; but in a great number of cases all basic temporal needs found satisfaction habitually, if not always, within the borders of an organization which, accordingly, deserved to be called "civil" in a rather full, though not unqualified, sense. In our time, dependence upon things, persons, and social structures lying outside one's own state or federal nation has become such a common and important occurrence that it may be wondered whether any society smaller than the world has the character of a civil society, except in a strongly qualified sense. Such a situation raises the problem of the world-state but does not demonstrate its possibility, and much less its ability to solve issues that cannot wait more than a few years.

We propose to terminate this inquiry with remarks on the causes of the common belief that civil government is an evil, though a necessary one, or, at any rate, the consequence of a deficient state of affairs.

1. In the exercise of civil authority, abuse is frequent and frequently grave. Frequent abuse is not necessarily a sign of intrinsic evil, but there is always a temptation to apply indiscriminately the principle connecting frequency and nature and to attribute an ethically evil nature to that which occasions abuse in many cases. If the frequency of abuse should render the very essence of government suspicious, it would be only logical to consider suspicious, also, science and art and technique and business and play and love. In truth, the ratio of failures is extremely high in all domains of activity which require virtue as an intrinsic condition of success. In civil government difficulties are more serious than elsewhere, and failures often entail dreadful consequences. Over and above lucidity, it may take some fortitude to realize the excellent goodness, the reverence-inspiring sublimity, of this institution, civil government, in spite of the overwhelming weight of its failures and abuses.

2. Among the purposes that civil government actually serves, the most obvious and consequently the best known is the repression of evildoers. The power of unconditional coercion is often treated as the defining feature of the state. If it were, evil alone would cause the state to be necessary. But,

in fact, coercion is only one instrument of civil government; a great deal of civil direction is accomplished through another instrument, viz., persuasion, which would be the only instrument of government in a society of ideally perfect people.

Aristotle defined the state in terms of completeness and self-sufficiency, not in terms of coercion. It may therefore seem strange that Thomas Aquinas, an Aristotelian, should refer to the power of unconditional coercion in the very first phase of his attempt to explain the necessity of the state. But beginning with the most obvious feature of the thing to be investigated is common and sound Aristotelian method. It is, furthermore, perfectly understood that the most obvious is not always the most profound. In an incipient investigation the methodological problem is to determine what feature is going to supply the safest approach and lead the mind most certainly to the core of the subject. Now, among the things that the state does and that the family cannot do and that the state alone can do, there is one the necessity of which is apparent to everybody: it is the training of youngsters, "dissolute and prone to vice," who do not listen to paternal advice but need "to be restrained from evil by force and fear." Thus we come to posit the need of an organization capable of using force for the discipline of tough characters and for the peace of all. The next question will be: Granted that an organization endowed with the power of unconditional coercion is necessary, what is the essence of the organization which is going to exercise such a power? This question is answered in terms of completeness and self-sufficiency, not in terms of coercive power; then it is easy to show that the state would retain its essence if circumstances were so favorable as to rule out all coercive procedures and threats.

3. Besides the identification of civil government with coercion, two common accidents contribute to the belief that government would be unnecessary in a society made of perfect

people. The first consists in a failure to distinguish between the substitutional and the essential functions of authority; if all the functions of government are thought to be of the substitutional type, government is logically deemed to belong to the period of immaturity of societies. The second consists in construing the ends of civil government after the pattern of the dominion of servitude, in which the end of government lies in the private advantage of masters. Whether the dominion of servitude can ever be a lawful institution remains to be seen; but that civil government should be aimed at the private good of the governing persons, and yet remain civil, is out of the question. The relation to the common good pertains to civil government in such essential fashion that governing for a private good means the perversion of polity into tyranny.

Notice that in both cases confusion arises from a failure to realize that civil government is defined by a relation to a certain kind of common good. It is by accident that the state has to exercise tasks which, because they are relative to some private good, would be exercised by private agents if the private agents concerned were not deficient. There is, in this connection, a striking dissimilarity between the father and the state. Duties of substitutional authority are altogether accidental in the case of the state and entirely normal in the case of the father. By accident, the state is guardian of orphans and tutor of the illiterate. But it is not by accident that a father is in charge of immature persons over a number of years.

4. Finally, let us again call attention to the illusion that the good will of each, if it were complete and enlightened, would suffice to guarantee the intention of the common good. This illusion is stubborn because it is hard to master the operation of the principles which, at the bottom of the question, seem to conflict but actually condition and supplement each other. The common good demands that particular persons should do full justice to the goodness of the particular good;

but, if such is the case, an over-all direction toward the common good is necessary. Thus the most essential function of authority springs, in the last analysis, from the *autonomic* goodness of the particular good. The autonomy of the homestead and that of the function matter highly for the common good, but, without over-all government, these autonomies would mean the disintegration of society. Thus autonomy renders authority necessary and authority renders autonomy possible—this is what we find at the core of the most essential function of government.

CHAPTER II

DEMOCRATIC FREEDOM

❊

ABUSES in government are such a frequent and serious disorder that protection against them is a problem of major importance for every society. Solutions are conceivably two: misgovernment can be forestalled by the wisdom and justice of those who govern, and it can be held in check by the resistance of those who are governed. These methods, of course, are not exclusive of each other. But there are societies in which the resistance of the people to bad government is institutionally organized and societies in which it is not. Let the first situation be called a "political" system, the latter a "despotic" one.[1]

---

1. Aristotle *Pol.* 1. 5. 1254b2, trans. Ernest Barker: "Whatever may be said of inanimate things, it is certainly possible, as we have said, to observe in animate things —and to observe there first [with any certainty] the presence of a ruling authority, both of the sort exercised by a master over slaves [δεσποτική] and of the sort exercised by a statesman over fellow citizens [πολιτική]. The soul rules the body with the sort of authority of a master: mind rules the appetite with the sort of authority of a statesman or a monarch." Also 1. 7. 1255b15; 12. 1259a37; 13. 1260a7; 3. 4. 1277a33; 14. 1285–a22; 4. 4. 1292a4 (on democracy ruling despotically); 7. 2. 1324a35; 3. 1325a25. Thomas Aquinas *Com. on Pol.* 1, les. 3; *Sum. theol.* i. 81. 3, ad 2um, trans. A. C. Pegis: "As the Philosopher says [1254b2] *We observe in an animal a despotic and a politic principle; for the soul dominates the body by a despotic rule, but the intellect dominates the appetite by a politic and royal rule.* For that rule is called despotic whereby a man rules his slaves, who have not the means to resist in any way the orders of the one that commands them, since they have nothing of their own. But that rule is called politic and royal by which a man rules over free subjects, who, though subject to the government of the ruler, have nevertheless something of their own, by reason of which they can resist the orders of him who commands. And so, the soul is said to rule the body by a despotic rule, because the members of the body cannot in any way resist the sway of the soul, but at the soul's command both hand and foot, and whatever member is naturally moved by voluntary movement, are at once moved. But the intellect or reason is said to govern

72

In spite of most uncongenial connotations, a despotic system is not necessarily iniquitous. The idea of enlightened despotism, popular among eighteenth-century intellectuals, is not absurd, it is only disquieting and suspicious. One feels suspicious about whoever claims to know better than the people the ways and means to make the people happy. Yet, so far as vaccination was concerned, Catherine the Great was right; cases of smallpox would have been more numerous if an ignorant people had been provided with adequate means of resisting the will of its sovereign. Almost inevitably, institutions calculated to prevent government from misgoverning or

---

the irascible and concupiscible by a politic rule because the sensitive appetite has something of its own, by virtue whereof it can resist the commands of reason."

We are using the division of government into political and despotic in a sense somewhat different from Aristotle's. As can be seen from the above-quoted text, Aristotle's division is tripartite, viz., into *despotic* or, as Barker puts it "of the sort exercised by a master over slaves," *political* or "of the sort exercised by a statesman over fellow citizens," and royal [βασιλική]. The difference between the despotic and the royal seems to be this: the despotic rule is exercised (1) over an agent without any power of resistance, (2) for the sake of the master (*Pol.* 7. 2. 1324a35; 1324b2); the royal rule is exercised over an agent without any power of resistance, but for the sake of the governed rather than for the sake of the king (*Pol.* 1. 12. 1259b10, trans. Jowett: "The rule of a father over his children is royal, for he rules by virtue both of love and of the respect due to age, exercising a kind of royal power"). Thus the notion of despotic rule, in Aristotle, concerns both a certain way of acting (order of efficient causality) and a certain end. This twofold reference is probably implied by the usual sense of the word δεσπότης, which means primarily not "despot" but "master (of slaves)." The meaning of "despot" in modern languages, especially since the theory of enlightened despotism, suggests that the teleological reference should be left out. A despot is a man who rules over subjects devoid of means of resistance; his rule may be for his own sake or for the sake of the governed—in the latter case government is royal in the sense of Aristotle.

Jowett and most translators render πολιτική ἀρχή by "constitutional rule." If we prefer the word "political," it is mostly because a constitutional regime is generally understood to include democratic, or at least representative, institutions; in fact, it seems that a political regime, in the theory of Aristotle, is necessarily democratic to a degree. There would be no term in Aristotle to designate the abstract concept of a regime which, through methods which may or may not be democratic, gives the governed a legally defined power of resistance to arbitrary government. Such a term is precisely what we need. "Political" is the best available.

overgoverning happen also to hamper good government.
Consequently, many constitutions provide for the suspension
of regular means of resistance when circumstances call for
drastic efficiency.[2]

By calling "political" the system which gives the governed
a legal power of resistance, Aristotle implies that a community
governed despotically is not in a genuine sense a state or a city.
The citizen is a free man.[3] Now his freedom is twofold, and a
man can fall short of it in two ways. So far as the *ends* of action
are concerned, the free man is not subject to authority, except
for his own good and for the common good; the slave, on the
contrary, is governed in view of the private good of another
man;[4] he falls short of freedom by being subjected to aliena-

2. See Clinton L. Rossiter, *Constitutional Dictatorship* (Princeton: Princeton University Press, 1948).

3. *Pol.* 3. 1. 1275a22; 6. 1279a21, trans. Jowett: ". . . the state is a community of freemen [ἡ δὲ πόλις κοινωνία τῶν ἐλευθέρων ἐστίν]."

4. *Pol.* 3. 6. 1278b33, trans. Jowett: "The rule of a master, although the slave by nature and the master by nature have in reality the same interests, is nevertheless exercised primarily with a view to the interest of the master, but accidentally considers the slave, since, if the slave perish, the rule of the master perishes with him. On the other hand, the government of a wife and children and of a household, which we have called household management, is exercised in the first instance for the good of the governed or for the common good of both parties, but essentially for the good of the governed, as we see to be the case in medicine, gymnastic, and the arts in general, which are only accidentally concerned with the good of the artists themselves." Thomas Aquinas *Sum. theol.* i. 96. 4, trans. A. C. Pegis: "Mastership has a twofold meaning. First, it is opposed to slavery, in which sense a master means one to whom another is subject as a slave. In another sense, mastership is referred in a general way to any kind of subject; and in this sense even he who has the office of governing and directing free men can be called a master. In the state of innocence [i.e., the state endowed with supernatural and preternatural privileges in which man found himself prior to the original sin] man could have been a master of men, not in the former, but in the latter sense. The distinction is founded on the reason that a slave differs from a free man in that the latter *has the disposal of himself*, as is stated in the beginning of the *Metaphysics*, whereas a slave is ordered to another. And so, that man is master of another as his slave when he assigns the one, whose master he is, to his own—namely, the master's use. And since every man's proper good is desirable to himself, and consequently it is a grievous matter to anyone to yield to another what ought to be one's own, therefore such dominion implies of necessity a pain inflicted on the subject; and

tion or exploitation. So far as the *cause* of action is concerned, the free man retains, in his relation to authority, the character of an autonomous agent; the subject of despotism (as well as the slave) falls short of freedom by being passive and instrumental.

In order to understand the distinctive features of democratic freedom, it is important to realize that a political regime may be thoroughly nondemocratic. Consider the relation of the old aristocracies to their kings: prior to the era of absolutism, aristocracies possessed such powers of resistance that the authority of the king often became merely nominal; even at the height of absolutism the nobility retained a number of privileges and liberties that the despotisms of our time would not grant to anybody. Clearly, there is no democratic relation between the hereditary king and the hereditary aristocracy. A still more striking example is supplied by the organization of the church: it is a typical case of political system in the sense defined above; yet it is not, by any means, a democratic organization. Such democratic features as can be found in it— e.g., a high degree of equality of opportunity—can be found in despotic regimes as well. Substantially, the "political" character of the church government is assured by an elaborate system of legal formulas which define with precision the boundaries of all rights and faculties. By virtue of these formulas the autonomy of the inferior is as much of an institution as the authority of the superior. At all levels, autonomy is guaranteed by statutes.[5]

Democracy has ways of its own, distinct from the statute,

---

consequently in the state of innocence such a mastership would not have existed between man and man."

5. J. E. Acton, *The History of Freedom and Other Essays* (London: Macmillan & Co., Ltd., 1907), p. 192: "No human laws were ever devised which could so thoroughly succeed in making the arbitrary exercise of power impossible, as that prodigious system of canon law which is the ripe fruit of the experience and the inspiration of eighteen hundred years."

though by no means incompatible with it, of procuring the political condition. This it does or attempts to do by either of two methods or by a combination of the two. In direct democracy there is no distinct governing personnel; the people governs by majority rule. In representative or indirect democracy *the governing personnel is subjected to the control of the people through the procedure of periodical elections.* The first method is the more unqualifiedly democratic, but it requires exceptional circumstances. In terms of historical reality, "democracy" almost always designates a system in which the representative method predominates.

Let us carefully refrain from begging any question concerning the efficacy of these methods. Let us, in particular, put out of our minds the notion that a society provided with democratic guaranties should or could discard the guaranties of nondemocratic description which other societies value. All that is meant, at this point, is that, concerning resistance to abusive government, democracy has methods of its own.

True, the ambition of democracy, from the very start, goes beyond the establishment of a political regime. For government to be political, it suffices that the governed be possessed of a legally guaranteed right of resistance; now, democracy cannot undertake to accomplish that much without pledging itself to accomplish much more. Political organization circumscribes government activities and procures freedom from abuse, but it does not imply that the people should step into the field defined as that of the government. When the political idea assumes the democratic form, the people asserts, over and above its freedom *from* abusive power, its freedom *to* govern itself. Keeping the goverment confined within a definite field is no longer held sufficient; the government has been taken over by the people. Such is democratic freedom, the defining feature of democracy.

In the formulas just used, one term calls for elaboration.

What is meant by "people" when it is said that in a democracy the people either governs directly or exercises control over the governing personnel? The discussion of this question will be divided into three parts, the first relative to the franchise, the second to the role of the majority, the third to parties.

UNIVERSAL SUFFRAGE

During the first ages of modern democracies it was commonly held that electors ought to be a selected group. Sex, property, and education were the grounds on which their selection was effected. Gradually, property qualifications came to be considered iniquitous; literacy came to be taken for granted; the political equality of the sexes was proclaimed. Exceptions to the principle of universal suffrage, though still very numerous, have, in our time, the character of abnormalities, and they are procured in most cases by fraudulent means. The principle of universal suffrage has won an almost axiomatic position in the political conscience of peoples. Modern dictatorships do not even try to dispense with it; they rather keep it within the limits of a farcical procedure. This double-sided fact has a twofold signification. It means, for one thing, that universal suffrage cannot be suppressed without a risky struggle against the forces of history, and dictatorships are unwilling to take such a chance. It means, secondly and more importantly, that, taken by itself, universal suffrage does not constitute a sufficient guaranty of democratic freedom. More than once men determined to crush democracy understood that universal suffrage, under appropriate management, would be more of an ally than a threat. True, what they retained and used for their purposes was an ungenuine process; but it is of great relevance to notice that sometimes such ungenuine processes can be substituted for genuine ones with striking success. Even though an election or plebiscite is known to have been thoroughly engineered by the men in power, a

magical prestige attaches to a high ratio of "Yeas." The enemies of democracy who boast of the popular support allegedly
evidenced by such elections and plebiscites pay tribute to the
persistence of faith in universal suffrage. What would they be
bragging about, if universal suffrage were known to be sheer
deception, as they used to say? It seems that the principle of
universal suffrage must be numbered among those propositions
which, at a given moment of history, have got hold of the
human conscience and, from then on, never can be rejected,
though they may call for reinterpretation.

The stubborn assertion of the principle of universal suffrage
is the more remarkable, since it is made in the face of weighty
objections. Good government is the work of excellent wisdom; it demands unusual virtue, intelligence, some education,
a great deal of experience, and many other qualifications
which cannot be expected to be possessed by any great number
of men. Universal suffrage, by giving all a share in the control
of the government, makes it mandatory for every man to become a statesman. No wonder if most find themselves in no
position to discharge the responsibility laid upon them. The
effect is the prevalence, in all parts of society, of the dispositions which are known to characterize the tyrannical ruler—
frivolity, arbitrariness, the blindness of passion. During the
great crisis of democratic faith—say, from the end of the first
World War to the violent suppression of most European
democracies by the Nazis—a few schools of thought specialized in showing that every misfortune or catastrophe happening in public life was traceable to the basic corruption born
of universal suffrage; the arguments were, seemingly, very
logical; they were easy to shape and to follow, their influence
was huge. As a matter of fact, not a few persons were surprised to notice that the suppression of democracy was not as
much of a solution to the problem of evil as they had expected
it to be.

Criticism of democracy in the twentieth century has been constantly carried out in a context of pessimistic expressions. This can be readily understood, since modern democratic thought, in its early phases, bound up its destiny with the then popular belief in the shallowness of evil, the goodness of nature, the inescapability of progress, and the imminent triumph of the rational order in society. "Democratic faith," an expression still much in use, conveys a feeling of nostalgia for the good old days. The optimistic vindication of universal suffrage never went into a complete silence. It may once again play a role of major importance, as a result of a needed reaction against the so-called "pessimism" of our time—gruesome, atheistic, putrid, histrionic. This vindication admits of three forms—statistical, sociological, and romantic—which generally, though not necessarily, operate as components of a single influence.

The statistical form of democratic optimism generally uses a metaphysical springboard and an a priori argument. Man's nature is held to be good, and, from the goodness of human nature, it is inferred that evil is comparatively rare in human action. To intrust government to a small minority, e.g., a family, a caste, a gang, or a clique, is risky, for evil may have a selective affinity for this minority and saturate it, while remaining infrequent in mankind at large. To intrust government, or at least the control of the governing personnel, to the whole multitude of citizens is safe, because in a great multitude evil is unlikely to command a majority. Experience, so it seems, confirms this expectation; monstrous characters, as compared with decent people, are few, and if they are interested in politics they have little chance to have more than a small number of candidates elected. They may hold a few seats in parliament at the extremity of each wing, make a nuisance of themselves, and do some good occasionally, through criticisms that more moderate persons would hesitate to voice; so long as the great number run the elections, government will be in decent hands.

This argument is made of heterogeneous elements and calls for attentive analysis. Let it be granted that human nature (in spite of what we know, by revelation, about its early adventures) is basically good. (How could it not be? A nature cannot cease to be good without ceasing to be identical with itself.)[6] Now, from the intrinsic goodness of human nature, *nothing can be inferred concerning the relative frequency of good and evil in the use of human freedom.* Ontological optimism does not entail moral optimism. It certainly does not entail moral pessimism either. It does not procure even a suspicion of what the ratio of good and evil in human action may be.

But, as soon as the content of human nature is philosophically considered, pessimism colors a priori expectations. The analysis of human powers reveals the condition of extreme insecurity which is that of rational life in man. A high ratio of failures is likely. The issue is to be settled by experience, but extreme care is needed in the phrasing of the question that experience is supposed to settle.

Although moral goodness and badness admit of innumerable degrees, the division of men into the morally good and the morally bad makes sense. It may be difficult to say who is a good man, just as it happens to be hard to say who is a

6. Thomas Aquinas *On Evil* 16. 2; *Sum. theol.* i–ii. 85. 1 (*Whether sin diminishes the good of nature?*), trans. A. C. Pegis: "The good of nature is threefold. First, there are the principles of which nature is constituted, and the properties that flow from them, such as the powers of the soul, and so forth. Secondly, since man has from nature an inclination to virtue, as was stated above, this inclination to virtue is a good of nature. Thirdly, the gift of original justice, conferred on the whole human nature in the first man, may be called a good of nature.

"Accordingly, the first-mentioned good of nature is neither destroyed nor diminished by sin. The third good of nature was entirely destroyed through the sin of our first parent. But the second good of nature, viz., the natural inclination to virtue, is diminished by sin."

good musician; but, just as it is possible to define the good musician and often to recognize him, so it is possible to define and often to recognize the good man, i.e., the man who is good not (or not only) as a flute-player or as a shoemaker, etc., but, absolutely speaking, as a man. The definition of the good man is frightfully exacting, for goodness implies achievement, accomplishment, completeness, totality, integrality, plenitude; goodness demands much—in a way, it demands all—but evil consists in privation and is completely brought into existence by any privation. Thus health implies the good functioning of all organs, but the malfunctioning of one organ suffices to cause disease and death. One single vice causes a man to be bad; a man is not good unless he possesses all the virtues. The answer of experience is unmistakable: the least that can be said is that we have no experience of a world in which the ethically good outnumber the ethically bad.

Not a few critics of democracy hold that such dark data entail the condemnation of universal suffrage. Granted that evil in human action occurs in a majority of cases, is it not clear that the wrong candidate will be elected? But if this argument were correct, the failures of popular choice would be characterized by impressive regularity, which is not the case. It does happen, not so rarely, that the candidate elected is precisely the better or the best. Considering, further, that among leaders appointed by nondemocratic methods the ratio of bad choices is never negligible and often frightful, it can safely be said that the frequency of bad choice by universal suffrage is far from equaling the ratio of ethically bad men among the voters.

Many would say that the contrast between the good man and the bad man, though relevant from the viewpoint of the moralist, means nothing to politics. True, civil government cannot afford to demand much along the line of ethical perfection; whenever it crusades indiscriminately, it destroys little evil and much good. Yet its ethical ambitions are great, its ethical dynamism is sublime, since it tends to promote total morality in all citizens, including generations of the remote future.[7] The notion of the ethically good man, with all its absoluteness, gives a sense to this movement and makes it intelligible. The contrast between the good man and the bad man is fundamental for the statesman as well as for the moralist; but from the standpoint of civil society it is supplemented —I do not say superseded—by the contrast between those men who are acutely antisocial and those men who are not. The latter section comprises, in addition to virtuous people, a great many ethically deficient persons. In other words, civil society, though concerned with the promotion of total morality, is very particularly interested in defense against crime. Above all, it is interested in keeping criminals away from governing positions. The danger is not purely theoretical; at all times the presence of murderers, perjurers, thieves, and sadists in governments has been very frequent. There is something slightly ironical about the worries of antidemocratic moralists, who are so much afraid that, for lack of enlightenment and virtue, universal suffrage may not intrust power to the most able and virtuous hands; for history shows how frequently the worst members of a community—men guilty of crimes punishable by death—attained positions of high leadership through such nondemocratic processes as birth, appointment by supposedly wise persons, intrigue, corruption, gang action, and civil war.

    7. Aristotle *Ethics* 5. 2. 22, trans. W. D. Ross: ". . . for practically the majority of the acts commanded by the law are those which are prescribed from the point of view of virtue taken as a whole; for the law bids us practice every virtue and forbids us to practice any vice." Thomas Aquinas *Sum. theol.* i–ii. 92. 1, 3, trans. A. C. Pegis: ". . . all the objects of the virtues can be referred either to the private good of an individual or to the common good of the multitude. . . . But law, as was stated above, is ordained to the common good. Therefore, there is no virtue whose acts cannot be prescribed by the law. Nevertheless, human law does not prescribe concerning all the acts of every virtue, but only in regard to those that are ordainable to the common good."

Although most men fall short of moral goodness, statistical data are rather comforting if reference is made to the dreadful dangers of criminals in power. In most societies criminals are but a minority; under most circumstances most people dislike the idea of being ruled by them. Ordinary people are not bad enough to judge that murderers, perjurers, etc., would be congenial rulers, or they do not have the kind of vice or neurosis that would make for such perverse judgment. Notice that totalitarian parties, even after having cultivated in the youth, over a period of many years, the determination to commit crime for the sake of the party, do not expose themselves to the hazards of genuine elections by universal suffrage. Their pedagogy works marvels when there is a question of training an elite of criminals. It does not do so well with the people at large. In order to win over the complicity of the masses, parties dedicated to crime need to use shrewd methods, paramount among which is the instrumentality of honorable men. Suppose that the extermination of a race is being contemplated. Not many constituencies would give majorities to candidates proposing abruptly to murder six or seven million persons never declared guilty by any court. During the early phases, in which elections are not yet entirely meaningless, the hope of the murderers rests upon the action of moderate and respectable men who never dreamed of sending any women or children to gas chambers but feel obligated to demand a quota for the Jews in a number of occupations, their complete exclusion from government positions, etc. A movement aimed at crime would have no success with the people if it were not started under virtuous auspices. With the help of honorable men, almost anything can happen. The determination of the people to keep criminals away from power does not work indefectibly. It is likely not to work when criminals have won the complicity of respectable men. It works in most cases. This is what is left of statistical optimism when its mythological foundations are dispensed with. Once more, keeping criminals away from power most of the time is not a negligible achievement, for history shows how often societies have fallen short of this modest blessing in the designation of their governing personnel.

Democratic optimism assumes a sociological form inasmuch as the identification of the voters with society is considered a ground for trust in universal suffrage. The underlying theory can be analyzed into two main parts. First, it is held that a multitude, acting in its own capacity as a multitude, possesses powers of perception and righteous direction that no individual can possess. Then emphasis is laid upon the consideration that only in universal suffrage are leaders selected by the whole of society. In hereditary government they are designated not by society but by the physical accident of birth, in restricted vote by particular individuals who may not be, by any means, identifiable with society; only in universal suffrage does society designate its leaders.

Here, as in the case of statistical optimism, an element of mythological belief threatens to conceal or distort an important truth. Erecting society into a deity, supreme and incorruptible, is a universally human practice which admits of an astonishing variety of forms. This product of the mythopoetic faculty is most recognizable in historical narratives of the romantic period where the People (always capitalized) appears at the proper time to straighten things out and put mankind back on the track of progress. It is not so clearly recognizable, but it is no less real, when the Absolute Spirit (in the sense of Hegel) with which society is identified finds a hiding place in a perfectly positivistic system of expression.[8]

8. On this see the criticism of Durkheim by Georges Gurvitch, *Essais de sociologie* (Paris: Librairie du Recueil Sirey, 1938), pp. 115–69, esp. p. 165: "La théorie de la conscience collective de Durkheim vient ici directement rejoindre la religion du 'Grand Être de l'Humanité' d'Auguste Comte et la théorie de l'Esprit absolu se réalisant dans l'Esprit objectif de Hegel."

According to some modern schools of positivism, a judgment that fails to win general assent cannot be held true, nor can a judgment which does win consensus be held untrue. This sociological notion of truth is commonly interpreted in a purely pragmatic or utilitarian sense, as meaning that the human intellect is but a biological instrument, successful when it procures adaptation to environment, unsuccessful when it does not. Yet, beyond utilitarian attitudes, it is easy to recognize the powerful appeal of a philosophy which places in society and its legally constituted organs of expression the supreme authority in matters of truth as well as in matters of justice. Anxieties caused by the defectibility of the individual mind cease to be intolerably hard if it is always possible, ultimately, to transcend them by sharing in the social life of the intellect, mysteriously identified with the self-revelation of the Absolute Spirit.

In all its forms the deification of society is a metaphysical operation. No wonder that it haunts positivistic systems—these are desirable places of safety, for, as soon as the metaphysical character of this operation is exposed, its weakness is obvious. Remove the screens erected by positivistic terminology, and it is clear that human societies, as well as human individuals, belong to the world of contingency which is ours, and that their judgments are subject to error. The great hope of early positivism, viz., that secular society would take over the part which used to be that of the church, has never died out; it is no longer voiced in dogmatic language; it is safely protected by a pragmatic and sociological reinterpretation of truth.

Assuming that the metaphysical situation is cleared up, the next task is to ascertain the power of society with regard to the kind of questions submitted to universal vote. Some questions are such that an individual is in a better position than a group to solve them, and others are better solved by a group than by an individual. At the extreme point of practical thought, i.e., in immediate contact with action, the judgment of one is, all other things being equal, better than that of many. At the extreme opposite, i.e., in the earliest phases of preparation for action, the co-operation of many is most obviously needed.[9] Deliberation and execution are the best available expressions to designate these contrasting phases of practical thought. Such contrast admits of a large amount of relativity, for it is often possible to distinguish, within a single phase, prior steps of deliberation and posterior steps of execution. With due allowance for this relativity, let it be said that in the phase of execution, considered as such, the intervention of many is unwanted; but in the phase of deliberation the multitude enjoys distinguished power. Let a line terminated on the right-hand side by an arrow symbolize the movement of practical thought, from the earliest phase of deliberation to the last executive proposition. The farther to the left an operation takes place, the more indicated it is that it should be performed by many. The farther to the right it takes place, the more indicated it is that it should be performed by few or by one. Most constitutions give the power of making laws to large assemblies but give that of issuing decrees to a small group or to one person; this is perfectly intelligible, since a law has the character of a premise rather than that of a conclusion, whereas a decree has the character of a conclusion rather than that of a premise.

Consider, now, the questions submitted to universal vote in common democratic practice; they all seem to belong, though in varying degree, to what can be called the "phase of deliberation." Roughly, the functions of universal suffrage comprise (1) the election of executive officers, (2) the election of assemblies whose main duties are (a) to make laws and (b) to control the executive power. Of these operations, the

9. On the faculties of the multitude the basic document is *Pol.* 3. 11.

closest to execution is the election of executive officers; yet it retains the character of a step prior to execution. The closest to the first principles of deliberation is the election of legislators; being a step prior to the making of laws, it is a step prior to a step still concerned with the premises of practical reasoning. In fact, the election of legislators is, of all political functions, the last to be taken away from the people. Dictators hesitate to confiscate it openly, for it requires too obviously the kind of contribution that a multitude alone can give.

That the multitude in charge of selecting the governing personnel should comprise all citizens follows from the nature of political society. Other societies are built on the basis of exclusive membership; not so the state, which is, by essence, the concern of all. Let it be granted, however, that under certain circumstances the genuine life of the city is better expressed by restricted than by universal vote—this happens as a result of such abnormalities as widespread ignorance, dictatorial power wielded over the masses by local chieftains, etc. Such situations are not so rare in our time; in the history of mankind considered as a whole their frequency is such as to conceal their purely accidental character.

To sum up: the sociological component of democratic optimism expresses truth, inasmuch as it asserts that the designation of political leaders normally belongs not to any individual person but to society. Again it expresses truth, inasmuch as it asserts that the participation of all in political elections is a normal condition for the integrally political character of elections. The qualification needed concerns situations in which the suffrage of all is, by accident, incapable of exercising its normal function as expression of the entire life of the community.

Assuming that a given situation comprises no particular obstacle to selection by universal vote, two conditions still have to be satisfied for the sociological character of this procedure to operate as a guaranty of service to the public welfare.

1. A multiplicity of individual acts does not necessarily add up to a social act. The act of casting a ballot can be repeated by many without the electoral result having the character of an effect traceable to the distinct reality and causality of the social whole as such. Many individual acts of voting constitute parts of a social fact, but the spiritual link, to be supplied by community life, may be missing. It would be of great interest and utility to investigate the circumstances and factors which cause an election to fall short of the social character needed for its full meaning. Roughly, whenever the maturation of the elector has taken place in individualistic isolation, the election is likely to be a multiplicity of individual acts rather than a social act. A society in which there is little traditional life, where young people are brought up in ignorance of their country's history, where local communities—those which are in immediate contact with personal life—have little influence on the shaping of character, where most human relations are controlled by economic self-interest, lacks, on election day, the guaranty that social causality may provide. The electoral result is not bound to be disastrous, but it is only by sheer luck that it happens to serve the common welfare, for, according to the nature of things and under normal circumstances, electing leaders is an act of common life.

2. Further, some collective or social processes are of such nature that their influence on an election would be detrimental or disastrous. Such are all sorts of mob phenomena. An election determined by collective hysteria is certainly a sociological result, an effect of collective life; yet it has little chance of being a wise election. A mob can be heroic, and there are moments of history in which what is needed is the heroism of the mob; but the thing that mobs cannot produce except by very rare accident is wisdom, and wisdom is what is principal-

ly needed for good elections. As the principal mob processes capable of having an impact on elections, let us mention fear, hatred, and enthusiasm. Elections are not indicated when such feelings are intense in the people. An election may be the work of social insanity—for there is such a thing—rather than that of social wisdom. Here is the weak point of socio-logical optimism: electors can be turned into a mob, and a mob can elect a Führer.

For lack of a better expression, we call the *romantic* compo-nent of democratic optimism the view that the more primitive part of society, which is also the larger, possesses, by virtue of its very primitiveness, some sort of superior wisdom. As is known, this view plays an important part in Rousseau, in the ideology on which the French Revolution throve, and in the Romantic movement in general. Accustomed as we are to scoff at romantic attitudes, we are not much aware of the operation of romantic primitivism in our own conceptions. Yet few men, today as well as in earlier ages, are entirely free from the postu-lation that soundness and virtue are principally found where the native hue of resolution is least sicklied o'er with the pale cast of thought. Think of our reactions to the calamities of the last decade; our burden would have been too heavy had we not assumed, though perhaps silently, that the great mon-strosities that we were witnessing were entirely traceable to distinguished men and that underneath corrupt aristocrats, debased intellectuals, pitiable victims of illusory virtues, robber-barons, plebeians-in-chief, etc., there remained the good people, misled into crime but free from criminal disposi-tions and invulnerable to the diabolic pedagogy of its masters. Who has never dreamed of the forces of evil being definitively curbed by the liquidation of some upper class, and of the liberation of the treasures of humanity—kindness, sound in-stincts, etc.— contained in the thick mass of the unsophisticated people? Such views are common among revolutionists and not foreign to conservatives: witness the willingness of the latter, in our time, to believe that the Russian people, in spite of thirty-three years of Bolshevik pedagogy, have retained all the virtues, including religion, that they are supposed to have traditionally possessed.

The legacy of the eighteenth century, in this connection, is ambiguous: one tradition depicts the ignorant barbarian as kindhearted and generous; another holds that good manners, the exacting laws of civilized conversation, the development of aesthetic taste, love for poetry and music produce abhorrence for the sight of human blood and an exquisite sensitiveness which renders crime repugnant and in the long run should make it impossible.

One thing can be held, at once, for certain: either of these views is unwarranted and misleading if it is asserted on principle and in systematic fashion. Not experience but our wish prompts us to assign either part of society as the main dwelling place of evil. True, realizing the presence of evil and its magnitude in our immediate neighborhood and in our own heart is often too much for our nerves; so we relegate evil, or the major part of it, into the social section that we suppose to be farthest away from our own selves. Let such wishful thinking be brushed aside and our minds be open to the full reality of the bad inclinations which are or may be particularly frequent in any part of society. The whole question is whether there attaches to primitiveness or, more precisely, to the kind of primitiveness found in the so-called "lower classes" of our societies any positive quality which may act, through universal suffrage, for the public welfare. The question is obscure, and it is not certain that questions of that kind admit of perfectly definite answers.

The great calamities of the twentieth century gave the few moralists who care for such interesting topics many opportunities to verify the old, but never popular, remark that men of refined culture are capable of distinguished cruelty. It would be arbitrary to suppose that the cruelty of the cultured person is worse than that of the barbarian, but it seems that the cultured person has his own way of being inhuman. The relevant thing would be to identify the distinct kind of inhumanity which seems to be conditioned by culture. As a first step toward such identification, let it be remarked that cultural refinement often favors the construction of patterns greatly at variance with existing reality and a feeling that these patterns ought to be realized regardless of the destruction that their realization may imply. Jointly, cultural refinement tends to dull emotions related to the preservation of existence. Anybody can dream of a utopian world, but intellectuals are particularly well prepared to envisage, in practical fashion, the sharp conflict with the forces of history, the awe-inspiring mutilations that have to be consented to if utopia ever is to assume real existence. The sentiment of awe is inseparable from a sense of mystery; but sophistication often suppresses the feeling that things are mysterious. Awe dries up and is replaced by eagerness to experience in the real world those things which were contemplated in the light air of rational speculation. A new sense for the absolute develops, but its object is man-made. Among the things to be crushed, the first is pity.

When idealistic absolutism combines with faith in a dogma, it is called "fanaticism." Not so long ago, say, until about the beginning of this century, it was rather commonly believed that fanaticism was what causes man to feel ruthless toward his fellow-men; it was hoped, accordingly, that the end of dogmas would be a decisive step in the conquest of cruelty. Agnosticism was considered the essence of humanitarianism. This is one of the ideological constructs which were dealt fatal blows by the two world wars and by the revolutions and repressions of our century. In times of social and political convulsions, a skeptical thinker, an agnostic intellectual, may reveal that his sense for the absolute, diverted from being by idealism, rendered acute by culture, and frustrated by doubt, has grown into a destructive frenzy.

Such perversions are unlikely to develop in people whose minds cannot afford to wander away from the real. A worker entertains such a relation to nature that all cheating in his calculations is inescapably punished by the operation of natural energies. Workers are possessed of occupational guaranties of loyalty to the real; for intellectuals, on the other hand, corruption by the ideal is an occupational risk. It may be illegitimate to assert anything over and above these propositions indicative of general tendencies. Should it be inferred that the influence of working people, who compose the majority in most elections, definitely favors the respect of human substance in government practices? It would probably be more accurate to say that their influence contributes to holding in check, when needed, the sort of destructiveness proper to the intelligentsia. Let there be no question of underrating the importance of this contribution; yet we are far from the romantic picture of the low strata of society as an inexhaustible storehouse of brotherly love. If other aspects of the people's primitiveness were analyzed, conclusions would not be more definite. Suppose that, instead of contrasting the refined culture of the upper class—or of part of it—with the lack of refinement in the great number, we should contrast the effects of poverty on the great number with those of wealth on the happy few. Since wealth is known to bring about corruption, it would be pleasant to imagine that wherever poverty prevails the mores are pure; but we know that this is not true. It can be safely said that the influence of the poor is likely to oppose the particular kind of corruption which thrives on wealth; such a conclusion is not devoid of significance, but it is devoid of glamour.

Thus in each component of democratic optimism we found a glamorous element of myth and a significant, though modest, element of truth. Modern criticism has exploded the myths, and in the resulting confusion the elements of truth have been lost sight of. Contrary to a common opinion, democracy does not necessarily require an optimistic vision of man; but it certainly requires the understanding of those genuine insights which combined with myths in the historical accident describable as democratic optimism. Enemies of democracy are greatly interested in maintaining the belief that nothing remains alive underneath the wreckage of the myths.

Strikingly, the criticism of democratic optimism, in spite of the pessimistic language in which it is couched, is often associated with a naïvely optimistic disposition. In social mythology the cheerful picture of the virtuous people is balanced by the description of the propertied class as an elite dedicated to lofty pursuits—above all, to the disinterested service of society. In this connection, also, the catastrophes of the twentieth century have proved instructive. They have taught us a great deal about the weak points of the upper class: the lack of realism, the hedonistic isolation from common suffering and common anxiety, the lack of a sense of history and the meaning of the present, frivolity and conceit, a readiness to make alliances with the worst elements of the rabble. Germany was delivered to Hitler by Franz von Papen— this will not be effaced from the pages of history. Most shocking of all was the realization that men describable as virtuous could become the accomplices of atrocious crimes in such a cloud of confusion that nobody knew—not even those involved—whether they were victims of monstrous illusions or had actually surrendered to evil. Together with a few progressive myths, this essentially conservative myth of the upper class has been disposed of by horrid experience.

And yet it is true that in a group describable as the upper

part of society a comparatively high rate of excellence is found. Society endeavors to place able persons in leading positions; it does not always fail; in so far as its effort is not frustrated, the frequency of merit is greater in the upper class than elsewhere. Society is entitled to expect particular service of this section of its membership where the ratio of excellence is particularly high. By giving each citizen equal power in the decisive act of selecting the governing personnel, democracy seems to deprive excellence of the weight that it should possess in order for society to be properly served by its best members. Regardless of their good will and desire to serve, men of skill and men of wisdom are restricted by the equalitarian law which, on election day, holds their ballot equal to that of any person not legally declared insane or criminal.

For the sake of thoroughness, we propose to disregard the shortcomings of the upper class and to keep in mind its aspects of excellence alone. The reasoning just summed up involves the postulation that excellent persons are deprived of all distinguished influence by the sheer fact that, at the ballot boxes, they do not enjoy any distinction. This postulation is often unexpressed, perhaps for significant reasons.

Now the experience of modern democracy makes it abundantly clear that various kinds of excellent people, though curbed by an equalitarian rule on election day, possess distinguished means of influence. Of all excellences, the one which succeeds best, or at least most obviously, in holding in check the equalitarianism of universal vote is property. Wealthy citizens, even though they be not members of assemblies, possess, by the very fact of their wealth, such power that authorities often have a hard time keeping them under control.

What holds notoriously for wealth holds less conspicuously and perhaps less regularly for other sorts of excellence. Geniuses, in our time more than ever, wield considerable power without having to go through the technicality of election. Men of knowledge do not constitute an aristocratic body legally possessed of privileges; but, as experts and technicians, they hold key positions from which they often exercise secretly a sort of dictatorship. If their idealism and ambitions were not curbed by the nonexperts that universal suffrage designates, human substance would soon be subjected to the most daring experiments.

But what about the man whose distinction is neither money nor expertness but virtue? He possesses an unusual amount of what is most needed for good leadership and for the selection of good leaders. Is he given a chance to render excellent service?

Let it be noticed, first, that some forms of virtue do not constitute a particular qualification for political leadership and do not even provide any particular ability to choose political leaders. Genuine virtue necessarily contains the root of political wisdom, but, for lack of appropriate circumstances, political wisdom very often fails to develop out of genuine virtue. In these cases it is simply not desirable that the virtuous person should be given distinguished means of political influence. His very virtue inspires him with a desire to remain average as a citizen. When, on the other hand, virtue is of such character as to constitute a title to a distinguished role in the city, two cases are to be considered. Either the virtuous person is actually in a prominent position, or he is not. If he is not, no conceivable system of government has any definite method for the enhancement of his influence. The significant problem concerns the person who, as an effect of his virtue, actually occupies a prominent position. Examples would be: high positions in business, in industry, in public administration, in the medical profession, etc., not infrequently reward skill associated with such ethical dispositions as integrity, loyalty, temperance, devotion to the public welfare, sense of duty, or sense of mission. In this gathering of distinguished citizens, political virtue reaches a high degree of concentration. Universal suffrage gives each of them a power equal to that of anyone, which looks like a harmful waste. But, in the case of recognized virtue as well as in the cases of property and skill, excellence possesses distinguished power independently of electoral results. By hypothesis, we are concerned with men whose moral qualities have already been given social recognition. They were promoted to high positions. They already possess unusual means of influence. Men of excellent moral character do not indispensably need to be given special treatment on election day. If only their virtue is socially recognized, they already have a distinguished opportunity to serve; and if their virtue is not recognized, nothing can be done.

It thus seems that conservative worries about the waste caused by the equalitarian rule of universal suffrage are excessive. Should it be recalled that any voting procedure treats equally men who are inevitably unequal? Imagine a carefully selected and highly exclusive body of electors, such as can be found in aristocracies. These men are generally appointed for life. Almost inevitably, some are too old to enjoy the fulness of their mental powers. On the other hand, there is no reason why there should not be a genius among them. Thus equal votes will be given to men ranging all the way down from genius to feeble-mindedness. But here, as well as in democratic organizations, inequalities which do not find expression at the ballots find expression elsewhere.

It is commonly objected that universal suffrage establishes the dictatorship of a power blind and deaf, devoid of intelligence and morality, material and nonqualitative in character, viz., the power of numbers. True, from the fact that the electoral result is expressed by figures it cannot be inferred that qualities had nothing to do with its determination. Democracy is said not to work satisfactorily unless it actually promotes the soundest trends existing in society. If the people's control through election fails to let qualities play the leading part, the conclusion to be drawn is that the society under consideration is not fit for democratic government (which does not necessarily mean that another kind of government would do much better).

The power given to the great number is itself, under normal circumstances, a qualitative disposition of the first importance. It means that men devoid of the qualities sanctioned by definite social distinction will not be constitutionally helpless. The common man has neither the distinction of property nor that of expertness nor any of the distinctions on the ground of which a person belongs to the upper class; he will be crushed unless the constitution of society attaches some power to the only distinction that he certainly possesses, viz., that of having numbers on his side.

At the beginning of this century some interpreters of the revolutionary labor movement went over to the theory that political democracy is a treacherous instrument of bourgeois domination, skilfully calculated to give the working class an illusion of power and to dissolve its action into such fake procedures as campaigning and electioneering, which inescapably result in a parliamentary majority sold to the interests of capitalism. According to this school of thought, the labor movement should keep away from political democracy and rely merely on the action of its autonomous organizations. A paradoxical intensity of determination was attained when some particularly radical syndicalists made alliances, against democracy, with extreme conservatives.

These experiments took place at a time when democracy was not seriously threatened. One thing that modern dictatorships made unmistakable is this: when the liberties of labor organizations are not protected by political democracy, they are soon suppressed. There is no question, for the working man, of choosing between the autonomous action of labor and political democracy, for, without the latter, the former is jeopardized. Unless competing parties are interested in winning the vote of labor, unions will soon disappear into some monopolistic organization controlled in all significant respects by whatever class or party controls the state.

To conclude: we did find an element of truth in each of the components of democratic optimism. But the decisive argument in favor of universal suffrage, viz., the need for a distribution of power to those who enjoy no distinction apart from their having numbers on their side, is related to pessimism. Experience shows that the operation of elites is not reassuring for those who happen not to be included in any recognized elite. Even if it were possible to designate infallibly, through a process which would have to be magical, men perfectly qualified for government, it would still be a good precaution to erect, in front of such a chosen few, as a check and a complement, the power of numbers. An elite, even if we suppose it to be genuine, can hardly escape the all too human temptation to think in terms of the elite and to ignore the problems of the many. It was noted, at the beginning of this discussion, that the principle of universal suffrage seems to have been definitively incorporated into the political conscience of modern societies. This happened in the midst of vociferous and scornful opposition, armed with never negligible objections. What is it that ultimately assured the victory of universal suffrage, if not in institutional practice, at least in the political and legal conscience? Beyond doubt, it was principally the realization that the great number of men are too much at a disadvantage unless there is a specific allocation of power to the many. There was a time when it was possible to believe that the destiny of the common man was safely intrusted to the wisdom of the upper class. That time is gone, apparently, forever.

THE RULE OF THE MAJORITY

In the introduction to the present treatment of democratic freedom, democracy was described as a particular form of political regime, viz., the regime which attempts to realize the political idea by placing the governing personnel under the control of the governed. Whether the democratic procedure is successful or not in keeping government confined within proper limits is a question that we left out of this initial consideration. In fact, no objection to democracy is more common than this: democracy easily gives birth to a particularly formidable kind of tyranny, that of the majority. Men in power, if allowed to believe and to make others believe that theirs is the government of the people, are prone to consider that their actions are indefectibly related to the common welfare; in other words, democratic origin inspires the governing personnel with a ruthless reliance upon their own judgment. Further, majority support gives government a power greater and harder to check than almost any power held by a minority; this is why one-party organizations, aware of the precarious lot which would be theirs if they were delivered to the consequences of their oligarchical character, try so hard to give themselves the appearances of majority government.

The danger of oppression by the majority is so obvious that the history of modern democracy is haunted by the ambition of including the minority in the controlling electoral body. The method calculated to achieve such inclusion is known as "proportional representation."[10]

10. See F. A. Hermens, *Democracy or Anarchy? A Study of Proportional Representation* (Notre Dame, Ind.: Review of Politics, University of Notre Dame, 1941). Attention must be called, in particular, to the writer's keen discussion of the concept of representation (chap. i). There was a time when the duty of the parliament was to represent the people before a king and his ministers, in other words, before an *already constituted*

100 PHILOSOPHY OF DEMOCRATIC GOVERNMENT

This method admits of many varieties, and more are devised every day, or so the story goes. But the general idea is simple enough. Let the government be likened to a pie; we are three, they are two; in the majority system we get the whole pie, and they do not get anything. It is not fair; the pie should be divided into five parts; the majority should get three and the minority two. This demonstration of proportional representation was proposed by sincere supporters of the system and cannot be interpreted as a malevolent caricature. True, the comparison between the government and a pie conveys the disquieting impression that the competing parties intend to observe the laws of fair play in the division of coveted advantages—as if they were planning to raid the treasury. Prior to elections the political problem concerns the establishment of power; but the answer of the proportionalists concerns the distribution of the advantages that the possession of power is expected to yield. The upholders of proportional representation are so worried about justice in the actual opera-

---

power; under such circumstances it was possibly desirable that all sections of the people should be represented in proportion to their importance. The representative assembly, so conceived, is an institution external to the structure of government and designed (1) "to limit the power of the prince in order to save the people from executive encroachment—in particular, from excessive taxes"; (2) "to give expression to the wishes of the people and to rehearse their grievances to the government with the hope of securing some positive action of redress" (p. 5). The general framework is that of a nondemocratic polity; the field of government is understood not to belong to the people; the representative assembly is part of the structure built by the people in order to keep a nondemocratic government confined within what is considered its field; at most, this assembly will exercise influence, by way of wishes, in a field which does not belong to it. But in democracy the field of government is in the hands of the people, and it is up to them to preside over the *establishment of a governing power.* Hermens remarks that the constant disregard of the proportionalists for the requirements of this fundamental operation—the constitution of authority—is influenced by the use of the word "to represent" and its derivatives with respect to assemblies which do not find a readily constituted power before which they would represent the people but have to *be* the legislative branch of government and to bring into existence—and to keep in existence —its executive agencies.

tion of government that they want an idea relative to *distribution* to preside over the phase of *constitution*.

They claim to eliminate majority oppression and guarantee equitable government by including the minority in the governing personnel. No wonder that new methods of proportional representation are continually devised; for the whole system is made restless by the character of its ideal. Majority plus minority equals unanimity. Unanimity is known to be a precarious thing. Under the appearance of justice, proportional representation signifies permanent uncertainty.

It is hardly necessary to recall the conclusions of our preceding analysis of unanimity as a means of procuring united action. Under the ideal circumstances of a society made exclusively of enlightened and virtuous persons, unanimity can work in so far as the means to the common good is uniquely determined. When the means to the common good is not uniquely determined—as a matter of fact, it is never uniquely determined in all its particulars and modalities—unanimity cannot be achieved except by luck. With regard to political assemblies where ignorance and ill will are frequent, it should be said without any qualification that unanimity is a casual affair. In so far as an organization tends toward government by unanimity, it delivers itself to the uncertainties of chance occurrences.

Imagine an electoral body divided into six million liberals and four million conservatives. Suppose that the assembly, elected according to a system of strict proportional representation, comprises sixty liberals and forty conservatives. Suppose that the principle of the equitable division of the pie is observed in the constitution of the cabinet, made, accordingly, of six liberals and four conservatives. This is already a picture of weak government; further application of the principle of proportional representation would make it weaker. What about premiership? Either the premier will be a man of the majority—but this would set a restriction on the principle of proportional representation—or we have to imagine such a clumsy procedure as a rotating system giving the premiership to a liberal for six days and to a conservative for four days out of every ten. But the principle of proportional representation would not yet be thoroughly applied. What happens when there is a question of passing a measure on which the parties disagree? A parliament may be divided into sharply distinct party organizations; a government may be constituted by a coalition of parties; conceivably, the presidency can rotate; but a measure cannot be split. The only choice is this: unanimous action or no action at all. Now unanimous action has the character of a compromise. Proportional representation causes weakness wherever it does not cause inaction.

Does it follow that no concession should ever be made to the principle of proportional representation? A really poor system may happen to be the best under particular circumstances. It is up to the prudence of the statesman to determine whether the circumstances do or do not call for some skilful combination of the majority principle and the proportional representation principle. Unanimity is a most uncertain way of procuring united action; yet there are situations in which the constitution of authority is impossible, so that action has to be united by way of unanimity if it is to be united at all. Such has been the case, so far, with regard to the over-all strategy of war coalitions; such is the case in the Security Council of the United Nations. If procedures based upon unanimity happen, in a few cases, to be necessary, procedures that are related to unanimity without going so far as to imply it are likely to be necessary in less infrequent cases. But let it be kept in mind that any concession to a system which embodies a tendency toward government by unanimity means increased danger of weak and uncertain measures, compromise, deadlock. Some decisions are of such a nature as to demand a wide margin of popular support. The rule of the two-thirds majority for certain measures, e.g., the ratification of treaties, may have to be consented to; but special action will be needed to compensate for the danger of a stalemate that this rule implies.[11] As a preventive measure, proportional representation seems to enjoy a distinguished place among the means of restraining the majority. True, it asserts a principle of equitable distribution when the political process is still in the phase of constitution, as a result of which the benefit of a possible check on oppression by the majority is outweighed by the evils of weakness and confusion.

THE PARTY SYSTEM

How does the role played by party organizations in the selection of leaders square with the democratic concept of people? When a presidential election takes place, the nation designates not the man whom they think to be the most qualified in an absolute sense but the man whom they think to be the best or the better qualified among a very small number of already designated candidates. The choice of the electors is narrowly restricted by the antecedent choices of the parties. Critics of democracy revel in describing the people as a captive sovereign caught in a narrow circle drawn by organizations

11. *The Federalist*, No. 22 (Hamilton) (New York: P. F. Collier & Son, 1901), p. 114: "To give a minority a negative upon the majority (which is always the case where more than a majority is requisite to a decision) is, in its tendency, to subject the sense of the greater number to that of the lesser. Congress, from the non-attendance of a few States, have been frequently in the situation of a Polish Diet, where a single vote has been sufficient to put a stop to all their movements. A sixtieth part of the Union, which is about the proportion of Delaware and Rhode Island, has several times been able to oppose an entire bar to its operations. This is one of those refinements which, in practice, has an effect the reverse of what is expected from it in theory. The necessity of unanimity in public bodies, or of something approaching toward it, has been founded upon a supposition that it would contribute to security. But its real operation is to embarrass the administration, to destroy the energy of government, and to substitute the pleasure, caprice, or artifices of an insignificant, turbulent, or corrupt junto to the regular deliberations and decisions of a respectable majority."

and committees in which private persons play the leading parts.

Yet it cannot be taken for granted without further inquiry that political parties are private organizations. Rather, the truth seems to be that, in some cases and to some extent, they act as organs of the people, so that a preliminary choice made by parties may have the character of a choice by the people. The problem is to determine under what conditions and to what extent parties act as organs of the people.

A first condition concerns their historical significance. It happens that through the operation of routine-mindedness, obstinacy, inertia, etc., a nominating organization retains, as an irrational legacy of the past, an importance disproportionate to the actual weight of the ideas and interests that it represents. A party may become a sort of rotten borough. It also happens that under the impact of transient circumstances the influence of a party grows far beyond its significance in terms of lasting reality or falls far below it. When none of these accidents happens, when there is a proportion between the power of a party and the historical substance that it expresses, its nominations are genuinely, though not unqualifiedly, acts of the people. A clear example is supplied by the Conservative and Labor parties in Britain today. These great organizations participate so deeply in the community life of the British that men chosen by them are, in a very deep sense, choices of the people. The vote of the majority decides whether the prime minister will be Mr. Churchill or Mr. Attlee; but, even prior to their re-election as members of parliament, it can be said that the people have designated these men as leaders of the government and the opposition.

In order that parties should assume the character of organs of the people, it is essential that they be widely open and allow for a continual stream of influence from without. A party which is so anxious to preserve the purity and strict discipline of its members as to remain voluntarily a minority or even a small minority and which is governed by a small group of leaders never exposed to the risks of election has no part to play in a democracy; it has all the essential features of an organization calculated to foster oligarchy.

Concerning the number of parties—a question devoid of glamour but not of importance, for the sound operation and the very survival of democracy may depend on such trivial issues—let it first be stated that democracy excludes absolutely the one-party system. If this system occasionally seems compatible with some amount of democratic control, it is so only to the extent that competition inside the party brings about effects similar to those normally expected of duality or plurality of party organizations.

The recent trials of democracy in several great countries, especially Germany and France, called attention to the danger inherent in a multiplicity of parties. The Anglo-Saxon two-party system has demonstrated its value as a factor of clarity and stability in government. One of the recognized reasons why proportional representation causes precarious and weak governments is that it favors the multiplication of parties. However, it must be granted that there is something non-democratic about the extreme restriction imposed upon the elector's choice by the operation of only a few parties. Suppose that each of the existent parties identifies itself with some major trend in the nation's history, that it is widely open to influences from without, and that it is provided with a sound internal organization. Even under such favorable circumstances the operation of the party system, and especially that of the two-party system, implies that the choice of the people is, to a considerable extent, restricted by private influences—this is, plainly, a nondemocratic feature.

We are, thus, led to examine a problem of great amplitude, viz., whether democracy can tolerate the operation of non-democratic principles and possibly benefit by it. This question is commonly answered in the affirmative in so far as it applies to modern democratic monarchies. Although the king of Great Britain and the Scandinavian kings may do little governing, they certainly play a very important part in the political life of their kingdoms. No matter how democratically inclined they may feel, these hereditary presidents of democracies, by the very fact that they are designated not by election but by birth, are nondemocratic characters. Yet few supporters of democracy would wish monarchy to be suppressed in these countries. The almost unanimous opinion is that, under the circumstances, monarchy is useful in several respects—that it is useful, in particular, for the protection of democracy. It is easy to see that by accident (but such accidents are frequent) a nondemocratic principle may serve democracy by holding in check forces fatal to it. One recognized drawback of democratic institutions is that they may occasion sharp strife among parties or factions. When people are sufficiently exhausted by such strife, the situation is ripe for the one-party system and dictatorship. Accordingly, one major need of democracy is protection against the destructive effects of domestic conflicts. That such protection, under definite circumstances, should be best procured by such a nondemocratic factor as a hereditary monarch is perfectly intelligible.

The same reasoning applies to the nondemocratic features of the party system. Let it be granted that even under the best circumstances the restrictions imposed upon the elector's choice by the antecedent choice of the party are, to some extent, nondemocratic. This does not necessarily mean that such practice is harmful to democracy. It may help democracy if it holds in check forces designed to harm it.

True, the problem with which we are concerned here is not peculiar to democracy. Any regime, in order to work well or merely to survive, needs or may need the operation of principles distinct from, and opposed to, its own idea. Ancient

monarchies were kept in existence through extensive conces-
sions to the aristocratic principle, and, in modern times, association with rather radical democracy is the only thing
which proved capable of assuring the survival of monarchy.
At this point it is pertinent to refer to the theory of the
mixed regime, worked out, among others, by Aristotle and,
with greater clarity, by Thomas Aquinas. The best regime
cannot be any *simple* regime, such as monarchy, aristocracy, or
democracy; it is a regime in which several forms are combined
in such a way as to promote the various aspects of the common
good, to each of which each political form is related in special
fashion.[12] Modern democracies can be described as mixed

12. *Pol.* 2. 6. 1265b33, trans. Jowett: "Some, indeed, say that the best constitution
is a combination of all existing forms, and they praise the Lacedemonian because it is
made up of oligarchy, monarchy, and democracy, the king forming the monarchy, and
the council of elders the oligarchy, while the democratic element is represented by the
Ephors: for the Ephors are selected from the people." Thomas Aquinas *Sum. theol.* i–ii.
105. 1, trans. A. C. Pegis (the title of the article is *Whether the old law enjoined fitting
precepts concerning rulers?*): "Two points are to be observed concerning the right ordering
of rulers in a state or nation. One is that all should take some share in the government,
for this form of constitution ensures peace among the people, commends itself to all,
and is most enduring, as is stated in *Politics* 2 [6. 1270b17]. The other point is to be
observed in respect of the kinds of government, or the different ways in which the constitutions are established. For whereas these differ in kind, as the Philosopher states,
nevertheless, the first place is held by the *kingdom*, where the power of government is
vested in one, and *aristocracy*, which signifies government by the best, where the power
of government is vested in a few. Accordingly, the best form of government is in a state
or kingdom, wherein one is given the power to preside over all, while under him are
others having governing powers. And yet a government of this kind is shared by all,
both because all are eligible to govern, and because the rulers are chosen by all. For this
is the best form of polity, being partly kingdom, since there is one at the head of all;
partly aristocracy, in so far as a number of persons are set in authority; partly democracy, i.e., government by the people, in so far as the rulers can be chosen from the people, and the people have the right to choose their rulers. Such was the form of government established by the divine Law. For Moses and his successors governed the people
in such a way that each of them was ruler over all; so that there was a kind of kingdom.
Moreover, seventy-two men were chosen, who were elders in virtue, for it is written
(*Deut.* I, 15): *I took out of your tribes men wise and honorable, and appointed them rulers;* so
that there was an element of aristocracy. But it was a democratic government in so far
as the rulers were chosen from all the people, for it is written (*Exod.* XVIII, 21): *Provide*

regimes with a predominance of the democratic element (at least according to constitutional law; for, so far as actual practice is concerned, the oligarchic element predominates in some of them).

To sum up: the association of democracy with nondemocratic principles may be expedient or necessary in two senses: (*a*) from the standpoint of the *entirety* of the common good, which in most cases is served better by a balanced combination of forms than by the exclusive reign of one form, and (*b*) from the standpoint of democracy itself, which may be well served by a nondemocratic principle acting as a check on its enemies.

THE INSTRUMENTS OF GOVERNMENT

The common confusion of authority and coercion is easily accounted for by the consideration that authority is more strongly felt and in all respects more noticeable when it proceeds by way of coercion. Yet it is perfectly clear that coercion is merely one instrument of authority; another one is persuasion. When it uses persuasion, authority is less apparent; but, as it often happens, the less remarkable is also the more frequent and ultimately the more important. Persuasion suffices in the great majority of cases. Frequent use of coercion evidences weakness.

It is sometimes difficult to trace the border line between what is coercion and what is persuasion. Threats often act as factors of persuasion; consequently, whenever there is mere threat of coercion instead of actual coercion, authority acts through a process participating in the nature of both instru-

---

out of all the people wise men, etc.; and, again, in so far as they were chosen by the people. Hence it is written (*Deut.* I, 13): *Let me have from among you wise men,* etc. Consequently, it is evident that the ordering of the rulers was well provided for by the Law." A thorough exposition of Aquinas' theory of the mixed regime is found in the admirable book of Marcel Demongeot, *Le meilleur régime politique selon Saint Thomas* (Paris: André Blot, 1929).

ments. For most purposes it is indicated to treat mere threat as a variety of coercion.

Another difficulty arises from a resemblance between persuasion and a particular form of coercive procedure, viz., psychical coercion. This difficulty will be considered later. Here we need definitions clearly verified in typical cases.

Roughly, a man is subjected to coercion when power originating outside himself causes him to act or be acted upon against his inclination. Kidnaping and arrest are basic examples. Persuasion, on the other hand, is a moral process. To persuade a man is to awaken in him a voluntary inclination toward a certain course of action. Coercion conflicts with free choice; persuasion implies the operation of free choice. Between the two there is all the distance that lies between determination from within and determination from without, plus all the distance that lies between freedom and merely determinate causality. But in experience it is not always easy, or possible, to say whether a process is from within or from without, free or determinate.[13]

The right to use coercion is often regarded as the defining feature of the state. This view calls for specifications. Notice, first, that minor forms of coercion are by no means a state monopoly. A distinction of the state is that the gravity of the coercive measures which it uses is determined by none except itself; extreme forms, viz., life imprisonment or death, are not excluded.[14] Further, since the state is not a voluntary association from which members can withdraw, it is not possible to escape state coercion by resigning. These distinguishing aspects of state coercion are fittingly conveyed by the expression "unconditional coercion." Secondly and more importantly, let us note that the power of unconditional coercion cannot

13. On coercion as opposed both to natural spontaneity and to voluntariness see Aristotle *Ethics* 3. 1. 1110a1; Thomas Aquinas *Sum. theol.* i–ii. 6. 5.

14. Aquinas *Sum. theol.* ii–ii. 65. 2 ad 2.

conceivably constitute the essence of the state. It results from
this essence and presupposes it. It is not the constitutive characteristic of the state, but only one of its essential properties.[15]

The functions of state coercion occasion a controversy of
great significance for the whole of political philosophy. In the
opinion of most, all that state coercion can possibly effect is
the safety of honorable people against evildoers. The problem
is whether, in addition to such effect, state coercion has a
pedagogical function whose beneficiary would be the evildoer
himself. Aquinas describes with great clarity the pedagogical
theory of coercion: by compelling mischievous characters not
to commit the bad actions toward which their will is inclined,
society creates in them, in spite of their ill will, a system of
good habits. These good habits, which by hypothesis are
mere products of coercion and are not in any way animated by
virtue, have something to do with virtue, inasmuch as they
remove obstacles to it.[16] Proud thinkers enjoy emphasizing the

15. In the hypothesis of a people free from evil, many would grant that authority
remains necessary but would deny that there is room for such a thing as state organization, for they hold the concept of state not to be realized when there is no use for coercion. True, if the essence of the state is constituted not by the power of unconditional
coercion but by the completeness (within the temporal order) of the good that the state
tends to procure, the essence of the state is fully realized in an organization designed
to procure such complete good, whether coercive instruments are needed or not. Further, in a people free from evil the state would not be deprived of the right to use
coercion. It would have no use for coercion, which is an altogether different thing. In
the midst of universal innocence and enlightenment, it would remain an organization
of such nature as to possess a right to use coercion, if need be.

16. Thomas Aquinas *Com. on Ethics* i, les. 1; *Sum. theol.* i–ii. 95. 1, trans. A. C.
Pegis (the title of the article is *Whether it was useful for laws to be framed by men?*): "As
we have stated above, man has a natural aptitude for virtue; but the perfection of
virtue must be acquired by man by means of some kind of training. . . . Now it is
difficult to see how man could suffice for himself in the matter of this training, since the
perfection of virtue consists chiefly in withdrawing man from undue pleasures, to
which above all man is inclined, and especially the young, who are more capable of
being trained. Consequently a man needs to receive this training from another, whereby
to arrive at the perfection of virtue. And as to those young people who are inclined to
acts of virtue by their good natural disposition, or by custom, or rather by the gift
of God, paternal training suffices, which is by admonitions. But since some are found

"from withinness" of virtuous action and the radical inability of coercion, which proceeds from without, to cause virtue. Such rhetoric thrives on shallow psychology and incompetent analysis of causal notions. In the sense in which a bulldozer cannot build a house, coercion cannot cause virtuous action; but, just as a bulldozer can remove an obstacle which, if not removed, would make the building of a house impossible or very difficult, so coercion can remove dispositions and habits incompatible with virtue and substitute for them habits which make the acquisition of virtue and its steady practice relatively easy. When coercion has succeeded in destroying such inclinations as extreme laziness, intemperance, and violent anger, no element of virtue has been brought into existence, but virtuous acts are much less difficult to elicit. Thus, to the question whether coercion causes virtue (a question generally asked with an accent of silly irony) it should be answered that it does, by acting not as an essential cause but as a remover of the obstacle (*removens prohibens*), a particular kind of incidental cause well known to philosophers and to men of common sense but not to proud thinkers.

It should be observed, further, that among the pedagogical effects of coercion some very important ones—probably the most important of all—are produced in entirely silent fashion. They concern not actual evildoers but decent people who never thought that they could commit a crime or a felony, yet these would become felons or criminals if they were not helped along the ways of good conduct by the ever present threat of

---

to be dissolute and prone to vice, and not easily amenable to words, it was necessary for such to be restrained from evil by force and fear, in order that, at least, they might desist from evil-doing, and leave others in peace, and that they themselves, by being habituated in this way, might be brought to do willingly what hitherto they did from fear, and thus become virtuous. Now this kind of training, which compels through fear of punishment, is the discipline of laws." On the relation between habit and virtuous voluntariness see Georges Desgrippes, *Études sur Pascal: De l'automatisme à la foi* (Paris: Téqui, 1935).

punishment in case of misbehavior. We know what happens to decent people when there is no more power to exercise the pedagogical tasks belonging to civil society. In wars and revolutions there are circumstances in which such outrages as theft, rape, and murder are sure to remain unpunished. Then many things happen which were believed impossible. Men who never stole a penny under normal circumstances send home heavy shipments of valuables; promiscuity prevails; instincts so perverse that one used to consider them rare accidents burst out where they were least expected ever to appear; only the strongest consciences—a small minority—resist the general trend. Few would be left if society did not soon resume its duty as a protector of conscience by associating the fear of punishment with the prospect of crime. Why are not these things clear to everybody? Why is there such widespread reluctance to acknowledge the service that coercion does to moral life? The answer seems to be that everybody would like to think that he and his peers, to say nothing of the rest of men, are so deeply established in virtue as not to need the additional help that coercion supplies. Nobody likes to grant that his good behavior is partly motivated by fear. Thus unwillingness to confess the extreme weakness of our nature gives birth to optimistic psychology. Another factor of illusion is the idea that virtue would not be genuine if fear had any part in its production—a view which proudly identifies virtue with the highest of its conditions and thereby ignores the law of development from the lower to the higher, which is that of all human perfection. Such association of optimism and purism is perhaps a characteristic of ethical idealism in modern times.

Concerning the relationship between coercion and violence, difficulties arise from lack of definiteness in the use of words. Yet it should be possible to work out precise definitions of these terms by considering the usages that present the strongest evidences of propriety. "Violence" is sometimes used as a synonym of "coercion." In this sense the arrest of a burglar by a police officer is an act of violence. Anybody can see that this is loose language, to be prohibited whenever scientific rigor is needed. Not the policeman, but the burglar, is violent. In fact, it is quite customary to designate by "violence" the unjust use of force. This would exclude as contradictory the concept of just violence. Yet this concept expresses distinct realities. Consider the entirely legitimate resistance of a private person to criminal abuse—is it not lawful violence? Shooting in legitimate defense is a just and violent means of protecting one's life. A war, no matter how just, is an act of violence, and so is a strike.

Thus violence does not coincide either with coercion in general or with unjust coercion. Plainly, it can be unjust, but it can also be just; its specific feature cannot imply determinately either justice or injustice. What is it, then, that distinguishes violence within the genus coercion?

The differentia of violence is best expressed in an entirely negative fashion: it consists in its not being the instrument of a man-made law. Such is the case with all abusive acts of force.[17] But such is also the case with just acts of force, like shooting in legitimate defense, a just war, or a just strike. The private person who fires a shot in order to protect his own life against a criminal acts, indeed, lawfully; yet he does not act in virtue of a commission given him by positive law and positive authority. What renders its action lawful is agreement with a merely natural law. The same consideration holds for a just war or a just strike.

On the other hand, the police officer who arrests an evildoer does not exercise violence. The force that he is using is

17. This proposition implies that a so-called "law," when it is abusive, is not genuinely a law. Force in the service of an ungenuine law is violence.

not only the instrument of natural righteousness but also an instrument of civil justice. A police officer, unlike the private person who, if no policeman was present, might have to elicit physically identical actions, acts by virtue of a commission received from a civil law and a civil authority. Think of the control of evildoers in the unsettled circumstances of the frontier. Evidently, it was not possible for honorable people to wait until regular police organizations and regular courts were established. Criminals had to be curbed without delay. The action of vigilantes was, no doubt, sometimes justified. But nobody would question that the substitution of regularly constituted police and courts for self-appointed or casually appointed guardians of life and property constituted indispensable progress in civilization. The word "civilization," so often used in loose ways, carries here a very precise sense which might well serve as a point of reference in our endeavors to ascertain what civilization basically means. The method of the vigilantes may be entirely just under the circumstances. No matter how just, it is not civilized, for its justification is effected directly by nature. Between nature and the private persons that have taken justice in their hands, no city stands as an intermediary. In civilization the righteous use of force derives its justification from nature through the city. There is this difference between the state of nature and the state of civilization that in the latter the demands of natural righteousness are not delivered to the interpretative whims of private persons; they are interpreted and directed toward their point of application by the wisdom of society. Circumstances which render violence necessary and just are primitive circumstances; all other things being equal, civilized circumstances are preferable. By unanimous agreement war is an uncivilized way of settling international disputes. If a time ever comes when military power is never needed except as the instrument of an organized human community, international relations, for the first time in history, will have assumed the form of civilization. It is clear also that compulsory arbitration is a method more civilized than the strike and the lockout.

This last example suggests the necessity of calling attention to a challenging accident. Labor sociologists generally hold that the procedure of compulsory arbitration should be avoided whenever it is not absolutely necessary, for experience shows that it increases the bitterness of labor conflicts. If this observation is accurate, it means that under certain circumstances the more civilized procedure may do less for peace than the more primitive one. This, of course, is mere accident, but the possibility and the conceivable frequency of such accidents should not be lost sight of.

Democracy is reputed to have a stand of its own regarding the two instruments of government—coercion and persuasion. It is said to favor persuasion in some special fashion. We propose to define the distinctly democratic part played by persuasion in the operation of political institutions.

1. According to a vague theory widely used for rhetorical purposes, coercion conflicts with the very essence of democracy. If this theory were formulated with precision, it would mean that democratic government should not use coercion at all.[18] Referring to the first chapter of this book, let us recall that what renders coercion necessary never has the character of an essential feature or factor, it is always some deficiency. In a community of ideally virtuous and enlightened people, government would be necessary, but not coercive procedure, for all would let themselves be persuaded that they ought to

18. *The Federalist*, No. 28 (Hamilton) (New York: P. F. Collier & Son, 1901), p. 144: "Our own experience has corroborated the lessons taught by the examples of other nations . . . that the idea of governing at all times by the simple force of law (which we have been told is the only admissible principle of republican government) has no place but in the reveries of those political doctors whose sagacity disdains the admonitions of experimental instruction."

follow the course of action prescribed by the government, even though another course of action might seem preferable to some. From the consideration that what renders coercion necessary is but an accident, we are tempted to derive the hope that coercion may one day fall into disuse. Here is the sort of fallacy in which the spirit of utopia is unmistakably recognized. Every utopia ignores some important aspect of history; this is why the realization of a utopia, when possible at all, costs a great deal of historical substance. In extreme cases utopia ignores contingency so completely as to suppose that whatever is devoid of essential necessity is also necessarily devoid of factual necessity and under appropriate management will disappear factually. The utopian element of Marxism discloses itself with striking naïveté in the celebrated page where Lenin speaks of coercion becoming unnecessary as a result of the good habits of social behavior contracted by everybody during the transitional period of proletarian dictatorship and terrorism.[19] The least that can be said is that the picture of such a faultless society does not have the slightest foundation in experience; in terms of practical thought, it does not possess even a shadow of reality. Further, any understanding of the conditions in which human freedom does exist evidences the inevitability of a large amount of evil in human society. No matter how impressive its scientific apparatus, a theory implying that a great number of men would act steadily in enlightened and virtuous fashion is to be dismissed as wishful thinking.

What moves many minds to indulge in such fancies is the vague belief that coercion is ethically evil. But, if this were the case, coercion should never be used, no matter how dire the threat to property, life, honor, and society. In truth, what is evil is not coercion but the state of affairs which ren-

19. V. I. Lenin, *The State and Revolution* (*Selected Works* [New York: International Publishers, 1935–38], VII, 93–94).

ders persuasion insufficient. Within such a state of affairs coercion is the lawful means to these worthy results—the security of honest people, the improvement of the guilty, the preservation and strengthening of precarious virtue in the wretchedly weak characters who make up the overwhelming majority of men.

2. It goes without saying that, whenever persuasion suffices, the use of coercion is unqualifiedly unlawful. At every particular moment there is, for a government, an upper limit to the effects that can be obtained through persuasion; beyond that limit coercion is necessary and good. But through education and improved organization it is always possible to push further up—though perhaps very slowly—the limit of what persuasion can effect. A steady determination to get the best out of persuasion may cause revolutionary changes; however, there is nothing specifically democratic about such a determination, for it is strictly required by justice in all systems of government.

3. It is often said that the toleration of violence is essentially undemocratic. It would be more appropriate to say that it is essentially unpolitical or uncivilized. Not to possess a monopoly on all major forms of coercion is no less a failure for a monarchy than for a democratic government. It is plainly the duty of every government not only to suppress unjust violence but also to foster circumstances under which no recourse to violence is justified.

4. The distinctive role played by persuasion in democracy follows from the implications of the elective method.[20] For the sake of clarity, let us assume that every political ruler, even though not elected, needs the consent of the governed to be confirmed in power. In the case of the hereditary king, this consent is normally expressed by the mere absence of opposi-

20. What is said in reference to elections and indirect democracy can easily be applied to plebiscites and other forms of direct democracy.

tion. Since, according to the institution of monarchy, it is up to the hazard of birth to designate the ruler, the burden of the proof rests not on those who maintain that the eldest son of the late king should rule but rather on whoever maintains that he should not. If there are no such obstacles as mental deficiency or extremely debased personality, succession in power is taken for granted. Its being taken for granted is precisely the sort of consent expected in nonelective government. It is only in case of strong opposition to the person designated by the law of hereditary succession that confirmation requires deliberation, inquiry, controversy, and a process of persuasion. Whenever such trouble takes place, the principle of hereditary succession undergoes a disquieting setback.

In an elective organization, designation is normally preceded by a process calculated to bring about the persuasion of the voter. If the electoral body is very small and composed of high-ranking people, usage may require the voter to shape his decision in solitude and without the help of any rhetoric; but this is a very exceptional situation. As a rule, a political election presupposes a political campaign. If the election is democratic, the process of persuasion preparatory to it concerns all the adult population; hence it has to be open and public.[21]

Thus the relation of democracy to persuasion can be described in three steps: (1) as a lawful and political regime, democracy systematically prefers persuasion to coercion and endlessly struggles to extend the domain of government by

21. Understandably, a feature required by a regime in which all are voters is also required in regimes of restricted franchise if the voting group (whether it be a majority or not) comprises a great number of persons. The democratic connection between open discussion and lawful designation is asserted by oligarchies in so far as the relatively great number of voters causes them to resemble democracies in some ways. Even when they were sharp in their opposition to democracy, bourgeois oligarchies of the nineteenth century needed this democratic feature—the open discussion of policies and persons—and occasionally they did not hesitate to release the energies of democracy in order to wrest it from a monarch and an aristocracy. Think of the Revolution of July, 1930, in Paris.

persuasion (which is not at all the same thing as to cherish the illusion that state coercion can ever fall into disuse); (2) as an elective regime, democracy rules that persuasion shall play a decisive role in the designation of the governing personnel; and (3) as democracy, it rules that attempts at persuading the voter shall take place in open and public discussion. Moreover, every democratic organization, no matter how large the part played in it by representation, retains (as we shall see in a later part of this book) some features of direct democracy. In so far as government is exercised directly by the people, i.e., without the intervention of a distinct governing personnel, what holds for the designation of rulers holds also for the exercise of government. Consider the case of a law submitted to referendum; it is passed or rejected according as its promoters have or have not succeeded in persuading the voters, and the vote, in democratic law, is held null and void if any of the contending parties was refused a chance to advertise its stand and to try its rhetoric.

The fact of great significance is that any system of designation which demands open discussion also demands freedom of expression. This is the proper angle from which to consider the relation between liberalism and democracy. Historically the two are often connected and not rarely disconnected. History knows of liberal democracies, of liberal and antidemocratic oligarchies, of democracies which were liberal in principle but not in fact, and of democracies which were extremely antiliberal both in fact and in principle (the last situation is best exemplified by Puritan rule in New England). We propose to inquire into the relation between democracy and liberalism considered as political essences.

A definition of democracy was proposed in the first chapter. As to liberalism, no more is needed here than a broad characterization in terms of tendencies. (Parenthetically, such a characterization is likely to express much more genuinely than a formal definition an entity like liberalism, which cannot be fully disengaged from the contingencies of history.) Let us describe, with regard to a few typical instances, contrasting attitudes, in one of which the spirit of liberalism is plainly recognizable.

1. Prices can be fixed by decree according to some sort of over-all plan; their determination may also result from multiple operations performed by buyers and sellers, all of whom are concerned with their own profits. Both methods are immensely older than the historical entity called "liberalism," and none of them belongs to liberalism in exclusive fashion. Yet it is obvious that the latter is, to say the least, the one that liberalism prefers.

2. Once upon a time it was held axiomatic that the only way to determine the proper rates of wages was to deliver the labor market to unchecked competition. True, wages happened to fall, not infrequently, well below the minimum necessary for biological survival. The closed-shop system, on the other hand, with all its disadvantages, makes for high wages. Although the liberal movement, in its early phases especially, was not short of generous men, the appalling poverty of the workingmen did not suffice to destroy, among liberals, the belief that, in the long run, all parts of society would draw the greatest benefit from a system which never forbade a worker to get hired for the highest wages obtainable under the circumstances.

3. Suppose that we are unanimous on such a subject as public decency; we still may disagree as to the best way to protect people against public expressions of immorality. Some think that motion pictures, magazines, etc., should be subjected to censorship, so as to forestall evil; others would rather recommend severe repression of actual felony; and others would maintain that the best method is to let everyone decide for himself what he is going to see or read. Liberals

hate the first method; they accept the second when the third does not seem to be practicable.

4. Suppose that we feel unanimously indignant at an abuse perpetrated by such a high-ranking person as, say, a general. Some would wish, nevertheless, that the case be smothered, even though this should mean freedom from punishment for the guilty one. Others think that abuse should be exposed and punished publicly. The former are afraid that crude acquaintance with their betters might jeopardize, in the mind of the people, respect for authority; others insist that the common man is too mature to be surprised by the revelation of human frailty in high places and so wise that his respect for authority will rather be increased by the realization that none can escape the rigor of law. The second attitude is that of the liberal, though not necessarily of liberals alone.

5. Suppose that we unanimously condemn the wilful murder of the innocent. We still may be divided as to how to deal with people who happen to think differently. Will they be allowed to conduct propaganda in favor of abortion and mercy-killing, or shall we demand of legislators that they promulgate an unmistakable definition of murder and punish ruthlessly whoever recommends acts falling under this definition? Some would say that, if the law permits the eulogy of certain kinds of murder, many people will soon be so confused as no longer to distinguish crimes, such as mercy killing, from the charitable actions called works of mercy. Others reply that silencing error never constituted an answer. The aim, so they say, is the eradication of error, which cannot be effected unless error is given a chance in open discussion; let it exhibit its true features, and minds will keep away from it. This is how liberals generally feel about freedom of expression.

In each of these instances the practice systematically preferred by liberals—let it be called the "liberal practice"—

happens to be supported by nonliberals or antiliberals under certain circumstances. One whose philosophy is entirely foreign to liberalism may well hold, within the framework of definite circumstances, that buyers and sellers ought to be trusted with the fixing of prices; that no pressure should be put on the labor market; that some amount of public immorality must be tolerated; etc. The thing that matters is the systematic character of one's preference, in other words, one's determination to favor a definite attitude by principle and without any need for a particular indication from the circumstances. A systematic tendency to adopt liberal attitudes evidences *the belief that the good of the social whole, or, as they generally put it, the greatest good of the greatest number, is best procured by the spontaneous operation of elementary energies.* This belief is characteristic of liberalism. Our problem is to determine whether democratic government is related to it in any essential fashion. Of course, we have principally in view liberal belief in matters of expression.

One thing is at once certain: democracy uncompromisingly demands whatever amount of free expression is needed for the process of electoral persuasion to be genuine. Consequently, any information that the people need in order to verify the trustworthiness of candidates will circulate freely; all facts and views relevant to the shaping of policies at the early stages of deliberation, when universal suffrage plays its part, will be subject to public discussion. But a great issue arises here, viz., whether the principles of political life should be delivered to controversy. By "principles" we understand, in the present connection, two sorts of propositions: (1) some propositions relative to the universal nature of society, which hold, in a variety of forms, for all societies and (2) propositions relative to the constant features and aspirations of a particular people or nation. That every citizen must enjoy guaranties against arbitrary arrest is a principle of the first description; that the federal Union of the American states is indivisible is a principle of the second description. In fact, democracy was often described by its adversaries as a regime entirely dedicated to the rationalistic examination and the never ending reconsideration of all principles; it is said, intelligibly enough, that restlessness plagues a society where this philosophic disposition prevails and that no organization can resist such pervading and radical power of destruction. Several democratic nations, in modern and recent times, went through endless periods of uncertainty. Our question is whether there is any necessary connection between such critical doubt and democracy.

One principle can be immediately asserted: there is an essence of the deliberative process which ought to be preserved under penalty of absurdity by all deliberative agencies. In essence, deliberation is about means and presupposes that the problem of ends has been settled. In the order of action, propositions relative to ends have the character of principles; they are anterior to deliberation and presupposed by it. The freedom of expression which is required by the democratic process of persuasion concerns all subjects that have the character of means and are matters of deliberation. Under fully normal circumstances the propositions relative to the very ends of social life are above deliberation in democracy as well as in any other system. Circumstances which make it necessary to deliver the principles of a society, its very soul, to the hazards of controversy are a fateful threat to any regime, democratic or not. A democracy may have to allow the questioning of the most indispensable principles, and such a necessity may be inflicted by the circumstances upon a nondemocratic government as well.

The free discussion postulated by the democratic process of persuasion would have no effect whatsoever on principles if it was always possible to distinguish clearly between that which has the character of an end (and should remain above deliberation) and that which has the character of means to be deliberated on. Obviously, such a distinction is uncertain and confused in many cases, and, whenever it is uncertain, the benefit of the doubt goes to freedom. In short, although the democratic freedom of discussion does not for any essential reason involve the first principles of political life, it inevitably entails what may be described as threatening digressions in their direction. Liberalism, understood with philosophic thoroughness, implies that principles themselves are thrown into the universal competition of opinions. Democracy does not imply liberalism, but it does demand a discussion of means freely conducted in all parts of society. In so far as it is impossible to trace a clear line between means to be deliberated on and ends or principles to be kept above deliberation, democracy implies a state of affairs in which accidents favorable to liberal attitudes and doctrines are likely to be more frequent than elsewhere. It would be inaccurate to speak of an essential connection between liberalism and democracy and equally inaccurate to deny that they are connected in some fashion. The connection between them is not an essential one; it is the kind that results from frequent relations of an incidental character. This frequency is not essential, but it has a foundation in essences. Preserving principles may be more difficult in a democracy than in nondemocratic societies. In democracy more than in any other regime it is a problem to assert principles in such a way as not to jeopardize the free discussion of means, and to insure free discussion of means without jeopardizing the principles without which social life no longer has end or form. The risks proper to democratic practice demand that the assertion of principles be more profound, more vital, and more heartfelt than elsewhere. Unless this assertion is embodied in the living essence of community life, it will be nonexistent.

Bureaucratic procedure cannot do a thing about it. A democratic society that loses its spirit is readily delivered to disintegration, for it no longer has any means of asserting its principles. The current objection which describes democracy as incapable of organization because it is continuously belabored by the restlessness of universal criticism holds for every democratic society that has lost its spirit. It is true that, to the forces of criticism inevitably released by the democratic process of persuasion, academic and bureaucratic statements of principles are no match.

In recent years the decline of the democratic spirit has occasioned the rise of a sort of coercion in which it is easy to recognize the most radical enemy of democracy. The best-known examples of coercion are physical processes, and, since it is sound method to use in the first place the best-known examples, all our references, so far, have been to physical processes. The time has come to consider the psychical forms of coercion. What distinguishes persuasion from coercion is not precisely the psychical nature of the former as opposed to the physical nature of the latter, but the essential part played in persuasion by the freedom of the subject on whom persuasion is exercised. When the means of influence operate determinately, there is necessitation from without, i.e., coercion, regardless of whether the means are physical or psychical. Great difficulties, however, result from the fact that psychical coercion often bears appearances which make it hardly distinguishable from persuasion.

Of all processes of psychical coercion, the clearest and those which it is fitting to use as points of reference are hypnotic and posthypnotic suggestions. It seems that contemporary research has disposed of popular beliefs concerning the extent of the power wielded by the operator. An order conflicting sharply with deep-rooted tendencies of the subject will not be carried out. This shows that the power of the operator is contained within rather narrow limits, but, within those limits, it plainly acts by way of coercion. Other facts of psychical coercion, more complex and more confused, have been known for generations to the students of mob psychology. More recently we have come to understand that propaganda, when carried beyond a certain point of intensity, becomes a process of psychical coercion.[22] Significantly, nobody can say where this point is found. Moderate propaganda is a process of persuasion. It is the normal instrument used by various parties in order to obtain votes for their candidates or for the measures that they recommend. A few speeches, a few leaflets, a few newspaper articles, balanced by speeches, leaflets, and articles in the other direction of about the same intensity and in about the same number, leave the voter free to form an opinion and to govern his action according to his prudence. But if propaganda is intense and succeeds in gaining a monopoly in a community, it is likely soon to become a process of coercion that can be likened to hypnotic suggestion in more than one respect. It can even do what hypnotic suggestion is declared unable to achieve, i.e., to drive habitually honest people to crime.

Propaganda built into a process of psychical coercion is an indispensable instrument of the totalitarian state. It replaces, in sufficiently disintegrated societies, the spirit of communal action, which holds the principles of social life above deliberation and criticism. Propaganda acting as psychical coercion and coupled with terrorism is the specific device of the totalitarian state in its self-given task of putting an end to the individualistic disintegration of societies. Propaganda, acting as psychical coercion, is also the most effective means used by the totalitarian party to come into power in apparently legal fashion. The big thing for such a party is to obtain a monopoly

22. See John W. Meaney, "Propaganda as Psychical Coercion," *Review of Politics*, January, 1951.

in some sections of society, no matter how restricted at the beginning. When propaganda is not checked by any contrary propaganda, it easily reaches the degree of intensity at which it no longer appeals to free choice but sets in motion determinate mental processes, as hypnotic suggestion does. The means of intensive propaganda supplied by modern techniques are a unique threat to the process of persuasion which is essential to democracy. Between moderate propaganda, which is a process of persuasion, and intensive propaganda, which is a process of psychical coercion, nobody can trace a clear line. The result is that psychical coercion, exercised by way of intensive propaganda, generally does not admit of legal identification. An election would be declared null and void if it was known that a considerable number of citizens has been subjected to violence or to the threat of violence. But no election was ever declared void because one party, through clever use of meetings, radio speeches, posters, leaflets, etc., succeeded in driving away from the mind of each voter all schemes of action except those favorable to the party. Of all conceivable forms of coercion, the only one which certainly conflicts with the essence of democracy is precisely the one which bears the greatest resemblance to the democratic process of persuasion. Thanks to such resemblance, it is sometimes possible to put an end to democratic control through operations which seem to be regular procedures of democratic control.

THE DEMOCRATIC TRANSFORMATION OF THE STATE

In the introduction to the present study democracy was described as a particular form of *political* government and a method of protection against government abuse. We now propose to examine the efficacy of this method. Modern democracies were brought into existence through victorious opposition to systems reputedly characterized by misgovernment and overgovernment. The blame of tyranny thrown at the old regimes concerned both wrong direction of government activity and the quantity of it. Democratic rule was expected to demonstrate its worth by refraining from any of the costly encroachments which aroused the people's anger against the kings. At the bottom of this early democratic hope we find the plausible argument that, since excess of government is painfully felt by the people, rulers subjected to periodical election cannot help governing as little as possible. Actually, over a long period, government did not make itself very noticeable in the daily life of most citizens in democratic America. On the other hand, French democracy soon gave birth to what was often described as the first embodiment of modern totalitarianism, i.e., the Jacobin rule.

At this point the notion of overgovernment needs to be elaborated. Let us keep in mind that, according to the beliefs commonly received in the early phase of modern democracy, government is bad whenever it is not strictly needed for survival, and perhaps even when it is strictly needed. Aversion to overgovernment was associated in the early democratic conscience with the dogma that government is no more than a necessary evil or, at best, the remedy for a deficient state of affairs. It is of decisive importance to determine whether the invalidation of this dogma leaves any ground for such aversion. Granted that government is necessary and good, independently of all deficiency, by virtue of the very nature of society, is there any ground for the proposition that government activity should be at all times kept down to a minimum, no matter whether circumstances demand that this minimum be high or that it be low?

The meaning of this problem can easily be specified through a simple example. A group of pioneers has settled in a valley. One purpose of this new community is to develop the valley into rich farm land. In the selection of the means, either one of the following arrangements may obtain: (1) The valley is owned collectively, and work is managed in a unitary fashion. Every decision of importance is made by the valley authority; if the system admitted of a thoroughly consistent realization, functions, teams, and persons would be mere instruments operated by the power of the community. (2) The valley is owned collectively, and all important decisions are made at the top of the organization; but, within the supreme agency, the heads of each function enjoy a large amount of initiative. The over-all directing board considers only the issues which cannot conceivably be settled within the limits of a particular function. (3) The valley is divided into fields, and each field is intrusted to an individual family, which exercises sovereignty within it, so far as family life and farming are concerned. Public utilities may be directly managed by the valley authority, but the spirit which produced private ownership of the land is likely to promote also a large amount of self-rule in the organization of each administrative department. The question under examination is this: Assuming that the various methods of management yield the same amount of crops, is there any definite reason to prefer management by the larger unit to management by the smaller unit?

The answer was foreshadowed in our inquiry into the most essential function of authority. Again, the reason why the direction of society toward the common good is not sufficiently effected by the enlightened good will of perfect citizens is that the particularization of interests, of activities, and of capacities is itself an element of the common good. The common good itself demands that not all interests, activities, and capacities should be common but that diversity should be produced in the two orders symbolized by the *function* and the *homestead*. The metaphysical law which demands such diversity demands also that no task which can be satisfactorily fulfilled by the smaller unit should ever be assumed by the larger unit. The principle of autonomy is implicitly asserted in the argument designed to establish the principle of authority.[23] It is perfectly obvious that there is more life and, unqualifiedly, greater perfection in a community all parts of which are full of initiative than in a community whose parts act merely as instruments transmitting the initiative of the whole. Abundance of life in all parts of the community is such an important phase of the common good that direct management by the whole is preferable only when the difference with regard to fulfilment of a task is very great. If, for instance, the exploitation of the valley under collective management means sufficiency for all and private exploitation causes general destitution, let the principle of better fulfilment prevail and management be collective. If, on the other hand, production is but slightly greater under collective management, let management be private, for a slight increase in production does not balance the loss which is suffered when men, instead of having affairs of their own to manage, on which to think and to deliberate with hope, with responsibility, with the dignity of initiative and choice, and with a continual urge to be alive, have but to take orders and carry them out in the management of common affairs.

Management by the smaller unit is often, but not always, the more efficient and the more orderly. Transfer of tasks from smaller to greater units is often indicated by the circumstances of modern economy. When such issues arise, it is of the utmost importance to remember that the values which concentration jeopardizes are among those which matter most for the fulness of rational life in persons and in the community. Any institution designed to centralize deliberation, decision, and command tends to bring subordinate persons down to the level

23. Leo XIII, *Rerum novarum:* "Let the State watch over these societies of citizens united together in the exercise of their right; but let it not thrust itself into their peculiar concerns and their organization, for things move and live by the soul within them, and they may be killed by the grasp of a hand from without."

of the slave, as described by Aristotle: he is an intelligent instrument, but his power of understanding hardly exceeds what is needed to grasp an order and to execute it.

Every power is exposed to the temptation of including in the domain that it directly rules things which might, without obvious disadvantage, be left out of it. In the government of a business enterprise and in any managerial office, those are declared excellent administrators who succeed in distributing functions to units and subunits in such a way as to retain only the over-all issues which do not admit of distribution. An organization enjoying such perfect order is really alive; waste is eliminated, and the highest authority has but to effect the direction of a life that is plentiful. One reason why good administrators are few is that the organization of autonomy demands the kind of effort that men fear most, i.e., the effort aimed at nondestructive simplicity. It is comparatively easy to struggle through long workdays with particular cases and minute details. It is also comparatively easy to simplify things by destroying a good part of their reality. But it is difficult to effect the kind of simplification which, under more rational, loftier forms, preserves everything and fosters a tendency toward plenitude; by virtue of such simplicity, authority is fully true to its essence and associates itself with autonomy in entirely normal fashion.[24]

The reluctance of men in power to foster or even to tolerate autonomy is known to be greatest when the power which they hold is that of the state. The history of all nations shows

24. Thomas Aquinas *Sum. theol.* i. 103. 6, trans. A. C. Pegis (title of the article: *Whether all things are immediately governed by God?*): ". . . since things which are governed should be brought to perfection by government, this government will be so much the better in the degree that the things governed are brought to perfection. Now it is a greater perfection for a thing to be good in itself and also the cause of goodness in others, than only to be good in itself. Therefore God so governs things that He makes some of them to be causes of others in government; as in the case of a teacher, who not only imparts knowledge to his pupils, but also makes some of them to be the teachers of others."

that states have a tendency to take over, whenever they can, functions that used to belong to smaller units of public administration, such as provinces or counties, or to private organizations, such as business enterprises, or to families, or to the church. Prior to the experience of modern democracy it could be considered with verisimilitude that state imperialism was a proper effect of monarchic or aristocratic government. Great hopes derived from the belief in the purification of the state by democratic control. Institutions calculated to hold in check the power of the state often are obstacles to efficiency and prove harmful in many respects; dispensing with them would be immeasurably beneficial if only the destructiveness of state imperialism was no longer to be feared. The argument used by Bossuet to vindicate the absolutism of the king got hold of the democratic conscience. The king, according to Bossuet, must be absolute, that is, free from bondage, because, if he is not, he cannot do the things that his function demands.[25] With regard to the possibility of abuse, Bossuet chooses the first of the conceivable solutions mentioned in the first lines of this chapter: "Misgovernment can either be forestalled by the enlightened wisdom of those who govern, or it can be held in check by the resistance of those who are governed." He trusts that the enlightened justice of the good kings will steadily outweigh the damage wrought by the bad ones. In the theory of the democratic transformation of the state, democracy is like the good king of Bossuet: enlightened and just, it can be trusted with means of action which could not be safely put in other hands.[26] But

25. Bossuet, *Politique tirée des propres paroles de l'Écriture Sainte*, Book IV, a. 1 (*Œuvres complètes* [Paris: Lefèvre & Didot, 1836], X, 347): "Without this absolute authority, he [the prince] can neither do the good, nor curb the evil: his power must be such that nobody may hope to escape it: and the only safeguard of particular persons, against public power, must be their innocence."

26. Élie Halévy, *Histoire du socialisme Européen* (Paris: Gallimard, 1948), p. 30 (the writer refers to the English radicals of the 1830's): "The old diffidence of the Whigs

Jacobin rule soon demonstrated that there is such a thing as a democratic absolutism. In so far as the old regimes were political organizations (even the power of Louis XIV was limited in many respects), there were some guaranties that the state would remain confined within the field delivered to its activities; the aristocracy and various autonomous organizations were particular about these guaranties. In democratic revolutions the people storms the field of government, after which institutions designed to keep the government within its field are sometimes allowed to decay; they are reputed no longer to be indispensable, since power is in the hands of an agent who, by a privilege that the king of Bossuet never possessed, can do no wrong.

With regard to this all-important issue of the democratic transformation of the state, much can be learned from Proudhon's attitude of relentless opposition to democracy. This attitude contains a paradox which is not completely explained by the consideration that, as an anarchist, Proudhon opposes all governments. For one thing, he is not an unqualified anarchist; in the last phase of his career the doctrine of anarchy matures into a system of federal government. Further, it is not only because the democratic state is a state that Proudhon treats it, according to the circumstances, with diffidence or with aversion. In spite of all that he has in common with the democratic movement, Proudhon has a very precise reason for criticizing democracy more than any other polity: in his judgment the belief in the democratic transformation of the state gives absolutism a particularly redoubtable chance.

In his early works Proudhon predicted and recommended the complete supersession of the state by the rational organization of economic relations. But toward the end of his career

---

toward the state was due to its aristocratic and oligarchic constitution; as soon as universal suffrage took it away from the hands of a caste, the radicals assumed that it could procure the interest of the greatest number."

he asserted that the state is indestructible, and his policies changed. A never ending struggle for the elimination of the state would be an absurd waste of energy. The real duty is to keep the state confined within the functions that belong to it irreducibly and to hold in check its always threatening tendency to trespass, to encroach, to invade, and to destroy. Although he no longer questions the everlasting necessity of the state, Proudhon continues to consider it with extreme diffidence. He is used to erecting human facts, when they prove strikingly permanent, into essential necessities; at least, he likes to speak the language of essential necessity whenever he deals with facts whose permanence is of great human significance. The state, accordingly, is described as possessed, on account of its very essence, with a tendency toward absolutism. What Proudhon means by this word resembles what we have come to know under the name of "totalitarianism," although he could not have had the slightest suspicion of the dimensions of crime in the totalitarian state. The tendency to monopolize, to effect direct management of an ever increasing multitude of functions, to assume continually increased powers, is not an accident connected with a particular form of government, such as hereditary monarchy; for every state, democratic or not, participates in the character of the prince and there is no withering-away of the state. The salvation of society depends on institutions provided with a power of resistance equal to the imperialism of the state. Among these institutions private property plays a distinguished part.[27]

A critical examination of this theory should comprise, in the first place, a vindication of everything that pertains to the essence of the state. This has been done in the preceding chapter. Let us merely recall, first, that the state is essentially defined not by coercion but by the completeness of the com-

27. P.-J. Proudhon, *Théorie de la propriété* (a posthumous book) (Paris: Lacroix, Verboeckhoven et Cie, 1866), p. 137.

mon good that it pursues, so far as the temporal order is concerned, and, second, that state coercion admits of being used
in an entirely ethical manner. Once more, what is wrong is
not coercion but the state of affairs which makes it necessary.

None of the necessary features of the state implies any imperialistic tendency. But we do not have to consider only the
essence of the state and of its instruments, the psychology of
the men in power ought to be considered also.[28] In this respect
the least that can be said is that the men who run the state are
constantly subjected to the temptation of developing imperialistic covetousness and lust for absolute power. When we speak
of "good" statesmen, we generally have in mind the kind and
degree of goodness that history shows to be achievable by
statesmen in not exceedingly rare circumstances; then even
good statesmen are by no means free from the temptations of
absolutism. In so far as they are enlightened, they are likely
to be aware of these temptations; and, in so far as they are men
of good will, these temptations are likely to be resisted. But
their enlightenment is not perfect, and their good will is
sometimes weak. Now a huge amount of evil can be done by
fairly enlightened men of rather good will through the operation of propensities of which they are not completely aware.
In fact, the state will be, most of the time, in the hands of men
whose lights are vague and whose virtue is, to say the least,
uncertain. From all this it clearly results that the state ought
to be treated as a kind of permanent aggressor that continually threatens the very substance of society. Whoever dares to
say such things seems to attribute to the state some sort of
evil essence. Perhaps Proudhon did not succeed in removing
such a risk; or perhaps he did not care. Is it so difficult to
understand that effects traced by some to the absurd fiction of
an evil essence of the state can be fully accounted for by the

28. On the psychology of the men in power see Bertrand Russell, *Proposed Roads to Freedom* (New York: Henry Holt & Co., 1919), pp. 128–29.

psychological dispositions that power inevitably produces in the men who hold power?

In the contemporary struggle between democracy and the totalitarian state, not a few persons were rendered hesitant or were even perverted into unconscious betrayal of their principles by the consideration that a democracy, after all, can be a totalitarian state. Let us ponder over the meaning of this apprehension. To say that democracy cannot be totalitarian because a state which has become totalitarian is no longer democratic would probably be true, but it would be of little relevance. It would probably be true, for the features of the totalitarian state prove incompatible with the definition of democracy. Contemporary experience shows that no totalitarian state can stand the test of an election and that totalitarianism demands the one-party system. But the relevant question is whether democracy can give birth to a totalitarian state, albeit at the cost of its own destruction. The traditional propensities of Jacobin democracy command an answer in the affirmative.

The illusion of the democratic transformation of the state is completely dissipated when it is understood that, in order to save society from state absolutism, it is not enough to incorporate into the structure of the state a system of checks, balances, and constitutional guaranties. Not even the ultimate check constituted by the control of the people over the governing personnel suffices; this control may not be genuine and it may also become the accomplice of state absolutism, for the passions which make for absolutism may get hold of the people itself, even though to its disadvantage.[29] In democracy as well

29. Jefferson never lost sight of the danger of absolutism in the democratically controlled state (*Notes on Virginia* [Memorial ed.; Washington, 1903], II, 162–63). The writer is surveying what he terms the "capital defects of the constitution": "All the powers of government, legislative, executive, and judiciary, result to the legislative body. The concentrating these in the same hands is precisely the definition of despotic government. It will be no alleviation that these powers will be exercised by a plurality

as in nondemocratic polities the absolutism of the state must
be held in check by forces external to the state apparatus. This
does not mean that the guaranties procured by democratic
forms are held ineffective or unimportant; they are important
but would soon disappear if they were not supplemented by
external institutions.

First among these institutions comes the freedom of the
church. Although the proper concern of the spiritual society is
eternal life, its liberty is such an obstacle to encroachments by
the state that every tyranny is eager to suppress it. According
to circumstances and to the idiosyncrasies of the rulers, the
campaign against the church as a stronghold of temporal liberties is conducted through bloody persecution, unbloody persecution, diplomacy, etc.

Next comes the freedom of the press. We saw that the
process of persuasion which is of the essence of democracy requires open discussion of all matters submitted to the people's
deliberation. Principles and ends are no matters of deliberation, but, as recalled, the border line is generally uncertain
between what is principle and what is conclusion, what is end
and what is means; let the benefit of the doubt be given to
freedom. Now, over and above its particular relation to democracy, freedom of the press is largely vindicated by the part
that it plays in the protection of society against government
abuses.

It is hardly necessary to elaborate on the services rendered to
public liberty by the private school, the independent labor
union, the autonomous co-operative, and, finally, by private

---

of hands, and not by a single one. One hundred and seventy-three despots would surely
be as oppressive as one. Let those who doubt it turn their eyes on the republic of Venice.
As little will it avail us that they are chosen by ourselves. An *elective despotism* was not
the government we fought for, but one which should not only be founded on free
principles, but in which the powers of government should be so divided and balanced
among several bodies of magistracy, as that no one could transcend their legal limits,
without being effectually checked and restrained by the others.''

ownership and free enterprise. True, several of these institutions may become highly destructive if their powers of initiative and expansion go beyond the proper limits. The freedom of the press may easily produce public immorality, slander, hateful strife, skepticism, the dissolution of the community spirit. The independent action of labor unions may, under crucial circumstances, place a dictatorial power in the hands of a minority, suspend the operation of the responsible authorities, and endanger public health, national defense, etc. And more than a century of socialist criticism has sufficiently advertised the evils that can be worked by private ownership and free enterprise.

Whenever an institution is provided with antinomic powers and causes much evil as well as a great amount of indispensable good, the task of human wisdom is to find a principle capable of safeguarding the good and forestalling the evil. This is a significant platitude. Let another one be uttered: if such a principle is expected to work without a high ratio of failure, disappointment is bound to follow. There is no reason why we should not improve indefinitely our understanding of the principles concerning the relations between the state and the church, the state and labor organizations, etc. But, no matter how properly understood and felicitously formulated these principles may be, their application will always involve uncertainty and risk. At this point a significant division takes place between two sorts of minds, those who accept with determination the prospect of never ending uncertainties, never ending trials and errors, incomplete successes, and new failures and those who decide that institutions causing so much trouble, opposing such obstacles to the reign of reason in society, entertaining in human history darkly mysterious regions, must disappear, regardless of the cost. Here is a choice whose consequences must be well understood. To take only one example: so long as

the labor unions are endowed with the right to strike, there
will never be any perfect guaranty of smoothness in the relations between labor and the rest of society; in spite of all measures calculated to keep striking within the limits set by the
public good, unwise labor leaders will occasionally take advantage of the loopholes of the law, put forward unreasonable
demands, pervert labor action into oligarchic exploitation,
threaten national economy through ill-timed campaigns, etc.
Legislative wisdom and appropriate contracts can do much to
curb such evils, but the only way to suppress them is to put
an end to the liberties of labor organizations. If the rate of
wages is decided by the agents of a state powerful enough to
keep the situation well in hand, nothing happens. The average consumer does not have to worry about being short of coal
in winter as a result of the independent action of a few private
persons. There is a general impression of orderliness reminiscent of the pictures of infallible regularity that technological
feats have imprinted on our minds. But liberty is gone and
death is coming.

At the conclusion of an inquiry into democratic freedom it
is fitting to ponder over the common opinion which sets in
opposition authority and democracy and, more generally, authority and freedom. According to this opinion, which is so
firmly established in many minds that the need to formulate
it clearly is almost never felt, authority and liberty, though
both necessary, oppose each other in such fashion that the
growth of one of them implies the decline of the other. Since
both are held necessary, they must be supplementary in some
way, but they are more opposite than supplementary. Circumstances may demand the strengthening of authority; so much
the better, then, if authority grows stronger, but let us know
where we are going and realize that liberty is being curtailed;
and, if the progress of society implies the growth of liberty,

let it be understood that a progressive society is a society in which authority is declining. In the same commonly held assemblage of thoughts, democracy is a device for the elimination of authority. It is liberty itself embodied in institutions proper to its genius. These views are not understood to imply that a community can do without authority; but if authority is held indestructible, then, in the same measure, democracy is held not to be entirely realizable. It is worth noticing that such views prevail among conservatives as well as among supporters of democratic progress.

From the previous analysis of the functions of authority (chap. i) it results that there is opposition between authority and liberty when the function of authority is substitutional, not when the function of authority is essential. This basic proposition can be developed as follows:

1. The progress of society and of liberty makes for the decline of authority so far as the paternal function of authority is concerned. Thus, for a community subjected to colonial rule, freedom means such a state of affairs that the foreign rulers can disappear without damage to the community, and do disappear.

2. A community is capable of greater freedom if it is capable of unanimity whenever the means to the common good is uniquely determined; it is more primitive or decadent and less capable of liberty if, even when the means to the common good is uniquely determined, it fails to achieve unanimity and needs to achieve unity by way of authority.

3. The progress of society and of liberty requires that at every given moment in the evolution of a community the greatest possible number of tasks should be directly managed by individuals and smaller units, the smallest possible number by the greater units.

But, with regard to the essential functions of authority, there is no conflict whatsoever between authority and liberty.

The more definitely a community is directed toward its common good and protected from disunity in its common action, the more perfect and the more free it is.

Between authority and liberty there is both opposition and supplementariness. Which one of the two aspects ultimately predominates? The answer is obvious, since opposition prevails in the substitutional domain of authority, supplementariness in its essential domain. Ultimately and absolutely, authority and liberty are more supplementary than opposite.

In order to interpret popular ideas concerning the conflict between democracy and authority, it is helpful to examine the various meanings of such expressions as "authoritarianism" and "authoritarian method," which are constantly used in opposition to "democracy" and "democratic method." Notice that, even in circles where democracy is held suspicious, the connotations of "authoritarianism" and related expressions are not particularly good.

1. Of all perversions of political authority, the most obvious and the most detestable is the subservience of public power to the private interest of the men who hold power. In many contexts the word "authority" and related words are understood to refer to the dominion of servitude. Civil government is so plainly unrelated, by essence, to government for the private welfare of the persons in power that it is hard to understand how it ever was believed that the use of civil government for private purposes could be anything else than accident and abuse. The explanation apparently lies in pictures received from old societies where public power was commonly vested in men also enjoying the situation of mastery. When civil power over the people and mastery over many slaves are found in the same person, the peculiarities of the second relationship have a good chance of being transferred to the first. The suppression of aristocratic privilege has done a great deal for the purification of the notion of civil rule. In order for this no-

tion to be fully recognized according to its nature, one more step in the direction of equal exchange is needed. So long as the upper class, which inevitably supplies a great part of the governing personnel, is commonly engaged in economic processes involving exploitation, there will be a temptation, for the public conscience, to misinterpret political rule as dominion of exploitation.

2. By the theory of paternal authority set forth in the first chapter of this book, we consider it entirely normal that authority should be treated as sheer abuse when there is reference to a paternal authority which outlives its necessity.

3. A similar view holds in the case of an authority which indulges in the tendency to extend beyond the narrowest possible measure the domain of the things to be managed directly by itself. Any infraction against the principle of autonomy can be described as authoritarian conduct and ought to convey unfavorable judgment, since it signifies that authority is operating beyond the right.

4. In the preceding three cases the contrast is not so much between authority and democracy as between authority and justice. When the meaning of the adjective "authoritarian" is set in special contrast to the kind of freedom that is the proper effect of democracy, the connotation of abuse has less propriety; for rejecting the democratic method is not always abusive; it may be the greater good under the circumstances. Democratic freedom essentially consists in the control of the people over the governing personnel through the procedure of periodical election; accordingly, any method which subtracts the governing personnel from the control of the people can be termed "authoritarian." Yet power not subjected to democratic control is not necessarily iniquitous.

5. We propose to describe, in the next chapter, a certain perversion of democratic thought and emotion which endeavors to eliminate the substance of authority and blames as au-

thoritarian every procedure in which authority asserts its genuine nature. The history of political ideas in modern times reveals the operation of a theory which destroys authority without burdening itself with the common paradoxes of anarchy. We shall coin a name for this theory. So far, for lack of a proper name, it has often been called the "theory of democracy."

CHAPTER III

AUTHORITY IN DEMOCRACY

✣

THE subject of sovereignty is one that every treatise or textbook of political science, no matter how elementary, has to discuss. Consequently, the state of the question in our academic and scholarly circles is particularly bad. With problems of extreme difficulty, the worst that can happen is that hasty and mediocre writers should feel obliged to contribute treatments for the satisfaction of not very exacting and not very industrious readers. True, the case of common teaching would not be so bad if great books had not set an example of uncertainty. This is not due entirely to the difficulties of the question; it is also due to the confusing influence of historical circumstances. The discussion of sovereignty often arouses passions which make a philosophic treatment impossible and substitute for it—most of the time surreptitiously—vindications of existing conditions or exhortations for the bringing-about of a new state of affairs. The writings of King James contain the ideology of British absolutism. More shockingly, Bossuet burdened posterity with a theory in which it is easy to recognize the ideology of the great historical movement which culminated in the monarchy of Louis XIV. Late eighteenth-century theories of sovereignty express the struggles fought by the American people against the British Crown or by the French bourgeoisie against king, nobility, and established church. The impression left by the literature on sovereignty is gloomy: distortion due to practical concerns can be feared almost everywhere.

Such factors of confusion make it particularly important to

state the problem in simple and clear terms. The common experience of civil societies shows that men obey other men. Disobedience is not infrequent, but it is impressively outweighed by obedience in any society that has not reached the last stages of disintegration. We have to interpret this great fact of political obedience. On what ground do some men claim a right to be obeyed? What are the reasons why they are not always disobeyed? Many would answer that they do not want to go to jail or to be shot down, and some theorists would maintain that fear and self-interest account sufficiently for the fact of obedience in civil society. Any human experience, any knowledge of history, evidences the shallowness of this explanation. The relationship which obtained between the police and the bootleggers in the era of prohibition exemplifies a situation in which fear and self-interest alone motivate obedience. Such a situation does not characterize civil society, it means the end of it. Things take place in civil relations, not exceptionally but regularly, as if some men had the power of binding the consciences of other men. The factual behavior of men in society testifies to the regular operation of an ethical motive of obedience. Not only in persons of lofty morality but also in those classified as average citizens there is a certain awareness of being obliged to obey public powers, at least a vague feeling that, things being what they are, men commonly considered as the agents of society have a right to give orders within the limits of their legally formulated functions. Now the proposition that a man can bind the conscience of another man raises a very great difficulty: far from being obvious, it is altogether devoid of verisimilitude. This is the very essence of the problem which we propose to examine; on the one hand, it seems to be impossible to account for social life without assuming that man can bind the conscience of his neighbor; on the other hand, it is not easy to see how a man can ever enjoy such power.

THE COACH-DRIVER THEORY

There is a way out. The difficulty can be explained away. It would vanish if it were possible to show that a man is never bound in conscience to obey another man. There is a theory according to which civil obedience is but an appearance and an illusion. If only traditional violences and superstitions were checked, the illusion would disappear and social relations would reveal their true nature, to the great benefit of all. Then it would become clear that the claim of man to be obeyed by his neighbor is in all cases unwarranted and deceitful. We obey ourselves alone. I really obey myself alone, and this is all that society needs and wants me to do. In society I remain as free as in solitude. Great caution must be used in giving this theory a name. No doubt Rousseau has written, about freedom and civil obedience, things which mean that, in the state as he conceives it, citizens are their own masters and obey but themselves. The theory we are in the process of describing represents an aspect of Rousseau's political philosophy; but to describe it, with no qualification, as Rousseau's theory of sovereignty might involve a risk of oversimplification.

This theory holds that the government is the servant of the people; but the same view is accepted in extremely diverse systems of political thought. It holds, further, that the men in power are delegated by the people, that they are given definite missions by the people, and that in the fulfilment of their missions they remain strictly subordinated to the people that delegated them. Thus the governing person is a leader entirely under the control of those whom he leads. Authority belongs not to the leaders but to the led. Or perhaps it should be said that real leadership, the one which is inseparable from authority, belongs not to the government but to the governed. *In so far as the governing person is considered a leader, his is a leadership without authority.* Because he is, in a way, leader, he seems to

have the power of directing judgments and wills, of binding
consciences—in short, he seems to exercise authority. Such
appearance is commonly exploited by tyranny. In truth, however, authority remains in the hands of the governed, since
it is only by virtue of their will and of the missions given to
persons of their own choice that the government exercises
leadership.

To call this the "theory of the sovereignty of the people"
involves intolerable confusion, for the same expression can be
used, and is used very commonly, to designate a widely different philosophy of civil authority. There is, in the theory
under consideration, something distinctive and unique which
ought not to be missed by the expression meant to designate
it; it is the statement that obedience of man to man, in political society at least, is mere illusion and violence, that the
citizen ought to obey himself alone, and that the leadership
exercised by the governing personnel involves no authority. The expression "sovereignty of the people" does not
bring forth this essential element of the theory. A proper
name for it is suggested by Paul-Louis Courier, a liberal, a
rebel in the petty bourgeois style, a Voltairean, a humanist
in perpetual revolt against church and state. He wrote that
in a liberal state of affairs the government is like a coach-
driver, hired and paid by those whom he drives.[1] The coach-
driver leads his patrons indeed, but only where they want

1. Paul-Louis Courier, *Lettres au rédacteur du Censeur*, Lettre X, 10 mars 1820 (*Œuvres*
[Paris: Firmin Didot, 1845], pp. 62–63). This letter is concerned with the freedom of the
press; the writer describes in humorous fashion the evils that its adversaries expect of
it: "If this abuse [i.e., the freedom of the press] should endure, every undertaking of
the court would be controlled beforehand, examined, judged, criticized, estimated.
The public would consider all business as their own; everything would arouse their
contemptible interest; they would check the records of the treasurer, supervise the
police, and scoff at the diplomatic service. In one word, the nation would manage the
government after the fashion of a coach-driver whom we hire and who is supposed to
lead us, not where he wants, not how he wants, but where we intend to go and by the
way that we find convenient. This is a thing horrible to imagine, contrary to the divine
right and the capitularies."

to go and by the ways of their own choice. The theory which reduces the role of the government to that of a leader without authority could appropriately be called "the coach-driver theory." Merely to assert that sovereignty belongs to the people is not precise enough; for it is not obvious, it is not even certain, that the sovereignty of the people suppresses obedience. By likening the government to a coach-driver, doubts are eliminated. Primitives traveling in a civilized country—as they used to do in eighteenth-century fiction—would perhaps believe that the driver of the coach is the real master and takes the persons on the back seat where he pleases; a similar illusion has been exploited by men in power throughout the history of mankind. It is only of late that the spell has been broken and that the governing personnel have been identified for what they are: purely instrumental characters whose duty it is, even when they shout orders, to fulfil the orders given them by the governed.

In the work of Rousseau the coach-driver theory is so supplemented as not to disclose too shockingly its paradoxical simplicity. Yet Rousseau has probably done more than anyone else to spead the ideal of an organization capable of doing away with the ethical substance of authority and obedience.[2]

2. J.-J. Rousseau, *The Social Contract* ("Everyman's Library" [New York: E. P. Dutton & Co., 1930]), Book I, chap. vi: "The problem is to find a form of association which will defend and protect with the whole common force the person and goods of each associate, and in which each, while uniting himself with all, may still obey himself alone, and remain as free as before." Book II, chap. i. "I hold then that Sovereignty, being nothing less than the exercise of the general will, can never be alienated, and that the sovereign, who is no less than a collective being, cannot be represented except by himself: the power indeed may be transmitted, but not the will." Better than any of the political writings of Rousseau, the *Émile* shows that the all-important thing is to substitute submission to impersonal forces for obedience to persons. See Augustin Cochin, *La Crise de l'histoire révolutionnaire* (Paris: Champion, 1909), p. 49: "Such is the precise and new meaning of the 'war against the tyrants' declared by the Revolution. It does not promise freedom in the ordinary sense of the word, i.e., independence, but in the sense in which Rousseau understands this word, viz., anarchy, deliverance from all personal authority, whether that of the lord to whom respect is due or that of

Persons concerned with real liberty soon recognized that the sovereignty of the people, as it appears to the readers of Rousseau, supplied tyranny with a new vindication of unprecedented efficaciousness. Rousseau and his admirers were perhaps less interested in what actually happens in social practice than in the purely interior and entirely spiritual process of interpreting relations among men. If a disciple of Rousseau has to choose between an unpleasant situation imposed upon him without any consent of his own and a pleasant situation to be accepted voluntarily out of a sense of obedience, he chooses the former as more consonant with his notion of liberty. The coach-driver theory exercised great influence upon the French Revolution, upon French democracy throughout its history, and upon all democratic movements inspired by French examples. It did not play a decisive part in the early ages of American democracy; the concept of natural law was then too strong to allow the voluntarism of such a theory to unfold its consequences and reveal its principle. From the time of Andrew Jackson on, the coach-driver theory has been an ideological factor of some importance in American history. It never won in America the same position of unquestioned supremacy that it did in several Latin countries.

This theory flatters an instinct of disobedience from which no human heart is entirely free. When this instinct is uninhibited, it may lead to anarchism. But if it is kept under control by an interest in good manners and a sense of respectability, it finds a fitting outlet in the coach-driver theory. Further, this theory draws considerable power from its apparent ability to explain a number of phenomena pertaining to regular democratic practice. Think, in the first place, of the direct government of the people by themselves as practiced, for instance, in New England towns and in some Swiss cantons. Although

---

the demagogue who exercises fascination. *If one is obedient, it will never be to a man but always to an impersonal being, the general will*'' (italics mine).

such government without a distinct personnel is seldom possible, it is reasonably held to constitute the fundamental pattern of democratic government. The archetype of democracy
is a government without a distinct governing personnel, without any representative assembly. No representation is needed:
the people gather, and they are the government. But, without
using any distinct governing personnel, democracy may use
agents. The people's assembly may appoint managers who are
not really men in authority; they are merely instruments, and
authority remains entirely in the hands of the people. Such
agents, managers, or secretaries employed by the people's assembly receive orders and do not—in spite, perhaps, of certain
appearances—give orders of their own. They can be properly
likened to coach-drivers who take the orders of their patrons
and lead them where they want to go. Against this background of direct democracy let us consider a democratic organization such as ours, with a distinct governing personnel,
elected legislative assemblies, and an elected president. Out-
wardly, at least, there are resemblances between this governing personnel and the managers hired, after the fashion of a
coach-driver, by direct democracy. We elect our representa-
tives on the basis of their programs. By doing so, do we not
order them to lead us where we want to go, that is, to the objective described in the program of our choice and through the
ways recommended by the program that we have chosen?
When new elections are held, we express either our satisfaction by re-electing our representative or our dissatisfaction by
voting for his opponent; it looks very much like hiring again,
or refusing to rehire, an instrumental character according as
he has fulfilled properly, or failed to fulfil, the orders that he
was given. A number of less fundamental but very significant
democratic practices seem to be properly accounted for by the
coach-driver theory. Think of the many means of pressure
used by the electorate, between election periods, in order to

have their will carried out. To write to your congressman that you want him to support a certain measure is perfectly intelligible if your congressman is, like the secretaries and managers of a direct democracy, a pure instrument that has no orders to give but only orders to take.

In order to test the coach-driver theory of sovereignty, we shall consider the case in which it seems to work most plainly and from which it derives most of its energy and prestige, viz., the case of a small community practicing direct, nonrepresentative government. Here are a few hundred farmers. Consider them, first, while they are not in session. Each of them, a private citizen, toils in his own field and minds his own business. When the assembly convenes, these men undergo a qualitative change. One hour ago they were scattered in their fields. Right now they have gathered for purposes of public business; they are no longer a collection of private citizens minding their own affairs, they are the people minding common affairs. It is crucially important to understand the qualitative nature of the change. *Between these few hundred farmers scattered in their fields, busy with their own private affairs, and the same farmers gathered in an assembly in charge of the community's affairs, the qualitative difference is just as great as between the President of the United States and any of us United States citizens.*

The best way to understand this qualitative difference is to consider the basic problem of civil obedience in relation to an assembly inclusive of all the people. The coach-driver theory serves the ideal of a situation such that each should remain, in society, as independent as in natural solitude and obey but himself. Does such a situation obtain in direct democracy? *Apparently* it does. These men who issue rules for common action by majority vote do not obey anybody except themselves. Suppose, first, for the sake of clarity, that the vote is unanimous; then everybody can say that the law is his own law and that, by obeying it, he obeys only himself. Suppose, then, that there is no unanimity but that I am among the majority; again I can, apparently, boast that the law which I shall obey is my own law and that, by obeying it, I obey only myself. But what happens when I am in the minority? Here lies the real test, and from the interpretation of my situation as member of a minority I shall infer conclusions concerning the proper interpretation of my situation as member of a majority or of a unanimous assembly.

Suppose that throughout a long period I was among the majority. What am I going to do the day I find myself in the minority? I may refuse to obey the law that I did not approve and declare myself a rebel; but then it will be clear that I have always been a rebel. A conspicuous rebel as member of a minority, I was already a rebel when I was member of a majority or of a unanimous assembly, since, even then, I was determined to disobey whenever I should happen to disagree. I never was a law-abiding citizen; I never abided by the law, except by accident. This makes it plain that the coach-driver theory does not supply a satisfactory explanation for the basic facts of political behavior even under the circumstances which would be most favorable to its operation, if such a theory ever could work. In a direct democracy where, by hypothesis, there is no distinct governing personnel, distinct persons are not governors but mere agents, purely instrumental characters. There is no question of obeying them, except possibly in incidental fashion, in the way in which the police chief would obey his subordinates in the enforcement of a traffic regulation that he made and that he can change. Such purely instrumental characters do not hold authority, *but the fact that authority is not held by any distinct persons does not mean that it is not held by anybody.* As shown in the first chapter of this book, the requirements of the concept of authority are entirely fulfilled in the case of a community governing itself directly, without any distinct governing personnel. Authority is not lacking; it resides in the community. The few hundred farmers meeting in assembly are, as a body, essentially distinct from what they were before they assembled and will be as soon as they return to private citizenship. Meeting in assembly, they are the government, and to this government each of them, on returning to private citizenship, owes obedience, regardless of what happened to him as a member of the people's assembly. Whether he belonged to a unanimous assembly, to the majority, or to a minority is entirely incidental. The thing that matters is that he is bound by the law that the people, acting as their own government, passed. Whether he voted for or against it makes absolutely no difference; he is subjected to it and ought to abide by it. This is the only way to interpret the fundamental data of political life so far as law and obligation are concerned. The coach-driver theory renders these data unintelligible by reversing relations between the essential and the casual. A citizen is considered law-abiding if, and only if, he considers his obligation independent from his personal opinion. If the law was passed in spite of his wish, his duty to abide by it may be unpleasant, but it is just as clear as if he had voted for it. In the coach-driver theory, on the contrary, my personal consent to the law is essential. I feel obligated to abide by the law if, and only if, I wanted the law to be what it is. Clearly, I abide by the law not on account of its essence as law but because of my incidental approval of it. If the coach-driver theory should ever be received in a spirit of strict consistency, society would soon be destroyed by secession. But this theory does not need to be applied with strict consistency in order to be effective. What generally happens is that the dissenter performs the acts prescribed by the law which he disapproves, but in a purely utilitarian fashion, merely in order to spare himself and others the inconveniences following upon the breaking of the law. Thus outward anarchy and the violent disruption of society are avoided. External order is not delivered up to the fortuitousness of unanimity. But the inner dispositions of minds and hearts toward the law are subjected to such fortuitousness; this weakens dangerously the unity of society and corrupts the character of political life by substituting a law of utility and force for the law of voluntary co-operation whenever I happen not to be in the majority. In a direct democracy as well as in any other organization the nature of society demands that man should obey man. The artifice calculated to do away with obedience threatens directly the principle of authority in its most essential functions, as expounded in the first part of this book. There we saw that the need for government is so rooted in the nature of society that government would be needed even in the ideal case of a society made only of enlightened and virtuous people. If government, as distinct from unanimity, is made necessary by the very nature of things, the obligation to obey has its roots in the nature of things, in the very nature of man and of human society. It is completely independent of my casual belonging to the majority or the minority. This is why the coach-driver theory is unlikely to be very popular where there is a strong belief in a law of nature independent of the whims of man.

Back to our initial question, let us remark, again, that there is something paradoxical about one man's having the power to bind the conscience of another man. Of course, a man cannot do such a thing. God alone can. And God can bind a man to obey another man. This he did by the creation of the human species, which is naturally social and political; for the necessity of government and obedience follows from the nature of community life.[3]

3. Leo XIII, *Diuturnum* ("On Civil Government") (1881), trans. presented by Joseph Husslein, S.J., in *Social Wellsprings: Fourteen Epochal Documents by Pope Leo XIII* (Milwaukee: Bruce Publishing Co., 1940), p. 52: "But now, a society can neither exist nor be conceived in which there is no one to govern the wills of individuals, in such a way as to make, as it were, one will out of many, and to impell them rightly and orderly to the common good; therefore God has willed that in a civil society there should

DIVINE RIGHT

Let us now turn to the subject so confusedly described as the "theory of divine right." The expression "divine right" is just as confusing as the expression "sovereignty of the people"; neither should be used except when the context removes all ambiguity.

The so-called "theory of divine right," as it has been known to the Western world ever since the seventeenth century, is related to the history of Christianity in such fashion that it does not seem possible to give an exposition of it except in terms of Christian history. According to Christian faith, God became man, and before he left this world he founded a society designed to maintain his life in men. The first leaders of this society were designated by him. Among them he distinguished one, Peter. Concerning the supremacy of the latter, disagreement came to a showdown early in the sixteenth century; from then on, part of the Christian world ignored the notion of one supreme leader appointed by Christ. Simultaneously, the other part of the Christian world became more and more articulate and firm in its acknowledgment of the supremacy of Peter and his successors. According to the upholders of Peter's supremacy, the head of the church enjoys a power which comes from God directly. The first person to hold this power was, moreover, designated by Christ himself. Here (i.e., in the case of Peter) we can speak of power by divine right with perfect propriety; for this power is in no way from man, it is from God alone, and even its conjunction with the particular person who holds it is effected by God. In the case of Peter's successors, the person is designated by man, the conjunction between power and person is effected by man, but

---

be some to rule the multitude. . . . But no man has in himself or of himself the power of constraining the free will of others by fetters of authority of this kind. This power resides solely in God, the Creator and Legislator of all things; and it is necessary that those who exercise it should do it as having received it from God."

power continues to be from God directly and exclusively. The successor of Peter, as well as Peter himself, is vicar of Christ and in no way whatsoever vicar of the church. Men have nothing to do with his power, except so far as the designation of the person is concerned. In spite of this designation by man, the expression "power by divine right" is perfectly appropriate.

We are considering here a spiritual society, a society which describes itself as not concerned properly and directly with temporal affairs, a society whose main ends are found in another world and in a future life, a society whose proper life and main ends are held to be supernatural. The Gospel states the principle of a distinction between this spiritual or supernatural society and the state or temporal society: There are, according to the Gospel, things that are Caesar's and things that are not Caesar's. But, between these two orders of things, the relation is such that the distinction, though intelligible and clear, cannot always work plainly. In centuries of universal faith as well as in times of widespread disbelief, clashes are frequent between the two powers. One effect of these uncertainties and adventures is that some ascribe to one power peculiarities, features, characteristics, and prerogatives proper to the other power. Not infrequently, people dreamed of a church organized and governed according to the pattern set by the temporal society. And not infrequently, people dreamed of a temporal power enjoying dignities similar to those of the church. We find in the Middle Ages theories implying that the pope is the vicar of the church as well as the vicar of Christ. History also records theories according to which the king is not the vicar of the people but only the vicar of God.[4]

Some extremists went so far as to maintain not only that the power of the king is directly from God but also that the

4. See *The Political Writings of James I*, with an Introduction by C. H. McIlwain (Cambridge: Harvard University Press, 1918).

designation of the king is effected divinely. The most paradoxical among these eccentrics was Filmer, who said that
kings and governors inherited from the patriarchs an authority received from Noah, from Adam, and ultimately from
God.[5] Such a reading of history probably did not convince
many people. On the other hand, the notion that great leaders, great makers of history, are singled out by God and taken
into governing positions through methods distinct from the
ordinary course of providential government is not uncommon.
Strikingly, momentous instances of such a belief can be found
in times and places where religious faith is not particularly
warm or orthodox. We have only to think of Napoleon and
Hitler. Of little importance in the history of political philosophies, the theory of divine designation sometimes played a
decisive part in political history. Its power is great when it
assumes the form of a myth capable of supplying a people, in
the midst of exalting emotions, with a practical explanation
of its manifest destiny.

The theory implying both (1) that the power of the temporal ruler is directly from God and (2) that God himself
designates the person of the temporal ruler deserves to be called
the "divine-right theory" in the most proper sense. Next to
it comes the theory which, though acknowledging that the
designation of the king, as well as that of the pope (with the
exception of the first pope), is effected by men, maintains that
the power of the king, as well as that of the pope, comes directly from God. This theory could also be described with
propriety as a theory of divine right, but the usual expression, "designation theory," is specific and satisfactory. The
designation theory is a more moderate, less paradoxical form
of the divine-right theory; it holds that in temporal power the
only thing traceable, *in any sense*, to human power is the
designation of the ruling person.

5. Robert Filmer, *Patriarcha*, published only in 1680.

THE TRANSMISSION THEORY

Another theory holds that the first bearer of civil authority is not the king or any governor but the people as a whole, the civil multitude. Whenever there is a distinct governing personnel, men have done two things and not one, as in the case of the pope: they have *designated* the ruling person, and they have *transmitted* to him the power given by God to the people. Let us emphasize that *transmitting* does not mean the same as *giving*. To say that God alone gives authority is the same as to say that God alone can bind the conscience of man.

The transmission theory is commonly attributed to Thomas Aquinas. True, the question does not belong to his *Problematik* and is not treated explicitly in any part of his work. The best approximation to a treatment of it is found in the *Treatise on Laws* of the *Summa theologica*. After having shown that law is a product of the reason—more precisely, a premise of practical argumentation (a.1)—and that it is essentially relative to the common good (a.2), Aquinas poses the question *Whether the reason of any man is competent to make laws?* The answer is commanded by the principle of proportion between end and cause. Since the end is the common good, the efficient cause ought to be, proportionately, the multitude or a person "holding the part of," "acting instead of," "being in charge of," the multitude. "Now to order anything to the common good belongs either to the whole people or to someone who is the vicegerent of the whole people. Hence the making of a law belongs either to the whole people or to a public personage who has care of the whole people."[6] In a later question of the same treatise he shows that custom can obtain the force of law; an

6. *Sum. theol.* i–ii. 90. 3: "Ordinare autem aliquid in bonum commune est vel totius multitudinis, vel alicujus gerentis vicem totius multitudinis. Et ideo condere legem vel pertinet ad totam multitudinem, vel pertinet ad personam publicam, quae totius multitudinis curam habet; quia et in omnibus aliis ordinare in finem est ejus, cujus est proprius ille finis."

objection to this statement is derived from the public character of the lawmaker: "... the framing of laws belongs to those public men whose business it is to govern the community ... but custom grows by the acts of private individuals. ..." Here is the answer of Aquinas (trans. A. C. Pegis):

The people among whom a custom is introduced may be of two conditions. For if they are free, and able to make their own laws, the consent of the whole people expressed by a custom counts far more in favor of a particular observance than does the authority of the sovereign, who has not the power to frame laws, except as representing the people. Therefore, although each individual cannot make laws, yet the whole people can. If, however, the people have not the free power to make their own laws, or to abolish a law made by a higher authority, nevertheless, among such a people a prevailing custom obtains the force of law insofar as it is tolerated by those to whom it belongs to make laws for that people; because, by the very fact that they tolerate it, they seem to approve of that which is introduced by custom.[7]

There cannot be any doubt that the transmission theory is in full agreement with the notion of political authority expressed here by Aquinas. These texts are most simply and directly interpreted by the theory that power belongs primarily to the people, who can use it to make laws for themselves, and that, if and when power lies in the hands of a distinct person, this person has the character of "one who substitutes for the people." The expression *gerens vicem* might suggest the coach-driver theory; but this is ruled out by Aquinas' general

7. *Ibid.* 97. 3, ad 3: "Multitudo, in qua consuetudo introducitur, duplicis conditionis esse potest. Si enim sit libera multitudo, quae possit sibi legem facere, plus est consensus totius multitudinis ad aliquid observandum, quod consuetudo manifestat, quam auctoritas Principis, qui non habet potestatem condendi legem, nisi inquantum gerit personam multitudinis; unde licet singulae personae non possint condere legem, tamen totus populus condere legem potest. Si vero multitudo non habeat liberam potestatem condendi sibi legem vel legem a superiori positam removendi, tamen ipsa consuetudo in tali multitudine praevalens obtinet vim legis, inquantum per eos toleratur ad quos pertinet multitudini legem imponere; ex hoc enim ipso videntur approbare quod consuetudo introduxit."

views on obedience and authority. Thus it can be said that his
only existent expressions on the subject of the origin of political power support the transmission theory. Yet, because
these expressions amount merely to a few sentences, because
the problem is not fully disengaged, and because the alterna-
tive solution (i.e., the designation theory) is not envisaged,
to state with no qualification that the transmission theory
is that of Aquinas would perhaps be more than the texts war-
rant.

But the transmission theory is supported in unmistakable
terms by the great commentator on Aquinas—Cajetan. Besides
a short commentary on the above-quoted passage of the
Treatise on Laws, the ideas of Cajetan are found in two "Opus-
cula."[8] The first of these, "A Comparison between the Authority of the Pope and That of the Council," completed on
October 12, 1511, was occasioned by the schismatic Council
of Pisa, directed against Pope Julius II. Cajetan discusses in it
Gallican theories already held in the fifteenth century in connection with the Council of Constance, especially the views
of Ockham and Gerson, who upheld the supremacy of the
council over the pope. King Louis XII of France submitted
Cajetan's opusculum to the University of Paris and intrusted
the duty of refuting it to a young and skilful doctor, James
Almain, who wrote a pamphlet entitled "On the Authority
of the Church, or of the Sacred Council's Representing Her,
against Thomas de Vio, Dominican" (1512), to which Cajetan
answered in a second opusculum, "Defense of a Comparison
between the Authority of the Pope and That of the Council,"
completed on November 29, 1512.[9]

As the adversaries of papal supremacy use arguments drawn

8. Thomas de Vio Cardinalis Caietanus, *Scripta theologica*, Vol. I: *De comparatione auctoritatis papae et concilii cum apologia eiusdem tractatus*, Vincentius M. Iacobus Pollet editionem curavit (Rome: Apud Institutum "Angelicum," 1936). Numbers refer to a convenient division of the book into short paragraphs.

9. Information from V. M. I. Pollet's Preface.

from alleged analogies between church and state, Cajetan is led to stress differences and to emphasize the unique relation to God that obtains in the supernatural and supra-temporal society. In the history of ideas concerning sovereignty, circumstances, most of the time, made for confusion; here they happen to make for distinction and precision. Cajetan is dedicated to showing what is unique in the power of the pope and by what features it is distinguished from any other power.

At the beginning of the first Opusculum (chap. i) Cajetan declares that the adversaries of the pope's supremacy should not draw any argument from the condition of monarchs "established by the Senate and the free people": the power of the pope was established by Christ. Later, after having abundantly developed the theory that the pope acknowledges no superior on earth and that the church is in no way superior to the pope, Cajetan examines the question of the deposition of a pope guilty of heresy.[10] That a heretical pope should be de-

10. On the subject of the heretical pope, let us quote Charles Journet (from Fribourg, Switzerland) in his important book *L'Église du Verbe Incarné* (Paris: Desclée de Brouwer, 1941), p. 596: "Pour bien des théologiens, l'assistance que Jésus a promise aux successeurs de Pierre les empêchera non seulement d'enseigner publiquement l'hérésie, mais encore de tomber, comme personnes privées, dans l'hérésie. Il n'y a pas, dès lors, à introduire de débat sur la déposition éventuelle d'un pape hérétique. La question est tranchée d'avance. Saint Bellarmin, *de Romano pontifice*, lib. II, cap. XXX, tenait déjà cette thèse pour probable et facile à défendre. Elle était pourtant moins répandue de son temps qu'aujourd'hui. Elle a gagné du terrain à cause, en bonne partie, du progrès des études historiques, qui a montré que ce qu'on imputait à certains papes, tels Vigile, Libère, Honorius, comme une faute d'hérésie, n'était au vrai rien de plus qu'un manque de zèle et de courage à proclamer, et surtout à préciser, en certaines heures difficiles, la vraie doctrine.

"Néanmoins, de nombreux et bons théologiens du XVIème et du XVIIème siècle ont admis qu'il fût possible que le pape tombât, en son privé, dans le péché d'hérésie non seulemont occulte mais même manifeste.

"Les uns, comme saint Bellarmin, Suarez, ont alors estimé que le pape, en se retranchant lui-même de l'Église, était *ipso facto* déposé, *papa hereticus est depositus*. Il semble que l'hérésie soit considérée par ces théologiens comme une sorte de suicide moral, supprimant le sujet même de la papauté. ...

"Les autres, comme Cajetan, Jean de saint Thomas, dont l'analyse nous paraît plus pénétrante, ont estimé que, même après un péché manifeste d'hérésie, le pape n'était

posed is for him not doubtful. He mentions the opinion that a pope who falls into heresy ceases, thereby, to be pope, so that no deposition is needed but merely the official sanction of his no longer being the head of the church. Cajetan speaks of this opinion with respect, but holds it untrue. He thinks that the heretical pope is still pope and has to be deposed, just as the heretical bishop is still bishop and has to be deposed. But how is it possible to grant the church the power to depose a man who is still pope without granting her *power over the pope*, which is precisely the thesis which Cajetan wants to refute? By this extreme difficulty Cajetan is led to work out instruments of unprecedented accuracy for the treatment of the problem of sovereignty.

His theory is that, although there is not on earth any power superior to the pope, yet there is on earth a power which in the extreme case of a stubbornly heretical pope can play the part of an instrument in his deposition.[11] "You must consider that

___

pas déposé, mais qu'il devait l'être par l'Église, *papa haereticus non est depositus sed deponendus.* Cependant, ont-ils ajouté, l'Église n'est pas pour autant supérieure au pape ... ils font remarquer d'une part que, de droit divin, l'Église doit être unie au pape comme le corps à la tête; d'autre part que, de droit divin, celui qui se manifeste hérétique doit être évité *après un ou deux avertissements (Tit.*, III, 10). Il y a donc une antinomie absolue entre le fait d'être pape et le fait de persévérer dans l'hérésie après un ou deux avertissements. L'action de l'Église est simplement *déclarative*, elle manifeste qu'il y a a péché incorrigible d'hérésie; alors l'action auctoritaire de Dieu s'exerce pour disjoindre la papauté d'un sujet qui, persistant dans l'hérésie après admonition, devient, en droit divin, inapte à la détenir plus longtemps. En vertu donc de l'Écriture, l'Église *désigne* et Dieu *dépose*. Dieu agit avec l'Église, dit Jean de saint Thomas, un peu comme agirait un pape qui déciderait d'attacher des indulgences à la visite de certains lieux de pelerinage, mais laisserait à un ministre le soin de désigner quels seront ces lieux. L'explication de Cajetan et de Jean de saint Thomas nous ramène ... au cas d'un sujet qui, à partir d'un certain moment, commence à devenir en droit divin, incapable de détenir davantage le privilège de la papauté. Elle est réductible, elle aussi, à l'amission du pontificat par défaut du sujet. C'est bien, en effet, le cas fondamental, dont les autres ne représenteront que les variantes" (by courtesy of Desclée de Brouwer, Bruges).

11 *De comparatione*, chap. xx: "Rationabilis sententia quod Papa factus Haereticus subest potestati ministeriali Ecclesiae, et non auctoritativae super Papam.

283. "Ad cujus evidentiam altius ordiendo, tria praemittenda sunt: primo, quod in

three aspects are found in the pope: The papal power, the person (say, Peter), and the conjunction of the two, viz., the papal power in Peter, from which conjunction Pope Peter results." Then, "if we discern the proper causes and apply them to their proper effects," we understand that the papal power (*papatus*) proceeds from God immediately, that Peter proceeds from his parents and ancestors, and that the union of papal power and Peter proceeds immediately not from God but from man, except in the case of the first pope, who was appointed by Christ. Thus, what is caused by man, in the case of the pope, is the *union of a person with a power which is not, itself, caused by man in any sense whatsoever*. Such union does not take place without election by men and the consent of the elect. The case is absolutely unique. The power exercised in the deposition of the heretical pope does not imply that the pope acknowledges any superior in this world; the power which deposes the heretical pope is not concerned with the papal power, which is directly from Christ; it is concerned merely with the *union* existing between the papal power and a man-designated person.

This is a very clear exposition of what was to be called later

---

Papa inveniuntur tria, scilicet: papatus, persona, quae est Papa, puta Petrus, et coniunctio utriusque, scil. papatus in Petro, ex qua conjunctione resultat Petrus Papa.

"Secundo, quod discernendo et applicando proprias causas suis propriis effectibus invenimus, quod papatus est a Deo immediate, Petrus a patre suo, etc. coniunctio autem papatus in Petro, post Petrum primum a Christo immediate institutum, non est a Deo, sed ab homine, ut patet: quia hoc fit per electionem hominum. . . .

"Tertio, quod . . . Petrus Papa, qui ex consensu suo et electorum causatus est, ex consensibus eisdem, scil. suo et electorum, ad contrarium dissolvi potest. . . .

"Ex his tribus praemissis habetur primo absque haesitatione certum, quod Petrus Papa, et in fieri et in corrumpi, dependet a potestate humana, non superiore nec aequali potestati Papae, sed minore. . . .

"Habetur secundo certo certius, quod aliud est posse supra coniunctionem Petri et papatus construendam seu destruendam, et aliud est posse supra Papam. . . . Unde potestas supra Papam non invenitur nisi in Domino Jesu Christo, potestas autem supra coniunctionem papatus et Petri invenitur, in terris, et merito, quia papatus opus Dei immediate est, coniunctio autem papatus et Petri opus nostrum."

the "designation theory." The role of man in the constitution of authority is limited to a designation when, and only when, the thing caused by man is merely *the union of a particular person with a power which does not come from man in any sense whatsoever.* The power to cause such conjunction does not by any means constitute a power *over* the ruling person. No wonder that such a theory is popular among rulers; but Cajetan makes it plain that it holds only in the case of the supernatural society. Even if a king happens to be appointed by God, contrary to the ordinary course of events, he does not enjoy a power independent of anything human; such power belongs to the head of the church alone. This is what Cajetan makes unmistakably clear in the second Opusculum. His opponent draws an argument from the power of the king. Cajetan answers:

Concerning what is added on an [allegedly] similar situation of kings, let it be said that kings are not proximate and immediate ministers of God, but, without any doubt, they are God's ministers by being the vicegerents of the multitude. Very different is the situation of the pope: he is not the vicegerent of the multitude but of Jesus Christ. Consider now the following four cases: (1) that of a king created by the people like Saul, according to the method which obtains so long as the situation remains within the limits of the natural law; (2) that of a king given by God, like David; (3) that of a pope made by Christ, like Peter; (4) that of a pope elected by the church, like all the other ones. Such is the difference [between pope and king], so far as representing the people is concerned, that the king, whether created by the people or given by God, represents the people and its power. [Saul and David], although they differ from each other in the way in which they become [kings], since the former is appointed by the people and the latter by God, do not differ with regard to the nature of their function and power. Just as a physical organ—say, the hand—if it happens to be produced by God miraculously, is the same as when it is produced by nature, so a political organ—say, the king—when it is created by God, is exactly the same as if it was created by the people, and consequently, whether he is made king by God or by the people, he represents and exercises the power of the people, and he is said to be the vicegerent of the people, not immediately that of God. But the pope, whether made pope immediately by Christ or immediately by the ministry of the church, has the same nature and the same power: and he does not represent the power of the people of the church, he does not represent the people of the church itself, but represents immediately our Lord Jesus Christ and it is of him alone that he is, immediately, the vicegerent.

The foundation for such difference between king and pope is that the royal power, by natural law, resides primarily in the people, and from the people is transferred to the king; but the papal power is above nature, and by divine law resides in one person; it does not reside, first, in a community.[12]

Further, "in relation to the natural end [God] gave power to the community, not to one person; but in relation to the supernatural end, he gave power to one person, not to the community." To the objection that, if the power of the church is not above that of the pope, it follows that church institutions are not so perfect as temporal institutions "because civil society can depose a tyrannical ruler, and the ecclesiastical society could not," Cajetan answers by denying the consequence and argues that "each society, viz., both the civil and the ecclesiastical, can depose a tyrannical ruler, but according to different methods: civil society, which is perfect and free, by exercise of power [*potestative*] and by human providence, the ecclesiastical society through the power of her Father, by means of persevering prayer, when it is really necessary."[13] Cajetan adds that the second method is better than the first, for the first is fallible but not the second.

12. Nos. 562–64: "Et ratio diversitatis in rege et Papa est, quia potestas regia naturali iure est in populo primo, et ex populo derivatur as regem; potestas autem papalis supra naturam est, et divino jure in persona unica, non in communitate primo est."

13. No. 801: ". . . utraque politia, scilicet tam civilis quam ecclesiastica, potest deponere tyrannice regentem ipsam, sed diversimode; quia civilis perfecta et libera potestative et per providentiam humanam, ecclesiastica autem per potestatem sui Patris, per orationis perseverantiam, quando vere oportet."

About three generations after these writings of Cajetan, another important theological document was produced, on the subject of sovereignty in temporal society, by St. Robert Bellarmine. In his "Discussions on the Members of the Church" (Book III: "On the Laymen")[14] he raises the question whether political power is an ethical thing and can be held by Christians. He has in mind the Anabaptists and Trinitarians of the time, with special reference to a statement made in 1568 by a group of ministers in Transylvania. After having shown (chap. vi) that political power is necessary and that its honesty is sanctioned by Holy Scripture, he makes the following remarks:

Firstly, the political power considered in its universal essence, without going down to the peculiarities of monarchy, aristocracy, or democracy, proceeds immediately from God alone, for it follows necessarily upon the nature of man; consequently it proceeds from the one who made man's nature. Further, this power is of natural law and does not depend upon the consent of men; for, whether they like it or not, they must be governed by somebody, unless they want the human genus to perish, which is contrary to the inclination of nature. But the law of nature is a divine law; thus government was established by divine right. . . .

Notice, secondly, that this power has for its immediate subject the whole multitude. Indeed, this power is of divine right; but divine right did not give it to any particular man; therefore, it gave it to the multitude. Moreover, apart from positive law, there is no greater reason why, out of many equals, one rather than another should dominate; therefore, power belongs to the whole multitude. Finally, human society must be a perfect republic; therefore, it must have the power of protecting itself, consequently the power of punishing the enemies of peace, etc.

Notice, thirdly, that this power is transferred from the multitude to one or several by the same law of nature. Since the republic cannot exercise this power for herself, it is bound to transfer it to one per-

14. Bellarmine, *Controversiarum de membris ecclesiae,* lib. III: *De laicis sive secularibus,* chap. vi. (*Opera* [Paris: Vivès, 1870], III, 10–12).

son, or to a few. Thus the power of the princes, considered in its genus, is also of natural and divine right, and the human genus could not, even if all men were gathered, make a decree to the contrary, viz., decree that there be no princes or governors.

Notice, fourthly, that distinct kinds of government, taken in their peculiarity, concern the law of nations, not the law of nature, for it is up to the consent of the multitude to establish above itself a king or consuls or other magistrates. If there is a just cause, the multitude may change a kingdom into an aristocracy or democracy and conversely, as we read that it happened in Rome.

Notice, fifthly, that it follows, from what precedes, that this power, considered in its particular forms, proceeds from God indeed but through the intermediary of human deliberation and choice; the same holds for all the other things that pertain to the law of nations. For the law of nations is, as it were, a conclusion deduced from natural law by human discourse. From this, two differences between the political and ecclesiastical power can be gathered: (1) one concerns the bearer of power, for political power resides in the multitude, but the ecclesiastical power resides immediately in one man as in its bearer; (2) the other concerns the efficient cause, for, whereas the political power, considered universally, is of divine right but, considered in its particular forms, pertains to the law of nations, the ecclesiastical power is in all ways of divine right and immediately from God.

This page of Bellarmine calls for two comments: (1) Bellarmine uses the expression *jus divinum*, "divine right," in a broad sense which can hardly fail to be confusing. Strikingly, the same man holds in the same page what he considers a divine-right theory of political authority and what most modern interpreters would describe as a theory of the sovereignty of the people. This gives an idea of the ambiguity of both these expressions and of the care with which they must be used. (2) Some readers of Bellarmine understood that for him the transmission of power from the whole people to a distinct governing personnel is itself a natural and divinely established obligation. The people, in whom political authority resides primarily, would not, in this interpretation, have the right to retain and to exercise for itself the authority which resides primarily in it. Bellarmine's theory, in short, would rule out direct democracy. Just as the nature of a society demands that there be political authority, so it would demand that political authority be intrusted to the hands of a distinct governing personnel.

In the first chapter of this book we tried to make it clear that the necessity of government is one question and the necessity of a distinct governing personnel an entirely different one. Our particular concern for clarity was motivated by a custom or tradition which associates the two problems, lumps them together, and treats them as if they were one. This customary view was attributed to Bellarmine, but it does not seem to be borne out by the present text. Plainly, Bellarmine does not have in mind, as he is writing this page, any example of direct democracy; he plainly has in mind the incomparably more frequent situation in which the common good demands that power be placed in a few hands. When the situation is such—and it is such in most cases, in fact, in all the cases of which Bellarmine can think—the duty to pursue the common good, which entails the duty to obey political authority, entails also the duty to put it in the hands of a distinct governing personnel, and the people are bound, under the circumstances, to transmit power, just as they are bound, under all circumstances, to obey civil power. All that Bellarmine demonstrates is that the transmission of political power from the multitude to the distinct governing personnel is not a matter delivered to the free choice of the multitude when, as he puts it "the republic cannot exercise such power for itself." Whether this situation is universal and whether there is no conceivable case in which the republic can manage political power for itself according to the requirements of the common good is a question that Bellarmine really does not consider. Notice that

Jefferson expresses himself, on the subject of distinct governing personnel, in terms very close to those of Bellarmine.[15]

The most systematic discussion of the question is found in
Suarez.[16] King James bitterly blamed Bellarmine for having
asserted that authority is not granted by God to the kings as
immediately as it is to the popes; he holds that the king receives his power not from the people but immediately from
God. Suarez' discussion is presented as a vindication of Bellarmine's theory against the criticism of King James. It is
relevant to note that, according to Suarez, the theory of Bellarmine is old and commonly received, whereas that of King
James is new and personal.

First of all, the writer is going to explain what is meant
when it is said that a certain power is immediately from God
or that God is the immediate cause and author of a certain
power. Such propositions imply that God acts as proximate
cause. His action as first and universal cause does not distinguish any particular power; for there is no power not given by
God acting as first and universal cause. Let it be said, for instance, that when the king appoints a person head of a city or
of an army, the power is from God as first cause, yet it is not
immediately from God but from the king (example mine).

Power is said to be immediately given by God, in unqualified
fashion, when God alone, acting through his will is the proximate

15. Thomas Jefferson, Letter to the Abbé Arnond, July 19, 1789 (*Works*, Ford ed.,
V, 103–4): "We think in America that it is necessary to introduce the people into every
department of government as far as they are capable of exercising it. . . . 1. They are
not qualified to exercise themselves the Executive Department; but they are qualified
to name the person who shall exercise it. With us therefore they chuse this office every
4 years. 2. They are not qualified to legislate. With us therefore they only chuse the
legislators. . . ." Let this quotation not be held to imply any stand with regard to the
controversial issue of a possible influence of Bellarmine on Jefferson.

16. Suarez, *Defensio fidei catholicae et apostolicae adversus anglicanae sectae errores*, lib.
III: *De summi pontificis supra temporales reges excellentia, et potestate*, Cap. 2: "Utrum prin-
cipatus politicus immediate a Deo sit, seu ex divina institutione" (*Opera*, XXI [Vene-
tiis, 1749], 114 ff.).

and essential cause that gives power. This is how we shall understand terms in the present discussion for, otherwise, this discussion would be frivolous and useless.

Then Suarez states that there are two ways in which God can give a certain power immediately (immediately: that is, through the exercise of his own power and will alone): (*a*) The power that he gives entertains a natural and necessary connection with the nature of a certain thing, of which nature he is the author. Thus, when God creates the soul, he gives it immediately the intellect and the will, though these powers proceed from the soul's substance. In moral matters an example is supplied by the power of the father, "for the power of the father over the son . . . is given immediately by God himself as the author of nature; it is not a peculiar gift entirely distinct from nature, but it follows necessarily upon nature, once generation is posited as the foundation. Conversely, the subjection of the son to the father is natural, it is from God immediately, it does not proceed from any peculiar disposition superadded to nature but follows necessarily upon the rational nature thus brought into existence." (*b*) The power given by God is not necessarily connected with the creation of a thing, but it is voluntarily superadded by God to nature or to a person. An example would be the power of performing miracles. Another example is the jurisdiction given to Peter: "God conferred it immediately, directly, and *per se*."

At this point Suarez raises the question whether the statement of King James, viz., that God gives temporal power to the kings immediately, holds in any of the senses just explained.

But more specifications are needed. It is necessary to designate with precision the subject to whom God is said to give power immediately and the regime which is supposed to be brought about by this donation of power. The first specification is needed because power can be considered as residing in

the whole body politic or as residing in distinct members of
the community; moreover, power can be considered either absolutely or as determined by a certain form: monarchy, aristocracy, democracy. These propositions and distinctions should
make it possible to show how political authority is immediately from God and how, nevertheless, it is intrusted to kings
and to senates not immediately by God but by man. Here is
Suarez' thesis:

Primarily, the supreme civil power, considered in itself, is given
immediately by God to men assembled into a city or perfect political
community; this does not take place by a peculiar and, as it were,
positive disposition or by a donation entirely distinct from the production of such a nature; it takes place by way of a natural consequence from the first creation of such a nature: therefore, as a result
of such donation this [supreme civil] power is not placed in one person or in any peculiar group but in the whole complete people, or in
the body of the community.

To establish this thesis, Suarez emphasizes the naturalness
of political power. Had there been no revelation, man would
still know for sure that such power is absolutely necessary.
This naturalness and this natural certitude signify that such
power exists in the political community as a property following upon its nature, its creation, its natural establishment.

For if a special gift of God, produced over and above the creation
of society, and a grant not connected with nature were necessary, the
natural reason could not, by itself, be aware of such gift or grant,
which would have to be manifested to men by revelation, in order
that they should know it with certainty; but this is false, as it appears from what was said.

Political power can be said to be immediately from God, inasmuch as

those things which follow upon a nature are given immediately by
the proper and immediate author of this nature . . . ; now, this
power is a property following upon human nature, as cause of the

gathering of men into a political body; therefore, it is given immediately by God as author and manager of this nature.

Suarez repeats emphatically that there is no intermediary between God and the body politic. Far from denying that political power proceeds directly from God, Bellarmine presupposed it, "for he did not posit any intermediary between the people and God; but he stated that between the king and God there is an intermediary, viz., the people, through which the king receives his power."

That political power resides primarily not in any particular person or group of persons but in the community as a whole is demonstrated by the very naturalness of this power:

By the nature of things, this power resides only in the community, inasmuch as it is necessary to the preservation of the latter and inasmuch as it can be manifested by the judgment of the natural reason. But all that the natural reason shows is that this power is necessary in the community as a whole; it does not show that this is necessary in one person or in a senate; therefore, in so far as it is from God immediately, it is merely understood to be in the community as a whole, not in any particular part of it. . . . The natural reason cannot conceive of any cause by which political power would be determinately placed in one person, or in a definite group of persons within the community, rather than in another person or group of persons; therefore, in so far as it is procured by nature, political power does not reside immediately in any subject except the community itself.

The natural reason does not decide, either, that the political regime should be monarchy or aristocracy. But then does it not follow that democracy is of immediate divine institution? This consequence should be denied, of course, if by "institution" is meant a disposition of a *positive* character; if, on the other hand, what is meant is, as it were, a *natural* institution, then this consequence can and must be received. Between monarchy and aristocracy, on the one hand, and democracy, on the other hand, there is this great difference that the former cannot be established without a positive disposition, whether divine or human, whereas democracy can exist without any positive disposition;

but democracy can exist without any positive disposition, as a result of a merely natural establishment or process, without any addition being required except the negation of a new or positive disposition, for the natural reason states that the supreme political power follows upon [the gathering of men into] a perfect community and that, by virtue of this same reason, it belongs to the whole community unless it is transferred by a new disposition.

Natural law gives political power to the community but does not demand that this power should always remain in the community or be directly exercised by it. It remains in the community so long as the community has not decided otherwise or until a change is lawfully brought about by one having power;

thus the perfect civil community is free by law of nature and it is not subjected to any man external to itself; considered as a whole, it has power over itself, and, if no change takes place, this power will be democracy; yet, either through the will of the community itself or through the action of one having power or a just title, political power can be taken away from it and transferred to some person or senate. From which it can be concluded that no king ever had political authority immediately from God or through divine institution (according to the common law), but through the intermediary of human will and human disposition.

Then Suarez considers, in explicit fashion, what is now called the "designation theory," i.e., the theory according to which the multitude is concerned merely with the choice of the ruling person:

One might say that this argumentation proves only that royal power is not given by God to a person without the intervention of human will and human action; but this is not a sufficient ground to deny that this power is immediately from God. Apostolic dignity was given to Matthias through the action of the other apostles, yet it was given to him immediately by God; similarly, the Pope is elected by cardinals, yet he receives his power from God immediately.

This objection, Suarez says, does not invalidate, but rather confirms, the preceding demonstration, first, because the analogy does not hold, then because it was never asserted that *any* intervention of human will or action suffices to cause the gift of power not to be from God immediately. Such immediacy is excluded only when there are

peculiar change and transfer effected by a new human disposition. Thus human action or human will can intervene in two ways in the conferring of a power that has its origin in God: (1) By merely designating or appointing a person who comes to occupy a dignity founded by God, under the very conditions in which this dignity was founded, and without authority or power to change it, to increase it, or to decrease it. This mode has obtained, with regard to the pontifical dignity, by way of carnal succession in the old law; in the new law it obtains by way of the legal election through which the person is designated. . . . (2) In different fashion the conferring of power by man may consist in a new donation or disposition, going beyond the designation of the person; then, even if such power has a foundation in some anterior divine donation made to another one, nevertheless, the conferring which takes place later is absolutely speaking of human right and not of divine right; it is immediately from man, not from God.

As to the circumstances in which kings acquire power, Suarez knows of two procedures, which he does not put on equal footing: (1) "In the original disposition" power is granted through the voluntary consent of the people, which consent can be given gradually, as the people increases, in which case royal power and perfect community come into existence simultaneously; it also happens that a complete community elects deliberately a king to whom it transfers its power. Here the community is anterior to the king. "This procedure is in principle the most convenient and the most rational. At the death of the king, there is no need for new elections or a new consent: royal dignity is transmitted by virtue of the original consent.'' (2) It happens that free peoples are subjected to kings through war, either justly or unjustly. If the war waged by the conqueror is just, the subjection of the conquered is just also, it is a just punishment which has the same effect as a contract with regard to the transfer of power and must be lived up to like a contract. More frequently, war is unjust: yet the people may later consent to the rule originally imposed upon them by unjust conquest. Of such cases Bellarmine had given significant examples: ''the rule of the Franks has become lawful by universal consent, although, originally, the Franks occupied Gaul unjustly''; the same holds for Spain with the Goths; it holds for England; and it holds for the Roman Empire, ''which was founded by Julius Caesar, oppressor of his country, and yet later became so lawful that our Lord said 'Give to Caesar the things that are Caesar's.' ''

To conclude the exposition of the transmission theory, it is proper to examine whether the three authorities of Cajetan Bellarmine, and Suarez give a unified expression of it. This question should, in our opinion, be answered in the affirmative. The only point that might cause difficulty is whether the people has the right not to transfer sovereignty to a distinct personnel. As already mentioned, the theory that the people would always be under obligation to place powers in the hands of a distinct personnel seems to be born of a misreading of Bellarmine. Cajetan does not, to my knowledge, tackle the issue at all. Of the three, Suarez alone voices the theory that democracy comes into existence *by nature* as opposed to monarchy and aristocracy, which cannot come into existence except by positive disposition. But if the other two admit that the transmission of power is not obligatory under all conceivable circumstances, they imply thereby that there is one law-

ful regime, viz., direct democracy, whose coming into existence requires no disposition to be effected by positive human
act, over and above the natural possession of power by the
multitude. In so far as the scanty texts of Aquinas make for
interpretation in terms of the transmission theory, it can be
said that the same theory of natural democracy is implicitly
held, unless one assumes that the people is never allowed to
govern itself directly, which assumption seems contrary to the
expressions of Aquinas. If law is said to be issued *either* by the
community *or* by the vicegerent of the community; if, further,
it is held that "the consent of the whole people expressed by
a custom counts far more in favor of a particular observance
than does the authority of the sovereign, who has not the
power to frame laws, except as representing the people,"
there must be a conceivable situation in which the community
elicits its own laws without the operation of any vicegerent.
And if the power to make laws belongs primarily to the community itself, no special positive institution is needed to bring
about a situation in which the community makes use of this
power; the natural democracy of Suarez seems to be nothing
else than such a situation. On this issue the obvious difference
between Suarez and Aquinas is one of language: as is known,
the latter, following the example set by Aristotle, generally
uses the word "democracy" to designate a corrupt form of
government.

AUTHORITY IN DEMOCRACY

Among the obnoxious simplifications which fill the treatises
of political science, let us single out the proposition that the
divine-right theory is theocratic and the sovereignty-of-the-
people theory democratic. If theocracy means the ruling of
temporal society by the spiritual power, no theory of divine
right is theocratic. The common view that every lawful authority holds from God the power of binding man's conscience

is not theocratic but rather dismisses all theocratic claim by
supplying the temporal power with a complete justification.
And King James's theory is shrewdly calculated to exclude all
threat of theocracy by setting, between the king and God, a
relation equal to that which obtains between the pope and
God (at least equal, for the privilege of hereditary transmission can make it even better). As to the expression "sovereignty of the people," we know that it may refer to the coach-
driver theory, in which case there is nothing democratic about
the so-called "sovereignty of the people," for there cannot be
democratic government when the very essence of government
is negated; this lust for a situation in which the need of society
for leadership would be satisfied without the leader (who may
well be the community itself, expressing itself through majority vote) being endowed with any authority does not pertain
to democracy any more than to any other regime, although
it is in the democratic framework that it expects satisfaction,
so that democracy is particularly exposed to its destructive
power. If, on the other hand, the expression "sovereignty of
the people" refers to the transmission theory, it should be
mentioned that this theory was never understood to hold for
democracy alone. Historians often described the views of
Bellarmine and Suarez as expressions of the democratic theory
of sovereignty; yet neither of these thinkers meant to recommend democracy. They both had in view principally the
monarchical governments of their time; and against the disorderly claims of emerging absolutism they meant to define
general conditions of political sovereignty holding for every
political government, whether democratic or not.

This point should be stressed: the transmission theory is not
understood by its proponents to be distinctly democratic. It is
distinctly *political*, no more.[17] The implications of its *political*

17. The "free people" of which Aquinas speaks (i–ii. 97. 3, ad 3) seems to be a
people subjected to *political* government in the sense defined in chap. ii.

character are three: (1) it concerns the state, i.e., the complete or perfect *temporal* community; (2) it concerns the fully *legitimate* government of such community rather than what we call a *de facto* government, which must be obeyed for the single reason that, under the circumstances, disobedience would entail more inconvenience than obedience; (3) it concerns, finally, a government which is *political* in the sense defined in the second chapter of this book, viz., in the sense in which a political system is understood to imply a degree of autonomy and a legally defined power of resistance in the hands of the governed. If a despotic regime happens to be legitimate (as in the case, mentioned by Suarez, of a rule resulting from just conquest and not yet sanctioned by popular consent), the transmission theory of sovereignty does not apply fully; true, the normal characteristics of temporal society are but partly realized; for a society which can be lawfully ruled in despotic fashion is one that has not yet attained maturity as a complete temporal society or one that has lost the privileges of maturity through some perversion.

When the concept of temporal government is realized with all its implications, the transmission theory of sovereignty holds, regardless of whether government is democratic, aristocratic, monarchical, or mixed. It implies that the governed consent to the government which is theirs, but it does not imply that this consent is necessarily exercised in the democratic procedure of election. The constitutional powers of the British king and those of the French president are similar in several respects: the French president is elected by the people, though indirectly; the British king is designated by heredity; both enjoy the consent of the majority. In the case of the president, this consent is expressed by election; in the case of the king, without any election. Notice that the popular consent given to the British king without any voting procedure is at least as genuine, sincere, profound, and unmistakably established as the consent given, through election, to the French president. The transmission theory implies that the power which primarily belongs to the people and has been transmitted by it to a distinct governing personnel can be withdrawn from unworthy rulers. We saw how firmly Cajetan maintains that the church is unlike the state so far as deposition of the unworthy ruler is concerned. According to Cajetan, the deposition of the unworthy king by the people constitutes the exercise of a power superior to that of the king, and there is no power superior to that of the pope, except that of Christ himself; so that the deposition of the heretical pope has to be accounted for in a way essentially different from the way in which the deposition of the unworthy king is accounted for. Thus, whether the regime is democratic or not, the transmission theory holds that the people, after having transmitted power and having placed itself in a position of mandatory obedience, retains a power greater than the power transmitted; this power is to be exercised when, and only when, the governing personnel are gravely unfaithful to their task. Consider, for the sake of clarity, the case of a monarchy according to the old pattern, i.e., that of a monarchy associated with few, if any, democratic elements; according to the transmission theory, the people enjoys, in such a system, a power greater than that of the king; what difference and what relation are there between this power of the people in a nondemocratic state and the power of democratic control?

The transmission theory holds that the people still possesses, after transmission has been effected, a power greater than that of the governing personnel; yet, in an aristocratic or monarchical regime this power cannot be lawfully exercised except in extreme cases: this is not democratic control, which is periodically exercised without there being anything abnormal or extraordinary about the circumstances. The British can vote Mr. Churchill out of power without even implying that they are dissatisfied with his record; they may merely mean that, after the war has been won, they intend to turn to tasks for which another administration is better qualified. The common right of deposition, which the transmission theory grants to every politically organized people, cannot be lawfully exercised without extraordinary circumstances, without dire and immediate threat to the common good. Thus, between the two, the difference is obvious. It can be illustrated by a comparison with the laws concerning the ownership of earthly goods. Anyone, no matter how destitute, may become lawful owner of a loaf of bread in case of extreme necessity. Yet there is a great difference, with regard to the use of wealth, between the man who can acquire it by regular means, i.e., by paying for it, and the man who can acquire it only in extraordinary circumstances and through the extraordinary privileges of extreme necessity. The people who transmitted power within democratic forms exercise, whenever election time comes, a power which may be likened to that of the regular owner over his regularly possessed goods. The people who transmitted power to a hereditary king and depose their ruler on account of high treason or some extraordinary mismanagement exercise a right that can be likened to that of anyone to make use of earthly goods, in an extreme emergency, to preserve his life or that of those who belong to him.

No matter how clear the difference between the common right of deposition and the democratic right of control, it is hardly possible to give much thought to the former without inclining toward the establishment of the latter. If people envisage the removal of their ruler as a contingency likely to occur in not extremely rare cases, they are logically inclined to promote institutions that can handle the procedure of deposition in nonrevolutionary fashion; such institutions, almost inevitably, turn out to be the beginning of democratic control. But what are the peoples who fail to realize that the removal of bad rulers is a thing necessary in not exceedingly rare cases? Such peoples are those among whom a mythical representation of the governing personnel prevails, as in traditional Japan and also in nontraditional countries where many persons have come to believe that the genius of history is embodied in a definite party. Since there can be no question of deposing the genius of history, there is no use contemplating circumstances under which it might be necessary to get rid of such a party. Let the conclusion be that the concept of popular control inherent in the transmission theory and inseparable from it favors the promotion of democracy, although it is not distinctly democratic and finds application in every fully political system.

The features characterizing the behavior of sovereignty in democracy are still to be disengaged. Let us use, as a starting point, the trivial consideration that democracy alone admits of nontransmission of power. If the people, having received sovereignty from God, refrains from taking the human measures necessary for the establishment of monarchy or aristocracy, it finds itself constituted as a democratic society by its very abstention. Nontransmission of authority means democracy in its most typical form. Although a regime implying no transmission of power and no distinct governing personnel is a rare occurrence, it is plain that direct rule of the whole community through majority vote is the archetype of all democratic institutions and the fundamental pattern which must be referred to whenever there is a problem of understanding the democratic element in a mixed society.

What characterizes the democratic condition of sovereignty is that, in a democracy, sovereignty is never completely transmitted. But let us first consider in what sense sovereignty can be said to be completely transmitted in a nondemocratic regime. If the nondemocratic regime is political in the full sense of the term, the people remains capable of exercising a power superior to that of the king; but the act of transmission implies that such power can be exercised only under extraordinary circumstances and on account of a dire threat to the welfare of the community. Under normal circumstances the transmission of power to the king precludes the exercise of this popular power which is greater than that of the king. According to the theory of Cajetan, the king deposed by the people is deposed by a power superior to his; thus it would not be appropriate to say that, under extreme circumstances, the power transmitted to the king reverts to the people; for the deposition of the king as described by Cajetan, in a sharp contrast with the deposition of the heretical pope, implies the exercise of a power superior to that of the king; it implies that, *while the king is still in power*, another power superior to his, viz., the power of the people, steps in and puts an end to the power of the king. Are we back to the coach-driver theory? The temptation is great to say that the transmission of power is ungenuine and merely apparent. If the people retains a power superior to that of the king, it looks very much as if the king were only a secretary or manager hired by the people. To this difficulty let it be answered that, in order for the transmission of power to be genuine, it suffices that the superior power of the people should be suspended by the act of transmission and should remain suspended until circumstances of extreme seriousness give back to the people the right to exercise it. While royal power is normally exercised, the people remains in possession of a power superior to that of the king; otherwise, it could not, under extreme circumstances, depose the king by virtue of a power superior to his. *But the act of genuine transmission suspends the exercise of the people's power; subjection to the king is genuine; subjects are bound in conscience to obey the genuine power of the king.* The proper effect of the extraordinary circumstances under which the people can depose the king is to make it again lawful for the people to exercise a power which it never ceased to have but which could not be lawfully exercised under normal circumstances. The key to the interpretation of the case is the notion that the actual possession of a power does not necessarily entail the right to use it actually and that the suspension of the right to use a certain power does not necessarily entail the loss of this power. The following example may help to explain this important point.

Let us think of a constitutional ruler to whom the constitution gives extraordinary powers (e.g., that of issuing laws without parliamentary vote) in emergency situations. When an emergency materializes, what is it, precisely, that happens? Extraordinary powers are given to the governor not by the emergency but by the constitution. But the constitution gave such powers under such limitations that any claim to exercise them outside the emergency situation would be high treason. What the emergency effects is the releasing of powers given by the constitution under the provision that they are emergency powers and, consequently, cannot be lawfully exercised except in an emergency. Similarly, the people who transmitted power to a king would be guilty of criminal disobedience if they decided to depose the king for no extraordinarily grave reasons. It would be like a constitutional ruler fancying to exercise emergency powers when there is no emergency. Thus the superior power retained by the people does not jeopardize the genuineness of the transmission. Transmission is so genuine as to bind the superior power of the people, to tie it up in such a way that extraordinarily serious circumstances alone can untie it. The situation, so interpreted, does not resemble the relation symbolized by the coach-driver any more than a constitutional ruler endowed with emergency powers resembles an absolute despot.

This is, briefly, the sense in which transmission of power is complete in a nondemocratic regime. Its completeness does not mean that the power of the people ceases to be superior to that of the king. Such superiority cannot cease. It is due to the very nature of civil society and to the privilege of the civil multitude as first bearer of God-given power. In this very precise sense the sovereignty of the people is inalienable.

What distinguishes democracy is that in a democratic regime transmission of sovereignty is incomplete even in the sense in which it would be complete if the regime were nondemocratic. In other words, over and above this nontransmissible power that the people retains under all circumstances,[18] the people, in a democracy, retains the exercise of powers which are transmissible and would be transmitted if the regime were not democratic. *Democracy never transmits the whole of the transmissible powers. Every democracy remains, in varying degree, a direct democracy.*

Let us briefly survey the features which evidence, in common democratic practice, the partial nontransmission of sovereignty. If government by distinct personnel is made democratic by the control of the people over the governing personnel through the procedure of periodical election, the very definition of democracy (indirectly exercised) points to merely partial transmission of sovereignty. It cannot be said that sovereignty is entirely transmitted to distinct personnel when the basic understanding is that this personnel will render accounts at the end of a determinate period and be reinstated or not by act of the people's sovereignty. But, in addition to the basic procedure of control over the governing personnel through periodical election, democratic practice always retains some aspects of direct democratic government. One of these practices is the obligation of submitting some particularly important laws (e.g., constitutional dispositions) to referendum. Another one, so common that without it democracy, at least in modern societies, is inconceivable, and so

18. Again, we are considering a people satisfying the conditions of *political* government.

broad in its scope as to affect all aspects of political life, is the power of public opinion.

This is one aspect by which normal democratic practice bears resemblance to the coach-driver system. On account of this resemblance, this aspect of democratic practice can favor the inconspicuous corruption of democracy into masked anarchy. What are we requested to do when organizations pray that we bombard our congressman with letters to the effect that we want him to vote in such and such fashion? Bombardment of congressmen by letters from the electors may be interpreted in either of two ways, and this is why it is always a risky method. It may be interpreted as meaning that power of legislation and control over the executive has never been genuinely transmitted to the United States Congress, that this power has been retained by the people, and that, accordingly, congressmen are merely managers hired by the people for the enforcement of their will. This interpretation, familiar to all demagogues, violates the Constitution of the United States and constitutes an appeal to rebellion. It is fitting to recall here Bellarmine's proposition that the people is not morally free to transmit or not to transmit power. As explained, this proposition does not necessarily signify that Bellarmine ignores the lawfulness of direct democracy. It means that, when circumstances are such that a distinct governing personnel is needed, the people is obligated to create such a governing personnel and to transmit authority to it. Transmission of authority is not necessary under all circumstances. *There are circumstances under which a community can do without distinct governing personnel, but the thing which is never ethical and never political is insincere, ungenuine, unfaithful, apparent, and not real— in short, treacherous—transmission of authority.* A king may not be restricted by constitutional control; but, if he is, he cannot ignore constitutional control without violating the constitution and deserving the most severe punishment. Similarly, a people may not transmit sovereignty; it may, if circumstances allow, govern itself directly by majority vote and know of no distinct personnel except managers. But when circumstances demand that power be transmitted to a distinct governing personnel, when this demand of the common good has been sanctioned by fundamental law, every attempt at corrupting transmission of power into an ungenuine process is sheer revolt against the fundamental law of the country. Provided that those things are understood, public opinion has a noble part to play in the operation of democratic government.

The truth is that in every democracy, at least under modern conditions, the people retains the character of a deliberating assembly. The constitutional tradition of Great Britain provides for two assemblies, the House of Lords and the House of Commons; but a less articulate part of the constitution gives considerable power to a third assembly, viz., the people, as able to express its thoughts and wills through the common channels of public opinion. The Constitution of the United States was written with a higher degree of self-consciousness; yet it includes an unwritten part which gives considerable power to a third assembly, viz., the people of the United States. That the powers of this informal assembly should not be mentioned in any formal document is easy to understand and entirely normal. But, because of the informal character of this assembly and of the unwritten character of its powers, great uncertainties inevitably ensue, and it is in the shadow of these uncertainties that democratic government ceaselessly undergoes the temptation of being corrupted into a coach-driver system. Again, all the essential features of government are found in a direct democracy. In a society ruled by majority vote, without distinct governing personnel, everyone is bound to obey; it is only by accident that one happens to be in the majority and to follow one's own judgment as one acts according to the decision of the majority. *Nontransmission of*

*power does not destroy the essence of government; but ungenuine trans-
mission does.* We mentioned earlier that a citizen of a direct
democracy who is determined to abide by the law only when
the law is what he wants it to be always behaves as a rebel,
never as a law-abiding citizen, even when he performs—in a
purely material sense—the actions prescribed by the law.
Similarly, ungenuinely transmitted sovereignty implies constant rebellion, even when the laws and decrees issued by the
governing personnel are complied with. Practices calculated
to assure the influence of the people on the policies of actually
elected assemblies and executive agencies are ambiguous and
risky, which does not mean that they are not necessary and important. So long as letters addressed to congressmen, press
campaigns, petitions, and street demonstrations are merely
the expression of opinions held by the consultative assembly
established, in unwritten fashion, by every democratic constitution, all is normal and sound. If, on the other hand, such
expressions of opinion are calculated to deprive the men in
power of their right to command, of their duty to have a
judgment of their own, of their responsibility, of their conscience; if such practices are calculated to change, through
threat and bribe, into mere secretaries or managers or mes-
sengers or mandate-holders or coach-drivers, men who know
that they are under obligation to exercise authority, to have a
prudence of their own and to make use of it, to be governors
and not mere managers; men who know that, as a consequence
of transmission, they cannot give up the character of holders
of authority without criminal failure to fulfil their task: such
practices mean rebellion and treachery established at the core
of political life. They tend to corrupt political life into a com-
petitive system where all moral idea is absent. Promises,
formal and informal bribes, threats of all kinds, not excluding
physical ones, and soon slander and calumny become determining factors in public life. In such confusion there is no

guaranty that the majority's wishes should prevail; it is all a question of force, and the greater force may not be on the side of the majority. In most cases it is more likely to belong to the minority—often a handful of particularly rebellious characters—who control the means of pressure. Practices calculated to make the transmission of sovereignty ungenuine do not lead the people to any sort of direct democracy but rather to oligarchic situations that are totally unwished for, except by their beneficiaries.

It would be very helpful, if it were at all possible, to formulate rules and criteria concerning those practices which, if our analysis is correct, can be either an important phase of democratic life or sheer rebellion, destructive of democracy and of political relations. One proposition can be safely uttered: in such matters quantity is of decisive importance, and the species of an action changes according as this action is of moderate, or of extreme, intensity. The situation of a congressman who receives, once in a while, letters in which a few electors voice their opinions seems not to differ, except quantitatively, from that of the congressman who is constantly disturbed by telegrams, telephone calls, and special deliveries. In fact, as often happens in human affairs, a change in quantity entails here a qualitative change, and nobody can say exactly where the qualitative change has taken place. (Changes that take place surreptitiously are always suspicious.) If some circumstances ever make it necessary to wage an extremely intensive campaign of opinion, those circumstances are not of the same kind as the circumstances which justify a campaign of moderate intensity.

Let us try, further, to define the qualitatively different characteristics of moderate and intensive campaigns. With due allowance for the element of relativity implied in all such considerations, let it be said that the moderate campaign implies merely a determination to have a certain opinion known and taken into consideration. An intensive campaign, on the other hand, means determination to assure the victory of an opinion. Now, an assembly whose opinions are merely to be taken into consideration is a consultative, deliberative, or advisory assembly; but one whose opinions are meant to be final decisions, delivered for purposes of realization to executive agencies, is more than a consultative assembly, it is a legislating and governing one. In short, considering that in every democracy the people retains the character of an assembly that has normally a part to play in the government, let it be said that the transmission of sovereignty to a distinct governing personnel leaves to the people the character of a merely consultative assembly. Granted that, in addition to the Senate and the House, formally established by written constitution, the democratic organization of the federal government actually comprises a third assembly, informally constituted and not mentioned in a written document—that of the people of the United States— let our conclusion be that, whereas the first two assemblies are endowed with the power of decision, the third one is merely consultative in character. Campaigns of opinion, when they become intensive, treat the people as if it were possessed with a power of decision. This is the meaning of the qualitative change corresponding to the change of intensity: a moderately intensive political campaign treats the assembly of the people as a consultative assembly; an extremely intense campaign of opinion treats the people as an assembly endowed with a power of decision. A congressman who receives, once in a while, letters that let him know how various groups of electors feel about impending legislation and executive policies is a man in power who receives advice from people normally endowed with an advisory function. A congressman bombarded with telegrams, phone calls, and special deliveries, even if those messages contain no threats and no bribes, is treated as a man in charge of enforcing decisions described to him as made by the third assembly, that of the whole people. But if the assembly of the people retains a power of decision and if its power of decision is understood to overrule the judgment of the Congress, then sovereignty has not been transmitted to the Congress in a genuine way. In order for campaigns of opinion to avoid the character of rebellion, it is necessary that they should treat the assembly of the people as a merely consultative assembly. Then they will be but moderately intensive.

It remains to be considered whether it is ever lawful for a people that has transmitted authority to claim more than the character of a consultative assembly, to claim a power of decision. The answer is not dubious: after authority has been regularly transmitted, the people can make decisions only when it can and ought to exercise this power which is greater than that of the governing personnel and which cannot be transmitted. One way to exercise this power is by deposing the governing persons; this is an extreme procedure, almost never necessary in a democracy, since democratic institutions subject the governing personnel to periodical re-examination. Another procedure is intense opinion pressure. To conclude: Intense campaigns of opinion, which imply that the people has the power of decision, are lawful only when circumstances are so grave as to give the people a right to exercise, albeit in limited fashion, the power greater than that of the governing personnel which was suspended, but not nullified, by the act of transmission.

It should now be possible to analyze the expression "government by the consent of the governed"—a historic and glorious expression which will never fall out of use. It has several meanings, which cannot be distinguished in political speeches or even in statements of principles. Such is the paradox of political notions considered in their sociological existence; for it is in a state of confusion that they are most active and produce their most important effects. About all the clarity that these subjects admit of will be procured if instruments of clarification are available to whoever needs and cares to use them. To work out such instruments and see that they are kept in good order is what political philosophers are paid for.

1. The proposition that government requires the consent of the governed may mean that political association is an act of the reason and of the will; that political society is not brought about by instinct and infra-rational forces but by rational judgment and free will and, more precisely, by the good use of reason and freedom and by the qualities which render such use steady, i.e., wisdom, justice, and friendship. So understood, the theory of government by the consent of the governed expresses a truth of great profundity and consequence. It is particularly important to recall it and to understand it in a time like ours, since the social sciences, understandably, are influenced by the successful pattern of the physical sciences and consequently tend to represent human societies as a product of nature, in the sense in which nature means univocal determination and is spoken of in opposition to free will. The naturalistic concept of political society does not proceed only from the deterministic philosophy of human nature generally associated with materialism and positivism; it proceeds also from a conservative and traditionalistic reaction against the political voluntarism which has been and remains at work in the ideological and emotional movements connected with Rousseau and the French Revolution. In their righteous opposition to propositions which seemed to describe political society as a work of human arbitrariness, some traditionalists so emphasized the natural character of society as to make it appear a product antedecent to any activity of reason and freedom, a product, accordingly, foreign to morality, at least so far as its basic constitution is concerned.

2. The notion of consent of the people may refer to the designation of the governing personnel. What is signified, then, is that political leaders are not self-appointed but are designated by the people according to procedures which admit of great variety and of which the least formal are not necessarily the least genuine. Under extraordinary circumstances, when elections and even regular consultations of public opinion are impossible, a handful of men may declare that they are the government and not be rebels. Think of the circumstances which led to the constitution of governments-in-exile during the occupation of Europe by the Nazis. In order for such a creation of leadership to be better than sheer rebellion, the indispensable condition is that there be, in the historical situation, a demand for such creation. This demand may be at variance with the conscious wishes of the majority. Thus, initially, a governing agency may exist and operate without the consent of the people. Plainly, it does not possess fully the character of a government until the self-appointed leaders are confirmed in power by popular consent. So long as such consent has not been expressed, the men who claim authority do not possess, except in a rudimentary and uncertain fashion, the prerogatives of a political organization. A committee which claims to be the government, whose purposes and activities seem to be borne out by the historical situation, but which has not yet been confirmed by any expression of popular consent, is one of these nontypical forms that history produces in times of crises and revolutions. In order to behave properly toward such nontypical forms, either by recognizing them or by opposing them, individuals need an unusual amount of lucidity; they have to make a clear decision in a situation which is not clear. They have to draw a definite line of action in a situation which is not definite. The virtue which produces such lucidity when all is dark is the fortitude of the heroes.

3. The proposition that government requires the consent of

the governed may mean that the leaders of temporal society do not receive their power directly from God and that political power does not reside in any distinct governing personnel unless it has been transmitted to them by the people. So understood, the theory of government by consent of the people would be identical with the transmission theory as opposed to the designation theory. A difficulty arises with regard to situations in which plainly lawful government is exercised without the governed having effected any transmission of power. Think, for instance, of the power exercised in conquered territory by the conqueror; if the war was fully just, this power is also fully just, though badly exposed to abuse. Or think of some barbarous population reluctantly controlled by a colonizing power. In spite of frequent and grave abuse, it would be absurd to deny that power exercised under such circumstances may be perfectly lawful. It may be lawful indeed, but not political. It is paternal authority, substitutional authority, in the sense of our first chapter.

4. The proposition that governments derive their powers from the consent of the governed may imply a demand for the periodical exercise of popular consent through the phases of political life. So understood, this proposition refers to the peculiar situation of sovereignty in democracy; it may even be considered the very formula of democratic government. If it is posited that consent of the people ought not to be given once and for all but should be elicited anew as political life goes on, there are only two possibilities, viz., direct democracy and control of the people over the governing personnel through the procedure of periodical election, that is, representative democracy.

5. The formula under consideration may signify determination to avoid complete transmission of authority. In this case it refers, again, to a situation which is not common to all lawful and political governments but proper to democracy. It

refers to the fact that every democracy is, in a measure, a direct democracy and that in every democracy the people at large retains the character of a deliberative assembly which participates in the government by voicing its assent or dissent in several ways. Referring to what was said above of the people's assembly in indirect democracy, let it be mentioned that, so understood, the theory of government by the consent of the people must be held with discrimination and awareness of the risks.

6. The theory of government by consent of the people may mean that, all other things being equal, persuasion is a better instrument of government than coercion. It implies, then, that every government has a duty to seek the maximum of voluntary co-operation, to explain its purposes and methods, to educate the governed, to appeal indefatigably to whatever element of good will can be found in them, and never to resort to coercion unless persuasion proves impossible. Such interpretation is entirely wholesome and necessary, provided that it is unmistakably maintained that the use of coercion is fully legitimate whenever persuasion fails to accomplish some necessary purpose.

7. In the six preceding senses the notion of government by the consent of the governed expresses either (*a*) an essential condition of lawful government, (*b*) a condition proper to political government precisely considered as political, or (*c*) some condition proper to democracy. But in a seventh sense the formula is understood to mean that the governed are never bound except by their own consent, that they never obey except inasmuch as they please to obey—briefly, that they are never obligated to obey. So understood, the theory that government demands the consent of the governed expresses neither a political nor a democratic necessity but mere revolt against the laws of all community.

CHAPTER IV
DEMOCRATIC EQUALITY

*

OUR treatment of democratic equality will be centered about the problem of the relations between equality and freedom. The political history of the working class, in the framework of modern democracy, contains a powerful statement of this problem. Referring to a general picture best exemplified by Continental Europe in the nineteenth century, it may be said that, during the phase of democratic struggle against the old aristocratic and monarchical order, liberty and equality are considered inseparable. The Third Estate identifies itself with the people at large, and the growth of a Fourth Estate is not yet rumored. The will to be free and the claim for equality seem to be but two aspects of the same enthusiasm. The doctrinal weapon of the struggle is a universalist philosophy which, through emphasis on the unity of human nature, proclaims simultaneously the equality of men and the end of arbitrary authority. When the old order is defeated, the leading section of the Third Estate makes a statement to the effect that the revolution is over. But soon a split takes place within what was the Third Estate. The Fourth Estate has arisen, with a new claim for equality—a claim which sounds unintelligible to its former allies of the bourgeoisie.

As soon as the working class asserted its existence as a distinct sociological entity, interpreters of its consciousness, whether workers or nonworkers, strove toward a doctrinal expression of its needs and ideals. These efforts resulted in a multitude of constructions whose extreme heterogeneity makes it more remarkable that general usage, in spite of

195

strong objections, imposes upon them a common name: this name is "socialism."

It may not be possible to work out a definition covering all theories and movements which can be described, without arbitrariness, as socialistic. Yet some features appear with striking constancy, if not with complete regularity, in these theories and movements. One such feature is a new demand for equality. True, to describe socialist doctrines as universally equalitarian would be a very crude oversimplification. One of the first and most decisively important of them, Saint-Simonism, was conceived by men possessed with a strong sense of distinction and was antiequalitarian in many respects. But the Saint-Simonists stressed equality of opportunity to the point of ruling out the right of inheritance—a step that liberal revolutions never contemplated. As is known, Saint-Simonism was strongly influenced by Napoleonic patterns; this sort of equality appealed to workers just as it appealed to the soldiers of Napoleon.

Our time, which has experienced the worst counterattack of oligarchic exploitation in modern history, experiences also equalitarian trends of unprecedented power. Many a conservative has come to consider that all honest men have a claim on the goods that "our betters" traditionally cherished. The progress of equalitarian ideas is perhaps most significantly evidenced by the fact that equalitarian conservatism is no longer a paradoxical attitude. But the historical forces which promoted equality remain restless. The peaceful enjoyment of newly won equalitarian relations is made impossible by intense worries. This restlessness, to a considerable extent, results from doubts concerning the relation between equality and freedom. The formula which attributed basic unity of meaning to freedom and equality seems to have been lost as soon as the defeat of the old hierarchies was certain. Through feats of organization and skilful manipulation of words, governments, especially those inclined toward totalitarianism, try to stun the people and to dodge the issue. But the issue is too vital to be dodged, and confusion is entertained by the feeling that the cost of equality might be the surrender of much freedom.

The equality of men is an ideal subject for empty talk and barren controversy. In order to avoid at least the most irrelevant comments, it should be understood that the proper statement of the question cannot be: Are men equal or unequal? Let us rather consider such questions as these: In what respects are men equal and in what respects are they not equal? Among the forms of equality which it is in the power of man to promote, which ones should be promoted and which ones should not? The necessity of continual distinctions of aspects or points of view in the treatment of equality will be held axiomatic throughout this study.

EQUALITY AS UNITY OF NATURE

To ask whether men are *essentially* equal, in spite of all the accidents which cause inequality among them, is the same as to ask whether there is one human nature, common to all men. Anyone recognizes here a particular case of the problem of the universals,[1] to which logicians used to dedicate much labor and ingenuity. Without a reminder, no matter how brief, of the principles commanding this issue, such expressions as "human nature," "the unity of human nature," etc., would never have a definite sense.

The treatment of universality achieved decisive progress when Thomas Aquinas explained that the predicates "universal" and "individual" pertain not to the intelligible constitution of any nature but to the states in which natures exist,

1. John of St. Thomas *Cursus philosophicus, Logica* ii. 14. 2 (Turin: Marietti, 1930), I, 507, a 4): "Univocatio vero physica est aequalitas etiam in inferioribus contrahentibus superiorem rationem, qualis invenitur solum in speciebus atomis, quae equalitatem habent in individuis."

to their way of existence.[2] There are within each thing features which belong necessarily to its constitution, without which this thing would not be what it is and without the grasp of which it is not understood for what it is. Think of the plan of a building in the mind of the architect; when the phase of planning is over, the determination of the building with regard to situation, materials, arrangements, size, etc., is complete. The problem that remains to be solved is one of execution or realization; it concerns the difference between not to be and to be, it does not concern any of the constitutive

2. *On Being and Essence*, chap. iii, trans. A. A. Maurer (Toronto: Pontifical Institute of Mediaeval Studies, 1949), pp. 38–39: ". . . we can consider it [i.e., nature or essence] in two ways. First, we can consider it according to its proper meaning, which is to consider it absolutely. In this sense, nothing is true of it except what belongs to it as such; whatever else is attributed to it, the attribution is false. For example, to man as man belongs rational, animal and whatever else his definition includes, whereas white or black, or anything of this sort, which is not included in the concept of humanity, does not belong to man as man. If someone should ask, then, whether the nature so considered can be called *one* or *many*, neither should be granted, because both are outside the concept of humanity and both can be added to it. If plurality were included in the concept of humanity, it could never be one, although it is one inasmuch as it is present in Socrates. Similarly, if unity were contained in its concept, then Socrates' and Plato's nature would be one and the same, and it could not be multiplied in many individuals.

"Nature or essence is considered in a second way with reference to the act of existing [*esse*] it has in this or that individual. When the nature is so considered, something is attributed to it accidentally by reason of the thing in which it exists; for instance, we say that man is white because Socrates is white, although whiteness does not pertain to man as man.

"This nature has a twofold act of existing, one in individual things, the other in the mind; and according to both modes of existing, accidents accompany the nature. In individual beings, moreover, it has numerous acts of existing corresponding to the diversity of individuals. Yet, the nature itself, considered properly—that is to say, absolutely—demands none of these acts of existing. It is false to say that the nature of man as such exists in this individual man, because, if existing in this individual belonged to man as man, it would never exist outside this individual. Similarly, if it belonged to man as man not to exist in this individual, human nature would never exist in it. It is true to say, however, that it does not belong to man as man to exist in this or that individual, or in the intellect. Considered in itself, the nature of man thus clearly abstracts from every act of existing, but in such a way that none may be excluded from it. And it is the nature considered in this way that we predicate of all individual beings."

features of "that which was to be."[3] All the difference between the building as planned in the architect's mind and the
actually existing building concerns the way in which the
thing exists, not the system of features that cause it to be what
it is and to be intelligible as a definite sort of being. The actually existing building, in case of a real storm, shelters real humans, and the merely planned building shelters but imaginary
dwellers against imaginary storms. Yet it is, in various states,
the same building: same location, same size, same materials,
same arrangement. How is it that one and the same thing admits of conditions so different from each other as merely objective existence in the mind and actual existence in the world of
reality? What makes both conditions possible is that neither
pertains to the necessary constitution of the thing. Examine
this building in detail; you will find that it contains seven
bedrooms, one living-room, one kitchen, one dining-room,
etc.; but this inquiry, no matter how thorough, will never
yield, as one feature among other features, "merely objective
existence in the mind," "actual existence in the world of
reality"—such existential conditions are foreign to the constitution that causes a thing to be what it is. Similarly, the
analysis of a nature will never yield, as a feature to be included
in a definition or derived from it, the predicate "universal"
or the predicate "individual." Let "man" be the universal
under analysis; we may consider the features constitutive of its
definition; then the properties connected with its differentia;
then the properties connected with its genus; then its remote
genera, etc. We shall find such intelligible features as rationality, progressivity, sociability, morality, sensibility, life, cor-
ruptibility, etc., but never "individuality" or "universality";
these are not features, but existential modalities. A nature is

3. This phrase, τὸ τι ἦν εἶναι, is one of the synonyms of essence in Aristotle. The
use of the past tense, ἦν, may be accounted for by an unexpressed reference to the production of things in time. The thing produced in time *is to be* before it actually is; in actual
existence it may be considered as that which *was* to be.

not, of itself, either universal or individual, and this is why it is capable of assuming both the state of individuality in the real and, in the mind, a state of universality produced by a process of abstraction and positive unification.

Asserting the reality of a human nature, one and the same in all men, does not imply belief in any Platonic type. It is in the mind alone that human nature, or any nature, possesses a condition of positive unity. In the real the features which make up the universal human nature exist in the state of individuality, which means that human nature exists in James as identical with the individual reality of James. The same human nature exists in Philip in the state of individuality, which means that it exists in Philip as identified with the individual reality of Philip. (Yet James is not identical with Philip. As John of St. Thomas says, two things each of which is identical with the same third thing are not necessarily identical with each other if the third thing is virtually multiple: "But the universal nature is virtually multiple because it is communicable to several things; therefore, identity with it does not entail the identity of the individuals among themselves.")[4] Inasmuch as it is the same human nature, made of the same intelligible features connected with one another in the same system of intelligibility, which exists in the real as identified with James and as identified with Philip, James and Philip are one in nature and are equal in an essential and fundamental sense, regardless of the inequality of their individual properties.[5] From the very instant of their creation men are different

4. John of St. Thomas *Cursus philosophicus, Logica* ii, q. 3, a. 2, ed. Reiser (Turin: Marietti, 1930), p. 320, b, 11.

5. Thomas Aquinas *Sum. theol.* i. 85. 7, ed. Anton C. Pegis (New York: Random House, 1945): ". . . it is plain that the better the disposition of the body, the better the soul allotted to it; which clearly appears in things of different species. The reason for this is that act and form are received into matter according to the capacity of matter; and thus because some men have bodies of better disposition, their souls have a greater power of understanding."

and unequal in countless respects; yet it is highly proper that they should be described as created equal, for in each of them the same system of intelligible features supplies individual reality with ability to exist.

On the basis of such a philosophy of universality, to speak of the common nature of men makes sense; to speak of a natural foundation for the brotherhood of men makes sense; to speak of natural rights makes sense; to speak of rights belonging to all men on account of the unity of their nature makes sense; to speak of equal justice for all makes sense; but none of those things makes any sense in the framework of a consistently nominalistic philosophy.[6] If theoretical ideas were always allowed to unfold their consequences in the actual course of events, the universalism of the rights of man would not have come into historical existence at a time that was the golden age of nominalism. But the tendencies of a theory may be held in check by a conflicting moral environment. This is how the Declaration of Independence happened to be written by a disciple of Locke. In the course of the nineteenth century, changes in the moral situation gave nominalism a chance to assert its consequences with dreadful logic and efficacy. It is hardly possible for a man to pay more than lip service to a nominalistic concept of human nature so long as healthy feelings of justice and brotherhood entertain in his heart a strong sense for human unity. But if our heart is dedicated to the ambition of crushing a part of mankind, a theoretical analysis which renders meaningless the concept of the unity of nature is likely to be grasped with eagerness and to develop its implications with strict logic. The later phases of the process are illustrated by the view that there is a greater distance between the highest and the lowest human races than between the lowest races of men and the highest races of

6. See J. Maritain, "Human Equality," in *Ransoming the Time* (New York: Charles Scribner's Sons, 1941), pp. 1–32.

brutes; unrestricted exploitation of man by man would be rational and good so long as the exploiter is classified as a member of the highest race and the exploited as a member of the lowest.

At this point it is important to remove the tempting assumption that all practical consequences of man's unity of nature follow the same pattern and let themselves be formulated in precepts of the same type. In fact, two kinds of equalitarian rules are directly traceable to man's unity of nature. There are cases in which the just and the unjust are totally determined by those features which are common to all men. In such cases any consideration of inequality as a possible modifier of the rule is irrelevant and unethical; in such cases the rule of justice is unqualifiedly equalitarian. In other situations unity of nature commands an equalitarian tendency, a dynamism of equality, without, however, causing the consideration of inequality to be unjust or irrelevant.

1. Let us consider, first, the rights corresponding to man's tendency to survive. They are, in a basic sense, universal and hold equally for all men. Accordingly, the precept protecting human life against murder admits of no exception or qualification. In order that the universality and absoluteness of this precept should be unmistakable, careful phrasing is needed. Let it not be said that it is never lawful to put a man to death: this may be lawful if man is considered in the state of degradation produced by crime.[7] Notice also that exposing myself or

7. Thomas Aquinas *Sum. theol.* ii–ii. 64. 2, ad 3. The title of the article is *"Whether it is lawful to put sinners to death?"* Objection 3 attempts to exclude an answer in the affirmative by arguing that killing a man is an act wrong in itself. Here is Aquinas' answer: ". . . through sin man moves away from the order of reason and thereby falls away from the human dignity according to which man is naturally free and exists for his own sake [homo peccando ab ordine rationis recedit; et ideo decidit a dignitate humana, prout scilicet homo est naturaliter liber, et propter seipsum existens]; thus he falls, as it were, into the condition of servitude that belongs to brute animals and can be treated according as it is useful to others. . . . Thus, although killing a man still enjoying his dignity is wrong in itself, killing a sinner may be good [Et ideo quamvis

my neighbor to danger of death is by no means the same thing as killing, even though danger be so great as to make death humanly certain. Properly understood, the proposition that it is not lawful to kill an innocent person expresses a necessity everlastingly belonging to the constitution of a universal essence. Every case of seeming exception is due to the unnoticed absence of some condition included in the correct formula of the precept. When the specified conditions are realized, the prohibition has the same meaning, the same essential significance, in all conceivable cases. Men are given equal protection by such a law. Age, social position, abilities, etc., do not matter. The prohibition of murder is not relative to any of the respects in which men are unequal but to features pertaining to the unity of human nature. Murdering an ignorant person is just as much a murder as murdering a well-educated person; education does not matter and degrees of education make no difference. Murdering a colored man is just as much a murder as murdering a white man; the law prohibiting murder is in no way relative to such contingencies as color or other so-called "race" features. Murdering a cancerous patient is just as much a murder as murdering a healthy person; it is not on account of health that murder is prohibited but on account of universally human features, common to healthy and to diseased persons. Murdering an unborn child is just as much a murder as murdering an adult man; the phase of life in which murder takes place is altogether incidental.[8]

2. As another example, consider the law of justice in exchanges. This law is known to be the strict equality of the exchanged values. It is seldom easy, it is often very difficult, to

hominem in sua dignitatem manentem occidere sit secundum se malum tamen hominem peccatorem occidere potest esse bonum, sicut occidere bestiam]."

8. All this does not mean that the seriousness of murder can never be increased by the circumstances. If the person murdered is the head of a family, the crime of murdering is complicated with a crime against wife and children.

ascertain such equality with accuracy. Yet it is always possible to define upper and lower limits within which the desired figure is certainly comprised. The distance may be great between these limits, and there often is something tragic about the clumsiness of the instruments that we use, for lack of better ones, in our endeavor to determine what justice expects of us. But we do know with perfect clarity that the rule of commutative justice has absolutely nothing to do with the aspects of human reality in which humans are unequal. The value of a house is in no way modified by such diversities in the condition of the owner as his being an expert businessman or an orphan infant, a white man or a colored man, a genius or feeble-minded, a saint or a criminal, a wealthy man or a poor one.

These examples suffice to show that human equality as unity of nature determines, with regard to certain questions, answers that are absolute, unqualified, exclusive of the consideration of degrees—answers, in short, that are equal. The truths expressed by these absolute answers are the foundation of the equalitarian dynamism which we shall now attempt to describe.

3. It was just recalled that exposing to death an innocent person—who may well be myself—is a moral act essentially different from the act of murdering an innocent person. It is always unlawful to murder one's self; it is not always unlawful to expose one's self to probable or inevitable death. It is always unlawful to murder one's innocent neighbor. It is not always unlawful to carry out action of such a nature as to entail inevitably the death of many innocent people. Concerning the moral essence "murder of the innocent," whose character is strictly determinate and intrinsically evil, men enjoy equal rights. But what about such a moral essence as "exposing the innocent to danger of death, or, more exactly, to danger of premature death"? Should it be said that with regard to this

moral essence, which is not intrinsically evil and which is by all means less determinate, men are equal or not? Should it be said that public powers are obligated to see that all men enjoy equal protection against premature death? Do all men have an equal right to protection against the risk of dying prematurely?

In a still very recent past, man-killing economic inequalities were considered, in all societies, a matter of course and of everlasting necessity. Common opinion held that the shorter life-expectancy of the lower classes was an inevitable consequence of the structure of society, as determined by eternal laws. All men die some day; why should not death come earlier in one part of society? On this subject our conscience has changed and, no doubt, improved. We have come to understand that the grounds for the desirability of a long life-expectancy are the same in all classes. It is human nature which demands that human life be protected by the efforts of society; this demand holds equally for all the bearers of human nature. It does not follow that it is in the power of society to give, with no delay, equal protection to all. It does not follow that a society in which some sections of the population are much more exposed than others to premature death is necessarily iniquitous. But it does follow that society has an obligation never to fall away from the track leading to equal protection for all. Forty years ago a young man could not afford a case of lung tuberculosis unless his father had a considerable income. Tuberculosis in a poor family meant certain death. Today in technologically advanced societies young people attacked by this disease have almost an equal chance to recover whether the family is rich or poor, and this chance is very good. For some other diseases and conditions the prognosis still depends to a large extent upon financial means and is very unequally favorable according as means are great or poor.

Several aspects of contemporary history manifest, in the

most impressive fashion, the equalitarian dynamism contained in the unity of human nature. It is important to remark, however, that the assertion of such dynamism often is lawfully restricted and delayed. If, for instance, in order to hasten the day when the death rate will be as low in the poorest section of society as it is today in the wealthiest, we had to suffer an enormously increased weight of bureaucratic organization, at the cost of a considerable amount of liberty, there might be a duty to accept, as on the battlefield, loss of life for the sake of liberty and community.

4. The aspiration of the mind toward truth would call for considerations similar to those just set forth. From the fact that the mind naturally strives for knowledge, it follows that everyone has a right not to be perverted by the pedagogy of the liars, but it does not follow that all persons have a strict right to an equal amount of education. Besides the ability to receive education is unequally distributed as well as qualitatively diverse, it is absolutely impossible for society to give all who are able to receive education at all degrees an equal chance to get it. Now let the question be stated in terms of tendencies. Not so long ago even elementary education was the privilege of a small minority; it is today available to all, at least in the best-organized communities. Very few received secondary education three generations ago; it is today very common in several nations. Opportunities for higher education have enormously increased, though they still are far from universal. Thus, with regard to the distribution of knowledge as well as with regard to the protection of life, the history of modern societies shows the operation of an equalitarian tendency. The many, who in the past were denied the good of knowledge, have a right to demand that society should promote the availability of education. This does not mean that any intellectually inclined person is entitled to educational facilities just equal to those enjoyed by the best-treated stu-

dent of equal distinction, and it does not mean that, in order to hasten the day when anyone can acquire all the knowledge that his intellect is able to receive, the state should proceed recklessly, jeopardize freedom, overburden the taxpayer, give teachers wretched salaries and students wretched teachers, etc.

The equalitarian dynamism of human nature accounts for the fact that even in conservative circles social progress is held to be characterized, in a large measure, by the progress of equality. Conservatives seldom miss a chance to recall that social conservation, such as they understand it, is by no means incompatible with social progress. Though possibly not incompatible, social conservation and social progress are certainly opposite in some ways, for social conservation designates, among other things, the maintenance of advantages traditionally enjoyed by small minorities, e.g., the ownership of big land estates as the material basis for aristocracy, whereas social progress, according to conservatives and progressists alike, is inseparable from the promotion of equalitarian relations.

NATURAL INEQUALITY AND STRUCTURAL INEQUALITY

Let those inequalities be described as "natural" which originate in the physical constitution of men, in the use of their freedom, in the social environment. They concern perception, memory, intelligence, imagination, will power, fortitude, temperance, leadership, etc. By "structural" inequality, on the other hand, we understand the unique sort of inequality which results from relations of authority and autonomy.

Although the essence of authority is entirely realized in a community governed by majority vote, most communities use distinct governing personnel, and the constitution of authority, in most cases, places some men above other men. If, further, the principle of autonomy obtains, the larger unit runs only the affairs that cannot be run by any smaller unit, and

society is organically divided into several communities characterized by decreasing amplitude of scope. As an effect of this
distribution of power, social structure comprises a plurality of
levels. In Rousseau's theory, structural inequality is simplified; citizens, under the sovereign, are unorganized and equal—
a state of affairs highly favorable to rationalistic experimen-
tation on human substance. Contrary to a common opinion,
hierarchical order is not a proper effect of authority; it is
properly effected by the joint operation of the principles of
authority and autonomy.

Where there is need for a distinct governing personnel, it is
desirable that the best should be identified and placed in governing positions. But the difficulty of identifying the best is
everlastingly tragic. This difficulty is a particular case of a
problem familiar to logicians: the problem of recognition.
There are fields of knowledge in which a definition can be
completely satisfactory without supplying criteria for the recognition of the defined essence in the data of experience. We
understand the definitions of the circle and the ellipse and still
do not know how to distinguish a circle from an ellipse whose
foci are at a short distance from each other. Instruments increase our ability to perceive the difference between a distance
greater than zero (ellipse) and a distance equal to zero (circle),
but the most powerful microscope does not render our power
of discrimination infinite. Since, from the standpoint of theoretical science, a distance expressed in thousandths of a milli-
meter is just as significant as a distance expressed in miles, it
should be said with no qualification that mathematical definitions do not guarantee the recognition of the defined entities
in physical experience. Plainly, the problem of recognition is
irrelevant in mathematics.[9] For widely different reasons it is
also irrelevant in philosophic disciplines. The philosopher of

9. To remove a threat of non-sense, let it be emphasized that we are speaking of
recognition *in sense experience*.

nature, for instance, defines the plant and the animal as sharply distinguished by the indefinite qualitative distance separating the position of knowledge from its negation. But when the time comes to determine whether such and such a lower organism is a plant or an animal—say, a protozoon or a protophyte—the philosopher does not have much to say.

In other fields of knowledge a definition is worthless if it does not include criteria for the recognition of the defined. One of these fields is law. Among the factors which cause discrepancy between law and ethics, the most considerable may be this: an ethical definition is complete without criteria for recognition, but a legal definition would not work if it did not contain such criteria. Consequently, particulars of no ethical significance—such as the crossing of a state border—may enter into the legal definition of a crime. True, a tendency to reduce the discrepancy between the ethical and the legal is an important factor of legal progress; yet, be it only because of the need for obvious means of recognition in law, such a discrepancy often proves irreducible. The same need for clear recognition is felt in all techniques; the definition of a disease, for instance, does not satisfy the physician unless it includes rules of diagnosis. One of the general characteristics of positive science, as opposed to the philosopher's knowledge of nature, is a systematic endeavor to meet the requirements of recognition. The concept of time, for instance, does not mean anything to the physicist independently of rules for the measurement of time. Such epistemological systems as the positivism of the Vienna Circle or the operationalism of Bridgeman illustrate brilliantly the relation of the science of nature to the recognition of essences in any given empirical situation. Whether this feature of positive science results merely from an attraction exercised by technology or pertains to positive science as a distinct way of theoretical knowledge is a question of fascinating interest which obviously cannot be discussed here.

The ability to perform the duties of government is an object whose definition needs to be supplemented with means of recognition. This is the tragedy: any definition calculated to procure unmistakable recognition of the best is likely to be at variance with the true nature of political excellence. Immensely important phases of political and social history can be described as the effects of a conflict between our need for a genuine notion of the best and our need for steady recognition of those held to be the best. Most societies save face and preserve some sort of peace by forcing upon people the belief that men selected according to their criteria are infallibly the most qualified for governing positions. When such a belief is shaken, revolution threatens.

Let us survey some of the characteristics actually used by societies in their definition of the best. The first place belongs to divine origin as certified by tradition or some other sort of common assent. If a few persons, as in traditional Japan, are universally believed to be raised above ordinary mortals by participation in divine privilege, there is no quarrel as to who should govern. If the people or the most active part of it, as in Napoleonic France, believe in the divine designation of a leader, there is hardly any controversy as to who should lead. Race may also be a very handy criterion. Sometimes it works just as clearly as the distinction between black and white. Under circumstances exclusive of such obvious distinction, the old aristocracies drew great help from the willingness to believe that excellence is transmitted biologically and that hereditary titles are but an expression of transmissible excellence. Elsewhere the criterion is the ownership of land. Elsewhere it is wealth, with no further specification. Elsewhere it is spiritual character: there are societies ruled by priestly castes. Elsewhere excellence is attributed to military men, so that competition for power concerns merely rival juntas and leaves the good people unconcerned. In our time government by experts is a rather popular program. In most fields the identification of experts is commonly effected with a very low percentage of error. Were we agreed that we should be governed by the best physicists, there would be little argument as to who should govern. Political designations would involve no political campaigns. There is also in our time a tendency to classify cultural refinement—i.e., ability to talk about abstract painting and sophisticated literature—among the criteria of political ability. (Besides the fact that the relevance of such talent is particularly dubious, this criterion is not the handiest, for cultural refinement is not a thing that can be recognized without a very high ratio of error.) Lastly, one criterion for political excellence is party membership. This criterion is ideally clear; all that is needed is to go over a list of names kept up to date by a conscientious secretary. All our worries are over. We are almost back to the pacifying system of the divine origin. The party is the bearer of the spirit of history—an immanent god deemed entirely trustworthy by those who have been willing to listen for some time to the propaganda of the party. Of course, competition is not tolerated; the party which is supposed to embody the genius of the people, the meaning of evolution, etc., soon achieves monopolistic rule or disappears. The people vote, but, since they all vote for the same party, excitement is at an all-time low, and many remark that things have seriously improved over the time when they had to choose among some thirty-two party organizations, as under the Constitution of Weimar.

There is in Pascal a page marked by bitterness and melancholy about the utility of clearly recognizable signs of excellence: if it is firmly understood that the man with two lackeys has precedence over the man with but one lackey, trouble about precedence will never arise. One feature of Pascal's pessimism is the belief that human societies need such practices and that attempting to replace irrational conventions by rational rules would result in destruction and greatly increased suffering. Some irrationality is not too high a price to pay for peace. In our time many hold that the certainty and definiteness procured by one-party dictatorship outweigh the inconvenience of government by criminals. Such an attitude is plainly undemocratic. Pascal's resignation to the rule of the nonrational is undemocratic. Democracy has often been described as essentially rationalistic; in the present connection at least, its determination to follow the line of rationality is not questionable. *Democratic equalitarianism is a philosophy which refuses to buy peace at the cost of irrationality in the relation between natural and structural inequality.* But the views of Pascal are not without some foundation, and it must be granted that democracy, by refusing to indulge in the resignation recommended by Pascal, assumes a burden of uncertainty and exposes itself to a distinct danger of strife; when a people fails, over a long period, to meet this danger and to preserve concord, the conclusion to be drawn is that the *sine qua non* conditions of democracy are not all satisfied.

As a sort of counterpart to the arbitrariness of most oligarchic solutions, democracy is often tempted to reject the whole problem by postulating the equal ability of all, so far as political affairs are concerned. It seems that in some ancient societies the postulate of equal ability was held essential to the democratic polity.[10] When problems of government are simple, this postulate may not necessarily entail disastrous consequences, and its disadvantages may be balanced or outweighed by felicitous effects connected with the distribution of authority. The case is somewhat similar to that of hereditary monarchy. That a man designated by birth should be intrusted with great power is intelligible if the functions of his power are so simple

10. Aristotle even seems to consider that it pertains to the foundations of *political* government (*Pol.* 1. 12. 1259b5, trans. Jowett): "But in most constitutional states the citizens rule and are ruled by turns, for the idea of a constitutional state implies that the natures of the citizens are equal, and do not differ at all."

as to be within the range of average intelligence. One reason why hereditary monarchs, in modern societies, have to be contented with very little power is that the hazards of birth cannot be expected to bestow upon a man the gifts needed for the operation of such a complex thing as a modern state. The factor which forbids hereditary monarchs to wield much power also rules out the rotation of authority. The only case in which the postulate of equal ability and the principle of rotating leadership can still conceivably operate is that of a small rural community with a well-settled population. Community of traditions and of habits causes homogeneity; the job that can be done satisfactorily by one man of a certain age and experience is likely to be done satisfactorily by another man belonging to the same age group, and the rotation of authority has plain advantages; through it, all are given to understand that there is nothing personal about government, that government is, in all respects, a function of the community. The obnoxious illusion that power belongs to some persons after the fashion of a private advantage is destroyed by rotating leadership. A society in which all are supposed to be equally apt to hold governing positions and in which power actually passes from hand to hand may embody with exceptional purity the ideal type of the civil and political organization.

With the exception of the rare circumstances which permit rotating authority, the postulate of equal ability is so paradoxical that it is almost never spoken of. It haunts the democratic conscience without revealing its identity; over long periods it remains inactive, or its operation remains unnoticeable; it has outbursts of activity, during which it changes the face of the world, for better and for worse; it expresses a complex of thoughts and tendencies the components of which we propose to survey, beginning with the most primitive and ending with the loftiest.

1. Excellence customarily arouses envy; democratic equali-

tarianism may encourage this acutely antisocial feeling. Opposition to excellence and a systematic support of mediocrity are among the risks of democracy. These risks are well known and do not call for any elaboration.

2. Here is a true story: A physicist of genius was making a political speech at a public meeting. A workman was so impressed by the genius as to find the speech impressive. A man who disliked the speech said to the workman: "He knows more physics than you do, but in politics you are his equal." In fact, the physicist was not a particularly wise citizen; whether the workman was, as a citizen, equally unwise, still more unwise, or wiser we shall never know. The postulate of equal ability, as asserted here, was not really intended to mean that physicist and workman were equal in political wisdom or lack of it. It meant that the science of physics is in no way a cause or a guaranty of political ability; the craft of the mechanic does not, either, signify that its bearer is a man of sound judgment in political affairs. All other things being equal, the political judgment of the mechanic is just as good as that of the physicist. But it is not denied that other things may be unequal. The postulate of equal ability signifies here that political wisdom is not a specialty, not an expertness, not an art or a craft; that it entertains no definite connection with any particular way of life or social position: it is a *human* quality on account of which intellect and will are righteously disposed with regard to the goods of man, not with regard to the good condition of a thing, as in art. The postulate of equal ability recalls this all-important truth, but in a very clumsy way. For one thing, it suggests that political ability is a common possession; in fact, the small amount of it needed for a man to be a good citizen is too rare, and the virtue needed for a citizen to be a good statesman is among the most sparsely distributed gifts; genius for physical science is far more common. Moreover, the postulate of equal ability disregards the *instru-*

mental role played by several arts, skills, and techniques in the operation of political virtue. Sound judgment in politics is never elicited by historical erudition, but it often happens that judgment about a political affair cannot be sound without the knowledge of history. There is no such thing as a political art, for nothing in politics can procure the specification and unity of a single art; but political wisdom, which is virtue and prudence and not art, normally uses arts as its proper instruments. The skill of the stylist is certainly distinct from the wisdom of the statesman; yet, when Mr. Churchill, after the great battles of Egypt, said to the world: "It is not the end, it is not the beginning of the end, but it may be the end of the beginning," he accomplished through this clarification, helpful to millions, a victory which supplemented nicely that of his armies. "Instrumental" does not mean "unimportant." A man having the ethical dispositions necessary for political leadership may still fall short of qualification if he lacks the skills that are the necessary instruments of political judgment and action.

3. The postulate of equal ability often expresses, though not in appropriate fashion, the demand that the people be led by men in communion with it. The problem of the communion to be established between the governing personnel and the people, with particular regard to the largest and least wealthy part of the people, commands the understanding of democratic progress in our time. It is the most central of all the problems concerning *the democracy of the common man.* Its importance and its obscurity suggest a guarded approach.

First, let us realize, in Socratic fashion, our ignorance concerning the common man. In spite of recent efforts, the study of history has remained principally and almost exclusively that of very small minorities and persons of high distinction—kings and queens, ambassadors and generals, captains of industry, savants, leaders of opinion, literary gentlemen and other artists, etc. Consequently, in our considerations on good and bad government we have in view, principally if not exclusively, the way in which these distinguished minorities were affected.

Contrary to the opinion held by skeptics and cynics, government has not always been in the hands of men with no regard for ethical rules. History records a number of cases of government by persons of deep virtue and a few cases of government by saints. If the man in power is genuinely virtuous, he holds it axiomatic that the common good for which he is supposed to strive cannot be restricted to any portion of society. Genuine virtue includes exacting justice and produces special interest in the welfare of those who are most likely to be treated unjustly, i.e., the common men. Unqualified virtue is animated by charity and intensely concerned with the poor, who are known to enjoy special dignity among Christians. In fact, some statesmen were steadily motivated by the determination to see justice done to the exploited and decent means placed within the range of the poor. Referring to those whom we know best, i.e., those who belong to our time and to our societies, it is hardly possible not to be under the impression that, in spite of their justice and charity, in spite of their determination to serve the poor and the exploited, they remained in most cases and to a large extent the men of a small group, the men of a selected few, the men of that portion of society distinguished by such features as good manners, education, and property. These good men were unaware of what was going on in the lower strata of society. But what accounted for such unawareness? Did they not inquire? They did, and they had some notions about rural masses being barred from ownership of land by the imperialism of aristocratic landlords or of capitalistic companies. They did promote credit institutions which made it possible, at least when circumstances were particularly favorable, for farmers to buy land. They knew appalling figures concerning unsanitary housing in big cities; they did much to encourage the construction of decent homes at reasonable prices. *The proletarian revolutions of our time revealed the grotesque insufficiency of such measures.* The revolt of the masses led by chiefs of their own, plebeians-in-chief—sometimes outright criminals—revealed to the world that modern democracy had remained, to an unsuspected degree, the concern of the happy few. Facts came as a surprise which should not have surprised anybody, for they were recorded and available. True, they were known, but their significance was not realized. The familiar difference between "to know" and "to realize" ought to be kept in mind here. A statesman of high moral character cannot be ignorant of the dire needs and vital aspirations of the common man, but he may *know* and fail to *realize*.

Deep in the history of conservatism we find the belief that the best that can be done for the great number of men is to have them ruled by an elite of responsible leaders carefully prepared by specialists in education and character training. This view is not obviously absurd; it may hold in a number of cases; it deserves respectful consideration; it admits of perversions—especially by way of optimistic fantasies concerning the reliability of the distinguished few—but it is not essentially perverse. It is not essentially aristocratic, for the principle of government by the best is capable of a democratic form: it has the meaning of a democratic principle when the best are designated by the people and subjected to its control. But it is essentially conservative, and it is objectionable in so far as conservatism is objectionable. If society is ruled by an upper class—by an elite socially recognized, socially organized, having its own schools, its own books, its own leaders, its own manners—inevitably and in spite of all the wisdom used in the training of such an elite, rulers will not realize, except occasionally and in short-lived flashes, the suffering and aspirations of the common man. This elite will think merely of slow and inadequate reforms; its policy will be conservative. So far as the common man is concerned, government by this elite is government by outsiders.

The common man is not unwilling to acknowledge excellence. He is by no means reluctant to give recognition to merit in such domains as science and art; he is not always the enemy of the rich; in most cases he is strongly inclined to reverence moral superiority. But as soon as he becomes aware that he and his brethren can take care of themselves, he resents intensely the leadership of outsiders. Outsiders are understood to comprise not only men distinguished by such a doubtful mark of excellence as wealth and those distinguished by marks of excellence irrelevant in politics (like science) but also those whose mark of excellence is a reverenced ethical perfection. To account for this resentment by envy alone would be shallow psychology. Anxiety takes hold of any man who knows that his destiny rests in foreign hands. The outsiders who rule may be benevolent; but it is feared that they will prove obnoxious in proportion to their benevolence. A frank display of hostility would be preferable; then the common man would know that he must rely upon himself alone, that his leaders are his enemies, that his destiny, in this strife, is in his own hands. But an attitude of systematic hostility toward well-meaning leaders is impossible; because they are well meaning and not always wrong, it is not possible to resist them always. Often, or most of the time, they have to be treated as leaders, i.e., followed and obeyed. Such a situation is bound to arouse anxiety: here is a man who entertains toward his leader feelings of reverence, esteem, even thankfulness, who respects the legal relation that subjects him to his leader, but feels that disaster will come as a result of blindness. *A leader from outside is considered a blind leader.* Only a leader in communion with us can realize what we are, what we need, what we are able to accomplish. But, in order to be in communion with us, ought he not to be one of us? Here we can easily slip into this dedication to mediocrity for which democracy is blamed. In order to be sure that he is one of us, do not make him too literate, for most of us are poorly educated; do not make him wealthy, for most of us have no property; and do not make him too virtuous, for most of us are weak. If he is too much of a hero, he will expect too much of us, who are no heroes.

Blind leadership is the worst, no matter how well intentioned the blind leader may be. What, then, is the proper method of removing the sort of blindness that is supposed to affect leaders from outside? Referring to the theory of affective knowledge outlined in the first part of this book, let it be recalled that, besides judgment *by way of cognition*, there is such a thing as judgment *by way of inclination*. In the former case certainty is provided either by self-evidence or by reduction to self-evident principles; in the latter case, by steady agreement between the requirements of the object and the movements of the desire. (Such agreement means that the desire reacts by a positive tendency to an objective situation demanding affirmative judgment, by a negative tendency—aversion—to an objective situation demanding negative judgment.) Without such steady agreement, judgment by way of inclination is merely wishful thinking. The heart is not, for the intellect, a reliable teacher unless there is between the heart and the intelligible object accord, harmony, sympathy, resemblance of nature—in a word, connaturality. If the object to be known is, for instance, the rule of justice in this particular transaction, my liking and my aversion are means of knowledge if, and only if, my will is entirely just. The just will experiences attraction and repulsion according as justice demands, because the just will, in so far as it is actually just, is of one nature with justice. Consequently, whenever the proper way to know an object is affective, the *sine qua non* of genuine knowledge is the establishment of connaturality between the heart and the object.

Now, as shown in chapter i, rules of action in concrete, contingent, unique, unrenewable circumstances cannot be assured by any science. Science falls short of the contingent situation with regard to which judgment by inclination alone can attain certainty. Beyond the domain of principles, the political leader has to exercise judgment by way of inclination; he has, accordingly, to be connaturalized to the goods of the community that he leads. But these goods are determined only in part (they are determined only with regard to their more formal part) by the universal nature of man and of the political community. In respects of decisive significance they are determined by the factual reality of this particular people considered in all its concreteness; with all the peculiarities resulting from its unique history; with the unusual energies that it possesses by virtue of some prodigious achievement in the past; with all its weaknesses, deficiencies, oddities, abnormalities, and paradoxical features. Clearly, it is not only to the good of the political virtue that the statesman ought to be connaturalized but also to the good of this particular community, a creation of history that is unique and without any precedent.

Judgment by way of affective connaturality about persons and societies is a subject insufficiently studied by philosophers. But challenging remarks on this subject are found in moralists and authors; for them, affective connaturality is a familiar instrument of observation. An example is this celebrated page of Balzac: "Only one passion could drive me away from my habits of study; but was it not also study? I used to observe the mores of the suburb, its inhabitants and their personalities. . . . In me, observation had already become intuitive, it penetrated the soul without ignoring the body; more exactly, it grasped external particulars so adequately as to go immediately beyond them; it gave me the power of living the life of the individual on which it was exercised, and enabled me to substitute myself for him, just as the dervish of the Arabian Nights assumed the body and the soul of the persons over whom he said certain words. . . . While listening to these people, I was able to take over their life, I felt their rags on my back, I walked with my feet in their tattered shoes; their desires, their needs, everything passed into my soul, or my soul passed into theirs. It was the dream of a waking man. I became inflamed with them against the workshop bosses who tyrannized them, or against the bad customers who had them come again several times without paying them. To put aside one's own habits, to assume another self through the inebriation of moral powers, and to play that game at will, such was my recreation."[11]

The common man dislikes to be ruled by outsiders because he is afraid of a ruler who would not feel his (the common man's) rags on his back, whose feet would not be hurt by his worn-out shoes, and whose anger would not be aroused by the injustices that he undergoes in labor and business relations. Argument against government by distinguished personalities boils down to this: these people—"our betters," as the English put it—by the very fact that they do not belong to our community, are incapable of achieving the intuitive knowledge without which leadership is blind. The "best" are not trustworthy as men of government because they are supposed not to be capable of the intuitions the proper condition of which is communion with the common man. Thus no more is needed than a reconsidered definition of the "best."

In order, for instance, to be an adequate leader for a community of small farmers, most of whom are tenants, it is not strictly necessary that a man should be a tenant farmer, just as it is not strictly necessary to be clothed in rags and shod with

11. Honoré de Balzac, *Facino Cane* (1836) (*Œuvres complètes* [Paris: Houssiaux; Hébert et Cie successeurs, 1877], X, 61).

tattered shoes to feel on one's back the garment of the poor and on one's feet his shoes. An outsider can be inflamed with tenant farmers against the exploiters of the farmer. But then is he still an outsider? Through the power of affective con-naturality he has actually come to exist, to live, to suffer, and to think inside the community of the tenant farmers. *The thing which matters is not so much sociological belonging to a group as intentional communion with it.* A local aristocrat may happen to be in deeply intelligent communion with tenant farmers; there is no objection to his being their representative in parliament; but aristocrats do not happen often to be in communion with laboring masses, so that a nation in which the countryside is overwhelmingly represented by country aristocrats is hardly a democracy.

To conclude: rule by men from distinguished groups is unobjectionable so long as these men are able to achieve communion with all parts of the community. But communion with the common man in spite of group origin is a thing comparatively difficult and rare; accordingly, it is desirable, most of the time, that the leaders of a democracy should be members of the larger class. Increased ratio of common men among leaders seems to be the democratic way of providing leadership with one of the most anciently known and valued forms of political excellence. Old-time stories tell of cherished leaders, often of royal blood, whom the people considered as men of their own in the struggle against exploitation. Government by men foreign to the common man—one of the major causes of civil indiscipline in modern times—may have been but a symptom of a long crisis centered about the relation between wealth and political power. Beyond this crisis lies the democracy of the common man.

EQUALITY OF OPPORTUNITY

The theory of equal opportunity, understood in its current meaning, can be explained as follows: It is granted that the structure of society necessarily implies inequalities; it is granted that inequalities demanded by the structure of society are entirely just; it is also granted that the rewards of economic activity cannot be equal for all; it is even granted that it would not be fair that they should be equal for all, since merits are widely unequal; but it is asserted that inequality should sanction individual merit and never be determined by any consideration foreign to individual merit. The notion expressed by these words is vague, and, like many vague notions, it has a character of radicalism made inconspicuous, under most circumstances, by the counteracting influence of complementary notions.

Equality of opportunity rules out a number of privileges upheld by aristocratic societies. Thus commissions in the army and navy used to be a monopoly of the nobility. At the dawn of modern democracy no reform was more popular than the abolition of such privilege. Notice that in our time nobody would question that commissions in the army and navy, including the highest ranks, ought to be accessible to those who are best qualified for such duties, regardless of social origin. All agree that it is impossible to intrust, say, the supreme command of the army to a less able man for the simple reason that the more able man was not born into the appropriate social group. Modern societies cannot afford such a waste, to say nothing of the danger of breeding discontent. Thus some forms of equal opportunity are unanimously recommended. Up to a certain point, nobody objects to the principle of equal opportunity.

It might be said, in rough outline, that the bourgeois revolution, so far as opportunity is concerned, consisted in making public functions accessible to whoever succeeded in qualifying for them. But in the process of qualification itself, there arise many problems of opportunity. If a public function requires, for instance, high education, the highly educated commoner appreciates the fact that the nobility no longer has a monopoly

on this function. Now what about the commoner who possesses intelligence and will power, who has all the natural
gifts required for high positions but, for lack of money and
guidance, never was able to acquire knowledge and never had
a chance to use his great gifts? Here, also, there is a waste,
there is ground for discontent, and there is perhaps injustice.
Furthermore, apart from public positions, is it not the duty of
society to see that wealth, honors, and, most of all, leadership
should belong not to persons of uncertain ability designated
by birth but to the most able, regardless of their birth? Very
soon the principle of equal opportunity comes to demand the
suppression of the right of inheritance. This decisive step was
made by the Saint-Simonists, with lucid logic. The Saint-
Simonian spirit is filled with stiff pictures of hierarchy and
unequal distribution; but this strongly antidemocratic mind is
also rationalistic. An act of rationalization was effected when
it was determined that birth would no longer exclude an able
person from a public function; the next step toward rational
society is the suppression not of private property but of its
hereditary transmission. On this point the undemocratic doctrine of the Saint-Simonists agrees with tendencies common
among democratically minded Socialists. Léon Blum said that
he became aware of his socialist calling as he was attending a
comedy in which a person exclaims: "Property is hereditary,
and intelligence is not."

But if it is considered unjust and intolerably wasteful that a
poorly gifted child should enjoy all the privileges consequent
upon wealth, while a better-gifted child has to stand all the
handicaps consequent upon the poverty of his parents, consistency seems to demand that no child should, as a result of
his birth, enjoy any peculiar advantage or suffer any particular
handicap. If we merely suppress the right of inheritance, without any further provision, the son of a medical doctor still
enjoys, if he cares to be a medical man, facilities that the son
of a coal miner does not enjoy; and similarly, though less con-

spicuously, the son of a medical doctor cannot become a coal miner so easily and successfully as can the son of a coal miner. Who knows? Such inequalities of opportunity may be of decisive importance. The waste that they entail may be as significant as the waste suffered by aristocratic societies as a result of the exclusion of the commoners from many leading positions. The principle which brought about the end of aristocratic privilege and the end of hereditary property also tends to bring about the end of all privilege or handicap attaching to the hazard of birth. As the culmination of the process we have a picture which, prior to the era of totalitarianism, bore a character of utopian unreality but no longer does today: the care of the young generation belongs not to the family but to the broadest possible social unit. If the social unit in care of the youngster is small, too much inequality of opportunity is left; children born in a poor village would be too much at a disadvantage in the competition with children born in university cities. Thus not the family, not the town or county, but the state or some broader unit, if there is any (think of inequality of opportunity, so far as education is concerned, between youngsters who happen to be born in Mississippi and those born in New York!), would take care of the education of children. But education is only a part of the training that a youth obtains from society. The whole of his upbringing must be taken over by society. And, since a considerable part of upbringing is effected not at school but at home, the largest possible social unit would have to provide children with a home as well as with a school. This is done on a large scale by totalitarian organizations and on a lower, but perhaps increasing scale by all nations. Ideally, all newly born humans would be intrusted to a gigantic organization and placed in a pool, where merit alone would determine direction and promotion.[12]

12. When Olinde Rodrigues—one of the earliest Saint-Simonists and the only one who had been closely acquainted with Saint-Simon—left the Saint-Simonian school in disgust, this is what he had to say on this subject: "Logiciens impitoyables! vous

Here, as in the Republic of Plato—which may well be the everlasting pattern of a society planned according to the kind of rationality that rationalism cherishes—children do not know their parents, and each man of the preceding generation has an equal right to be addressed as father. Here the son of the coal miner is at no advantage with regard to coal mining, and the son of the medical doctor is at no advantage with regard to medical practice, and the son of the Greek scholar has no advantage with regard to proficiency in Greek studies over the son of the Latin scholar. Periodical tests make it possible to effect, at all ages, a classification of the growing multitude. It is not claimed that those tests are infallible: They admit of failure, but failures in such a rational system happen less frequently than with the random selections relied upon by traditional societies. Statistically and with regard to large numbers, the tests work. This is about as far as mankind can go along the line of the elimination of chance.

We have many reasons to be grateful to the Saint-Simonists. These antidemocrats, by the fact that they adhere so thoroughly to the theory of equal opportunity, reveal that this theory—or at least their version of it—does not proceed from the democratic principle. It is not so much a democratic theory as a rationalistic theory. Clearly, great destruction results in human societies from the casual course of events. It is only natural that we should be anxious to create, as far as we can, rational order in society; it is natural and sound, for instance, that we should want inequality of wealth and power or inequality of education to correspond to inequalities of merit rather than to conventional inequalities determined by the unverifiable behavior of remote ancestors. But at the end of

---

vouliez enseigner au nom de Saint-Simon qu'à l'avenir l'enfant, vagissant à peine, serait arraché au regard même de sa mère délivrée, aussi bien qu'à celui du père, pour abolir plus sûrement, selon vous, tous les privilèges de la naissance'' (*Œuvres de Saint-Simon et d'Enfantin* [Paris: E. Dentu, 1865], VI, 43).

the process we understand that, for having rejected the wastes and destructions consequent upon primitive forms of chance, we have come to cause the incomparably worse destructions and wastes consequent upon a combination of extreme rationality and of the most intolerable kind of chance, i.e., human arbitrariness. To estimate the waste involved in the perfectly rational organization of equal opportunity, just consider that all the beneficent energies attaching to the personal forms of motherly love would be wasted. If inequalities of opportunity are to be systematically avoided, the hired nurses who take care of infants in the pool run by the largest possible social unit would show to the youngster intrusted to them no feeling except the common tenderness that any woman normally shows to a baby. Anything over and above such common feeling would restore, within the rational pool, nonrational inequality of opportunity. This example is telling enough to render further elaboration superfluous.

It is extremely important to realize clearly, even though at the cost of tedious repetition, the character of the process which we are watching. It seems that one and the same principle brings about an early phase of unquestioned excellence and later phases of obvious destructiveness. Should it be said of equal opportunity that some amount of it helps, that too much of it hurts, and that it is up to the prudence of the statesman to draw the line between the moderate amount which helps and the excessive amount which hurts? But the duty of political philosophy is precisely to go beyond such empirical answers and to discover, in the plurality of the principles involved, the foundation of the solutions that prudence formulates in terms of the appropriate mean.

As interpreted so far, the principle of equal opportunity states that nothing matters except qualities of strictly individual character. Its consistent development leads to a condition of individualistic isolation which deprives all individuals of great goods. The question to be considered now is whether this principle is individualistic by essence, so that a nonindividualistic interpretation of it would be impossible.

Let us go over examples suggested by the preceding analysis. The principle of equal opportunity seems to exclude the right of inheritance because this right causes inequalities unrelated to individual merit. But if the right of inheritance is suppressed, all are deprived of the advantages procured by a system of economic circumstances favorable to conjugal faithfulness and paternal devotion, favorable to the stability of the home, and capable of giving man great comfort in his unequal struggle with time and death. When the theory of equal opportunity is so understood as to imply such destructions, it is impaired by a failure to list adequately the requirements of human life. By mistake the great goods connected with integration in a stable home were not counted among the goods for the possession of which there is a question of giving individuals opportunity and equal opportunity. The statement of the problem was biased from the beginning by the silent operation of individualistic preconceptions. The whole picture changes when it is realized that some of the things for which opportunity is sought are of such nature as to balance and restrict the principle of equal opportunity. Among the goods that I desire for all children is the advantage of being, if circumstances make it at all possible, the apprentices and the partners of their fathers in vocational life; this implies that becoming a farmer will be easier for the son of a farmer than for the son of a coal miner. The unoriginal proposition that some equality of opportunity helps and that too much of it hurts now assumes a meaning by which empiricism is transcended. The excess to be avoided admits of precise definition: so far as opportunity is concerned, equality is carried too far when it impairs the goods to which opportunity is relative; more specifically, a policy of equal opportunity begins to be harmful when it threatens to dissolve the small communities from which men derive their best energies in the hard accomplishments of daily life.

Let us consider, for example, the granting of scholarships to gifted students whose parents cannot afford the expenses of higher education. Through this practice, of unquestioned equity, many young men leave forever the environment where they had their early experiences and settle in an environment which will never be that of their parents and relatives. Such adventures are very often necessary, but whoever fails to see that they involve serious risk makes it known that he is a reckless and irresponsible thinker. Now, if there is risk, there is a problem of finding the circumstances under which resulting inconveniences will be remedied. Let it be said, in merely tentative fashion, that, so long as the change is entirely voluntary, the disadvantages of the uprooting are likely to be remedied by adequate ties with the new environment and by the maintenance, in a more spiritual form, of ties with the old environment. If, on the contrary, society systematically seeks to achieve the highest degree of fluidity; if a "rational" organization of public education puts pressure on the young men and their families in order that trades, vocations, and environments should be determined exclusively by individual talent, what really goes on looks like an orderly slaughter of the goods procured by integration in the family and other small social units.

We shall now try to outline the general measures that democratic equality demands, so far as opportunity is concerned.

1. Democratic equality forbids absolutely the legal exclusion of any person from any function on account of this person's group allegiance. A society in which army and navy commissions are given only to the sons of the nobility is undemocratic; a society in which no one can become the head of the state unless he happens to be the first-born son of the

preceding ruler is undemocratic so far as the function of head of the state is concerned; a society in which people marked by a certain color are excluded from certain functions is undemocratic.

2. Democratic equality requires, further, that society should take positive measures in order that group allegiance should never entail *factual* exclusion from any function. A society in which the sons of peasants or proletarians, no matter how bright, are denied the financial help necessary for higher education is undemocratic.

3. In the administration of measures designed to give merit a chance, the principle of the greatest possible autonomy should prevail; in other words, these measures should never be managed by public powers when they can be managed by private initiative, and they should never be managed by the larger unit of public administration when they can be managed by the smaller unit. Uniformity, far from being the object of systematic endeavor as in rationalistic politics, should rather be the object of a reluctant concession, never made unless it is obviously needed. Under conditions of autonomous management, the social aspect of personal destinies and the meaning of the person's incorporation in groups which may not be of his own choice are unlikely to be ignored. With proper attention given to the social aspects of personal destinies, the principle of equal opportunity loses the absolutism which would make it a first-class factor of atomization and a formidable wrecker of democratic communities.

EQUALITY VERSUS EXPLOITATION

It was recalled above that freedom has distinct meanings in distinct orders of causality. So far as the final cause of government is concerned, there is freedom when government is exercised solely for the common good or for the good of the governed; if government is exercised for the private good of those in power, the governed are slaves. The condition of slavery is thus defined by the union of two intelligible elements: (1) a legally recognized authority relationship (of master to servant), whose distinctive purpose is (2) the maintenance of the master's private good by the servant's labors.

Either element of this definition procures a foundation for a variety of degrees. As history shows, the direction imposed by the master upon the servant may be more or less comprehensive and more or less necessitating (1), and the part of the servant's labor dedicated to the master's private good may be smaller or larger (2). When both elements are at or near a minimum, the word "slavery" sounds improper; "servitude" and in some cases "serfdom" are preferable.

Among those subject to authority, the slave is thus distinguished by the *alienation* of his effort. A related idea is expressed by saying that he is being *exploited* by his master. Let us reflect upon the crucial concept of alienation, which, as evidenced by great intellectual catastrophes, is not free from confused interpretations.

There can be self-sacrifice and the last measure of devotion without there being any degree of alienation. (Socialism, in its fight against the alienation of human effort, too often took for granted the exaltation of the ego contained in the formulas of its predecessor, liberal individualism.) There is no alienation when I work for my wife and children, for they belong to me; no alienation when I work for the one I love, because the beloved is another self; no alienation when I work for our community, for I belong to it and it belongs to me and its good is not, by any means, alien to me. Above all, there is no alienation when I work for God, for he is more interior to me than I am to myself—a sublime truth familiar to metaphysicians and to mystics as well, but both Proudhon and Marx missed it completely. Whoever seeks his own self away from God undergoes precisely the worst kind of alienation. And whoever sur-

renders his self for the love of God finds himself in God and
eternity.

There is alienation in the case of the slave as just defined;
slaves are unpaid labor, which means that they are not recom-
pensed for their work but are merely given maintenance.
There is also alienation in the case of the ill-paid wage-earner.
By saying that he is ill-paid, we imply that his wage is not
equal to his work; thus part of his work is dedicated, in involuntary fashion, to the welfare of a private person, his employer. There is alienation in the case of the small truck-
farmer when market prices are so low that he cannot make a
decent living out of the sale of his vegetables. There is alienation in the case of victims of usury, including tenants who pay
too high a rent. There is alienation in the case of consumers
who pay excessive prices for any commodities or services.
These people are not slaves, inasmuch as the alienation of their
labors is not established by a legal relation of authority. We
thus come to understand that the exploitation of man by man
can be managed in either of two ways: (1) through an authority relationship sanctioned by law or (2) through unequal exchange. No legal formula compels the wage-earner to remain
under the authority of the employer; the small truck-farmer is
not under the authority of his customers, the debtor is not
under the authority of the creditor, and the tenant of a house
is not under the authority of the owner. But, like slaves, these
people undergo alienation when they have to be content with
processes of exchange in which they give more than they receive, which means that part of their contribution is, involuntarily, given for nothing to another person. It would be arbitrary to describe as slavery the situation brought about by
unequal exchange, but it often can be described as a sort of
servitude.

According to such a witness as Tocqueville, the history of
freedom is, to a frightful extent, the history of a conflict be-

tween freedom and equality.[13] Be that as it may, there is one case at least in which freedom and equality, far from conflicting, agree, coincide, and become indistinguishable from each other. It is the comprehensive case of freedom as opposed to servitude, of freedom from alienation, of freedom from exploitation. The work done yesterday by a slave may be done today by a free laborer; suppose, for the sake of clarity, that the latter receives a recompense fully equal to his service. Transition from the state of the slave to the state of the normally paid laborer signifies, undividedly, achievement of freedom and achievement of equality. If inadequate wage maintains inequality, the legal abolition of slavery and serfdom, for having failed to end exploitation, would be described as having failed also to end servitude.

In rough outline, the social history of modern times is dominated by two great revolutions. The first began in the late eighteenth century; its main parts are over, although it is still going on, and still has to go on, in some countries, for a long time. The second had hardly begun before the first World War; we know that it is going on; we know that it is still very far from termination; whether it is still in its initial stage or is already beyond it we do not know. Giving these revolutions names is an embarrassing duty. If the first is called the "democratic" revolution, a few questions are begged with regard to the second; and if the second is called "socialistic," more questions are begged. Let these terms be used, if indispensably needed, in purely conventional and provisional fashion. What relation there is between these two revolutions is by no means obvious. Some historians perceive mostly resemblances and continuities, others contrasts. Some would say that they are merely two phases of one and the same revolutionary process. They certainly have in common a feature of central impor-

13. *Democracy in America*, Part II, Book IV, chap. vii (New York: P. F. Collier & Son, 1900), II, 339 ff.

tance: in either case there is a question of putting an end to a system of exploitation or alienation.

The democratic revolution asserted with great vigor the proposition that political government is dominion over free men; it endeavored to destroy the myths and practices which had, to some extent, corrupted civil government into a master-to-servant relationship. It also opposed with success processes of alienation connected with the division of society into castes and orders, with slavery and serfdom. But it did little about processes of alienation that had no special connection with political structures, with the aristocratic constitution of society, or with institutional servitude. It even seems that in countless instances it released forces of exploitation that the old regimes used to keep under control.

As a result of the democratic revolution, which abolished slavery, serfdom, and feudalism, unequal exchange became the main factor of alienation. It was often noticed that liberalism brought down to a minimum gratuitousness in human relations. Such a thing as the free distribution of wealth, which played a considerable part in more primitive economic systems, was excluded from normal relations, except within the limits of a narrowing family circle. Beyond these limits the communication of wealth had to be effected by way of exchange alone. With economic transactions reaching unprecedented magnitude, alienation through unequal exchange assumed overwhelming importance at the time when alienation through legal bondage was formally abolished and factually declining.

It is axiomatic that exchange is just if, and only if, the exchanged values are equal;[14] then, and only then, the partners treat each other as equal; then, and only then, both are free from alienation and exploitation. Here justice is equality and freedom, and all is ready for the growth of friendship. On

14. Thomas Aquinas *Sum. theol.* ii–ii. 61. 2.

these principles there can be no disagreement among honest persons. But the question is pervaded by anxiety as soon as the problem of *recognition* is envisaged. What values are equal? What is the criterion of equality of value? Here are a farmer and a shoemaker; exchanging wheat against shoes is for them the most natural thing in the world. But what weight of wheat equals in value a pair of shoes? We certainly can define an *insignificant* amount of wheat and know for sure that it is inferior in value to a pair of shoes; and we can define a *huge* amount of wheat, such that nobody would doubt that it is worth more than one pair of shoes. Between the insignificant and the huge the distance is hopelessly wide.

We have already called attention to the difficulties of the problem of recognition in ethics. These difficulties cover the whole domain of moral life; we like to think that there are safe regions in which the right and the wrong are recognized without any special inquiry; this is an illusion, possible under ordinary circumstances, violently shaken in wars and revolutions as the identities of things and persons become uncertain. To know crime from virtue in time of war, I need to know whether this war is just; assuming that it is, I still do not know crime from duty so long as I do not know whether these shadows are enemies, friends, or nonbelligerents. Common behavior in wars and revolutions shows that when the problem of recognition becomes exceedingly difficult, most persons give up all interest in the answer and soon come to ignore and to deny the problem itself. Let us be allowed to express this hypothesis: the adventures of human conscience, with regard to equality of values, are partly to be understood as an effect of fatigue and discouragement. In the wars of our time resignation to indiscriminate destruction of life often resulted from the difficulty of determining who is a belligerent. For lack of a better criterion, fliers would treat as belligerent, at the cost of many innocent lives, anything that moves within a distance of twenty miles behind the enemy lines; such a rule of action shows that hope of finding a working criterion has been given up. We are suggesting that with regard to equality of values most men use or are ready to use, without circumstances being upset by any war or revolution, almost any conventional criterion, no matter how crudely inadequate, out of a sense of hopeless difficulty and out of a biological realization that life cannot wait and that exchanges must go on.

In an economy using money as an instrument and measure, the problem of the equality of values becomes the problem of the just price.[15] Among the methods employed in the determination of prices, that of the market enjoys an obvious privilege. It is assumed that the best possible way to obtain a fair estimation of the value of a service or a commodity is to leave it up to those whom it directly concerns, i.e., prospective purchasers and sellers. They meet in a public place and a deliberation goes on, with clashes and compromises, mutual pressure, mutual control, and control by the public. It is not claimed that this method enjoys any kind of indefectibility. It would be granted that in each particular case it probably falls short of the rule of justice; but it is held, not unreasonably, that casual influences work one day in one direction, another day in another direction, so that in the long run the rule of justice is approximated as closely as it can be by any human method. Under exceptional circumstances prices are fixed by government decree; this, too, is not a procedure free from risks, and it may be held that in many respects, especially with regard to the protection of liberty against government arbitrariness, the risks of the market system are lesser than those of price-fixing by government decision.

What does honesty mean to a businessman operating under the market system? Let us suppose that he is a person of un-

15. On the theory of the just price according to classical theologians see Albert Sandoz, "La Notion du juste prix," *Revue thomiste*, April–June, 1939.

compromising righteousness. In order to know what he has to do, to what sacrifices he has to consent, and what returns he can expect, he merely has to know about the situation of the unsophisticated market. The most common temptation of dishonesty regards operations calculated to sophisticate the market. One may, for instance, spread false news or overemphasize the significance of an actual fact in order to have prices go up or down at will. There is also sophistication of the market when a group of businessmen sell at abnormally low prices in order to get rid of a competitor. So long as the market price genuinely expresses the conclusions of a deliberation between prospective purchasers and prospective sellers, buying and selling at the market price is buying and selling at the just price, as far as it can be determined under the circumstances.

Since prices change, the system implies the possibility of making profits without performing any operation except purchase at a low price and sale at a higher price. This defines "commerce." But a tedious experience of idle discussions makes it necessary for us to elaborate on this definition. Economic subjects lend themselves so nicely to rhetoric and dogmatism that people who would not fail to grasp the meaning of an abstraction, say, in chemistry, can talk indefinitely to demonstrate that they have not understood the meaning of an ideal type in economics. When a physician says that some conditions demand a diet free from sodium chloride, he does not imply that the thing contained in the saltshaker is ideally pure sodium chloride; he does not even imply that it is in the power of any chemist to isolate one gram of NaCl without any admixture of any other chemical; all that he implies is that there is a relation between the ingestion of a chemical essence symbolized by NaCl and the evolution of a disease, so that, in so far as the patient ingests NaCl, whether in a pure form or in mixture, he can expect to undergo such and such symptoms. Now, when the century-old definition of commerce just recalled is voiced in certain circles, it is tempestuously objected that a merchant patterned after this definition is a mythical character impossible to find in the world of experience (a fiction of philosophers and theologians, just as NaCl is a fiction of chemists). It is argued that between the purchase and the sale the merchant produces space utility (e.g., if he moves grapefruit from Florida to Quebec) or time utility (e.g., if, just by keeping merchandise in his basement, he transforms new wine into old, or butter in July, when cows have plenty of milk, into butter in January, when milk flows less abundantly). If it were not for the literary habits of thought commonly exercised on such topics, it would be clear to everybody that *in so far as* a man creates space utility by moving a commodity from a place where it is plentiful to a place where it is scarce or time utility by keeping a commodity from a time when it is plentiful to a time when it is scarce, there is no question of describing him as a merchant; he is a producer of utility, just as is a woodcutter or a miner. The relevant question is this: Over and above compensations obtained for such services as woodcutting or coal mining or space utility-producing or time utility-producing, is there such a thing as a *profit* corresponding to no production at all, but merely to an advantageous difference between price at the time of the purchase and price at the time of the sale? If such a thing exists, commerce exists and is definable, and the description of its laws is relevant both in a theoretical sense and in a practical sense, whether or not there exist individuals specialized in commerce and determined not to produce any utility under any circumstances. The thing contained in the saltshaker is certainly not pure sodium chloride, and the thing contained in our atmosphere is certainly not pure oxygen. To deny the reality of commerce, as defined above, for the reason that most or all businessmen produce some utility is as good logic as to deny the reality of oxygen for the reason that in our atmosphere the molecules of nitrogen are the overwhelming majority.

For the sake of clarity, we are going to consider the abstraction of the pure merchant, just as a chemist considers the abstraction called NaCl without having to decide whether or not it is possible to realize this abstraction in a state of absolute purity. What does profit mean in relation to the law of commutative justice, which is one of strict equality between the exchanged values? This is the problem.

It is necessary to subject the commercial practice to a two-fold examination. Let us consider the merchant, first, in the exercise of an individual act of buying or selling. Provided that the rules of the game are observed, viz., provided that the market has not been sophisticated in any way, the purchase is just and the sale is just. So far as we can know, the money that he gave up when he bought was equal in value to the commodity that he acquired, and the money that he received when he sold was equal to the commodity that he sold. There is in the school of Aristotle a great deal of diffidence toward commerce even when it is not accompanied by any sophistication of the market, for the mover of commercial activity is the desire to make money, and this desire contains a threat, inasmuch as its immediate object does not impose on it any measure. If I desire such real wealth as food or shelter, the very nature of the thing desired involves a principle of measure: one house in town and one in the country are about as much as I can enjoy, and the amount of proteins and carbohydrates that I can use per unit of time is contained within very narrow limits. On the other hand, it takes no particularly perverse disposition to experience unmeasured desire for money. Precisely because money is means in the second power, means in view of means and instrument in view of instruments, it presents the desire with no specification and no measure. From this it follows that profit-making is always a disquieting and risky proposition. However, Aquinas and other great theologians explain that honesty can be preserved in commerce if specification and measure are supplied by the ends to which desire for money is subordinated.[16] Taking advantage of a difference in price on the unsophisticated market is an action which does not possess its justification within itself; it is not good of itself; but it is not, either, bad of itself, and it may receive from the appropriate end the justification that it does not possess in itself. Taking advantage of a difference in price in order to support one's family or to relieve the needy is a perfectly justified action. Its justification does not spring from its own nature; it springs from the end to which it is related. Such justification by the end is possible because there is nothing intrinsically evil about a purchase and a sale at the market price.

A distinct and supplementary approach is effected when we consider not individual acts of purchasing and selling but the general relation of the merchant to society. Let us suppose that a businessman reaches the end of a life characterized by skill and honesty. He never indulged in practices designed to sophisticate the market, but he was so skilful and so lucky as to gain much more than he lost. He has acquired a large amount of property through a series of operations each of which was absolutely fair. But, assuming that he has been a pure merchant, by no means a producer, it is plain that, if his career is considered as a whole and related to society, there has been between this honest man and society no real exchange. *All the wealth went one way. Through a succession of actions each of which was entirely lawful, wealth leaked out of society.* Exchange has been more apparent than real. Notice, further, that what happens most clearly in the case of the pure merchant, happens no less really in the case of the mixed character whose income is made partly of compensation for his services as a producer and partly of profit. The significant fact is that, in a system which identifies the just price with the unsophisticated market price, wealth leaks out of society through operations each of which is perfectly legal and lawful. The significant fact is

16. Thomas Aquinas *Sum. theol.* ii–ii. 77. 4.

that the market system makes for the permanent possibility of a leak without there being dishonesty on the side of any partner. The significant fact is that, if the operation of the genuine market is accepted as the safest way to approach the determination of the just price, burglars, robbers, brigands, and swindlers are unnecessary to cause wealth to leak out of society: the regular and perfectly honest operation of the system suffices.

To sum up: nobody questions that exchange is just if, and only if, the exchanged values are equal. The whole problem is to measure values in such a way as to know what values equal what values. The answer that the just price is identical with the market price, provided that the market is unsophisticated, may not be the last word on the subject, for the market system admits of one-way transactions and illusory exchanges. The least that can be said is that greater accuracy in the determination of the just price is highly desirable, if it can be achieved at all.

Since there is no reason why constructs should be less lawful and less useful in philosophy than anywhere else, let us indulge in the construct of a businessman of such unusually exacting conscience that he wants to sell merchandise for what it is, instead of following the common rule of taking as much money as possible from the customer within the limits of the unsophisticated market. His first concern is to determine his cost of production. Suppose that this virtuous man is an innkeeper and that the commodity whose cost of production he would like to know is the use of a particular room for one night. Let us try to understand what operations and what difficulties are involved in determining the cost of production of such a commodity. Some entries are very clear, some are essentially obscure. It is easy to know what figures should be entered for rent, fire insurance, taxes, interest, etc. The figure to be entered for wages is less certain, but, except in time of inflation, the margin within which it is contained is rather narrow. But I have also to enter my own salary, and here, according to the familiar paradox of prudence, there is no chance to know the truth except through the influence of virtue. The customary view is that I can look for the highest possible remuneration so long as it does not involve any violence to my associates or any sophistication of the market. To say the least, such a view cannot be expected to deliver the most accurate answer to the problem of the just price. The way to the answer is a deliberation in terms of human needs conducted in a disposition of entire generosity. Covetousness and pride would make me feel that no income is too big a reward for me; but temperance and humility cut the figure down. Fear would incline me to overdo the amount to be set apart for purposes of security—in fact, it is the craving for security more than lust for pleasure that causes the evil of boundless desire. Thus fortitude is needed in order that desire for security should not cause me to trespass the boundaries of the just price. The ultimate rule is an estimation of human needs, and this estimation cannot be effected without the unique light that proceeds from virtue. It goes without saying that it is only for the purpose of simplicity that we are imagining a solitary research by an individual conscience; such deliberations have to be conducted, so far as possible, by the wisdom of society. Yet ultimately there is always some amount of indetermination to be actualized by the operation of individual prudence, and it is not possible to disregard entirely, no matter how much we would like to do without it, the trivial consideration that there cannot be justice in society without a minimum of good will in the individuals who make up society.

Let human needs be divided, according to tradition, into those which are biologically determined (*necessarium vitae*) and those which are sociologically determined (*necessarium status*). With regard to the former, science and technology have brought about significant conditions of extraordinary novelty. For one thing, the appreciation of these needs has become subject to fast change; for another, the change always takes place in the same direction, inasmuch as the more recent view is more exacting than the less recent. Our children are reputed to need, in order to survive and to keep well, a huge amount of costly things which fifty years ago were considered luxuries or were totally unheard of. From the point of view of the present inquiry the most relevant fact is that the increasingly high estimation of biological needs entails equalitarian consequences. The case can be simply described as follows: Assuming that society is determined to assure the satisfaction of biological needs, let us compare a period in which biological needs are measured by 2 units with a period in which they are measured by 20 units. Since biological needs are, roughly, the same for all, higher estimation causes a greater amount of wealth to be distributed equally. As the estimation of the biological minimum goes up, technology makes it possible to procure this increasing minimum for all. So long as low production ruled out the distribution of the biological minimum to all, the estimation of this minimum was likely to be much below the truth; it is heartbreaking to declare, as necessary to life, commodities that one knows to be far beyond the range of most of one's fellow-citizens. Abundant production, whether it be a fact or merely a technical possibility, pushes up the estimation of the biological minimum by making the expert free to heed all the suggestions of experience.

With regard to the needs resulting from a social state of affairs, let us first remark that they are sometimes as imperative as items included in the biological minimum. For many men it is easier to do without their full ration of calories than to do without a white shirt. Thus no notion of luxury or futility should be systematically connected with the concept of merely sociological necessity.

Here is a telling fact: whereas the estimation of biological needs has steadily gone up in recent times and, by going up, has brought about equalitarian consequences of great significance, awareness of needs connected with social rank has declined in significant respects; and this also entailed equalitarian consequences. These two movements with one effect favor each other; that is, as more units of wealth are assigned to biological needs, fewer are left for needs of merely sociological character, and, as fewer units of wealth are assigned to "conspicuous consumption," more are left for the salvation of human life. What we mean is not that the total ratio of wealth allocated to sociologically determined needs has declined; in democratic mores the common people have social obligations which, taken as a whole, are extremely costly (decent apparel, good-looking homes, clean lawns, etc.); the significant change concerns the needs connected with high rank in society. The rationalism of democracy produces here its most certain and least harmful effects. So long as expenses declared necessary on account of rank are moderate (e.g., white collars for office workers), they admit of rational justification; but, in order to believe that one's social status imperatively demands a huge sacrifice of wealth—at the cost, possibly, of human lives—one's view of social hierarchy must be colored by mythological belief. The aristocracy-aping bourgeoisie of the nineteenth century gravely took over the nonrational postulates which made it possible to enjoy murderous expenses of conspicuous consumption with a feeling of mere submission to the eternal laws of the social order. It is worth remarking that little was accomplished, in this connection, by the democratic revolution, or by its first phase. A good sign that a new revolutionary phase is irresistibly going on is that it has become impossible for men possessed with a normal conscience to understand how pleasure can be found in meals as costly as those which were such an important part of social life for the upperclass gentlemen of the Victorian era.

This is how a philosophy of human needs—which implies, of course, a whole philosophy of human destiny—has a central part to play in the computation of costs of production. The social conscience of the nineteenth century revolted against the treatment of human labor as an item of merchandise. But if human labor ought not to be treated as an item of merchandise, no item of merchandise ought to be treated as a mere item of merchandise, for there is always, at the core of the cost of production, the recompense of human labor and the answer to human needs. Incorrect estimation of human needs, one way or the other, entails error concerning the cost of production, inequality in exchange, rupture of balance, alienation.

But suppose that the cost of production of a service or commodity has been exactly computed. The construct of the virtuous businessman can be of further help, for a question of no negligible importance remains to be examined. Is the just price equal to the cost of production? There is a strong appearance that it is. Once more, justice in exchange is nothing else than the equality of the exchanged values. Does not equality demand that the sum surrendered by the purchaser be no greater than the total cost of the commodity purchased?

If producers sold their products at a price equal to the cost of production, they would set a fine example of disinterestedness, but society would not be well served, for there would be no provision for two social needs of the most essential character, viz., *capitalization* and *free distribution*. The meaning of capitalization is clear, but in oral discussion of these ideas I have had many opportunities to notice that the expression "free distribution" fills minds with horrifying pictures related to that of the wealthy man showering bills, from a window, upon a cheering crowd. Free distribution is, indeed, fittingly defined in opposition to exchange. Wealth is made available to the consumer in either of two ways, according as the surrender of equal value is or is not the condition under which wealth is made available. In the first case there is exchange; in the second case wealth is distributed freely. Upset souls are generally pacified not by this definition or any definition but by examples leading to the realization that in the daily life of our societies a huge amount of wealth is distributed freely, that the survival of our societies without extensive processes of free distribution is absolutely inconceivable, and that an economic system in which wealth is made available by way of exchange alone has never existed (although societies tended toward it in the golden age of liberalism). Let it be recalled, further, that abundance causes exchange to be more insufficient than ever as means of distribution. As a matter of fact, we are constantly using a hundred ways of maintaining scarcity, for we know well that, under the circumstances, abundance or some forms of it would entail poverty.

Thus the hypothesis of the price equal to the cost of production leaves unanswered the question of capitalization and that of free distribution. It takes little imagination to find a solution to both these problems and to the problem of determining the cost of production as well: in an extensive system of state ownership, public powers fix prices and have a monopoly on capital and on free distribution. It is the government which distributes relief, education, family allowances, bonuses of all descriptions, and free room and board in its army and in its concentration camps. Nothing can prevent state bureaucracy from determining the just price of each item of merchandise as equal to the cost of production, plus a certain ratio for capitalization and another ratio for distribution. Wealth no longer leaks out of society through unequal exchange; any amount of money paid over and above the cost of production is assigned to functions of capitalization and distribution directly and exclusively relative to the public welfare. Alienation has come to an end. By keeping effectively all wealth within society, such a system properly deserves the name of "socialism."

It is important to recall the ideas which were commonly

held on the subject of the state at the time when socialist doctrines were constructed. The background of socialism in the
nineteenth century is constituted by economic and political
liberalism, a system in which the state apparatus is made
necessary only by deficiencies that are likely to be gradually
remedied. Roughly, the basic duty of the state is to see that
contracts are lived up to and to protect honest people against
mischievous men. Further, there is hope that, as a result of a
better understanding of the laws of society, there will be, in
the not too remote future, fewer disorders to correct and less
need for the coercive power of the state. In its daring expressions, bourgeois liberalism is very close to anarchism.

In uncertain relation to bourgeois liberalism, which is
mostly centered about economic life, a more popular trend of
thought, rooted in the French Revolution, cherishes the notion that the dangers of tyranny inherent in the ancient structure of the state can be safely excluded by democracy. Elimination of government may come later; within the explorable
portion of the future, what matters is that government should
be in the hands of the people and work for the people. Here are
the two patterns which exercised decisive influence upon the
treatment of the state in nineteenth-century socialism: let the
first be described as the theory of the withering-away of the
state, the latter as the theory of the democratic transformation
of the state.

The experiences of our century, inasmuch as they evidenced
the connection between state socialism and totalitarianism,
have made us receptive to the criticism of Proudhon, already
cited in the second chapter of this book. Not a believer in the
democratic transformation of the state, Proudhon shows that
the proper way to contain the imperialistic dynamism of the
state is to have it faced by a force possessed with equally
uncompromising imperialistic ambition. This force is property. It alone can preserve society from exhaustion by the de-

velopment of the state into totalitarian machinery. The last
thought of Proudhon on the subject would be nicely expressed
by the consideration that much should be forgiven to property
on account of what it does for liberty. To put into the same
hands the power of unconditional coercion which belongs to
the state and the power of ultimate decision concerning
earthly goods, which constitutes the right of property, is an
arrangement fateful to freedom.[17]

The problem of alienation through unequal exchange admits
of undemocratic solutions, in which mercantile exploitation is
replaced by incomparably worse forms of servitude. Democratic complacency, in our time, identifies itself with the opinion that dictatorships and totalitarian practices can be avoided
without the issue of alienation through unequal exchange
being treated in any thorough fashion. Confusedly, many like
to think that this is the kind of issue which ceases to be burn-
ing as soon as living standards are adequately raised. In several
countries social politics is a dialogue between an antidemocratic party which proudly asserts a solution of its own and a
democratic party which cherishes, without daring to voice it
too loudly, the hope that the question will be dodged indefinitely. *Yet alienation through unequal exchange is the thing that
democracy, in the second phase of its revolutionary development, has to
deal with, just as alienation through institutional bondage was the
thing that democracy had to deal with in its first revolutionary phase.*

Are there elements of a solution in actual democratic practice? Before attempting an answer to this question it is necessary to sum up the data of the problem.

We have understood that the market system is but a primitive method of approximating the just price. Even if controlled, in spite of verisimilitude, by unflinching honesty, the
market system implies a continual allowance for profits. (By

17. On this, see the essay of Georges Gurvitch, "Socialisme et propriété," *Revue de
métaphysique et de morale*, Vol. XXXVII (1930).

"profit" we mean any appropriation of wealth made possible by the market situation or by a relation between market situations over and above the recompense equal to the commodity sold or the service rendered.) Without trying to define a better method, we tried to show what better things a better method would do. It would treat the just price as a total made of (1) the cost of production and (2) a surplus for purposes of capitalization and free distribution. The part constituted by the cost of production corresponds to the interindividual aspect of exchange. The surplus is social by essence; its meaning is best expressed by contrast with the methods of state ownership: in a state-socialistic organization it is up to the central administration to save money for capital goods and to effect investments; it is up to the central administration to save money for free distribution and to effect the distribution. Private ownership embodies the principle of autonomy; it relieves the state of tasks that can be fulfilled by individuals, families, and associations, but it also assumes that private persons and private groups will actually perform duties which have to be performed anyway. For instance, subsidizing education on a broad scale is a thing which has to be done in any modern society. One way to get that thing done is for the state to collect through taxation all the money needed for the schools, plus a suitable percentage for the maintenance of the bureaucratic machinery and a few other forms of waste, and to distribute help to schools according to rules and whims which are those of the men in power. There is more autonomous life and there is less waste if money goes directly from private persons and groups to the schools. But when distribution is not effected by public powers, private persons and groups are intrusted with a social responsibility and cannot arbitrarily allocate to private pursuits the money needed for the schools.

With regard to the cost of production, the all-important item is human labor. Iniquity creeps in here. Should the conclusion arrived at by the market-place deliberation be my only rule, I would often undervalue my neighbor's labor to the point of making him destitute and overrate my own labor beyond all reasonable limit. (Such things happened commonly at the time when societies allowed themselves to be governed according to the dogmas of economic "science.") As an effect of the moral work carried out in the last three generations, it is now a common opinion that human labor is not an item of merchandise and that recompense for my neighbor's labor cannot be allowed to fall below the minimum needed for a decent life. This worthy step in the enlightenment of the common conscience still has to be supplemented by the realization that, on the other hand, the recompense for my own labor cannot be allowed to go up with no limit. There is somewhere an upper limit beyond which income no longer is a compensation for service but assumes the character of a one-way traffic of wealth. Just as we have come to outlaw destitution, which was still considered an inescapable phase of the economic cycle three generations ago, so a day will come when the conscience of the just will realize that the recompense of human labor, though admitting of inequalities, is comprised between a lower limit, which cannot be very low—for it takes a terrific amount of money to prevent children from dying and to bring them up decently—and an upper limit, which cannot be very high—for no aspect of the common good demands that any person should enjoy an income many times greater than his avowable needs.[18]

18. A great change has taken place, within the last century, in common notions concerning the ethical meaning of high profits and quickly made fortunes. Suppose that a writer composes a novel dedicated to humanitarian and, as it were, socialistic ideals, a novel designed to stir compassion for the poor, etc. It would not occur to him, in our time, that the hero of the novel should be a man who made a very big estate in a few years through the skilful exploitation of a device. Victor Hugo wrote such a novel, *Les misérables*, about a century ago. Toward the end of his life, Jean Valjean notices that his adopted daughter, Cosette, and her husband, Marius Pontmercy, have been led by false rumors to believe that the money given to Cosette as her dowry (a huge

Let us use as the background the picture of industrial societies during the golden age of laissez faire economy; against this picture it is easy to distinguish, in the democratic practice of modern societies, institutions and trends designed to promote equality in exchanges, to prevent wealth from leaking out of society, to procure greater accuracy in the estimation of human needs, and to assure the social use of everyone's surplus. The following examples should not be mistaken for the outline of a system; they are meant merely to suggest hopeful research.

1. The first place belongs to the labor union. Prior to the organization of working people, the labor contract was bound to be heavily unequal in the vast majority of cases. It would take a miracle of wisdom and disinterestedness for an equal contract to take place between two parties, one of which—the employer—can wait and cannot be replaced, whereas the other —the isolated laborer—can be replaced and cannot wait. But organized labor can wait and cannot be replaced. Its position is roughly equal to that of management. As an effect of this equality of position, genuine, i.e., equal, contracts can be negotiated between management and labor without any superhuman virtue being presupposed on either side. With due al-

---

one for the time, 600,000 francs) has been acquired dishonestly. On his deathbed Jean Valjean, who is dying a saint's death according to the religion of Hugo (humanitarian deism), dismisses their scruples: "I invented the substitution of rolled up snaps for welded snaps in bracelets; they are prettier, better, and not so dear. You can understand what money can be earned by it; so Cosette's fortune is really hers. . . . M. Pontmercy, have no fear, I conjure you. The 600.000 francs are really Cosette's. I shall have lost my life if you do not enjoy it! We succeeded very well in making glasswork. We rivalled what is called Berlin jewellry. Indeed the German black glass cannot be compared with it. A gross, which contains 1200 grains very well cut, costs only three francs. . . . I forgot to tell you that on buckles without tongues still more is made than on anything else. A gross, twelve dozen, costs 10 francs and sells for 60. That is really a good business. So you need not be astonished at the 600.000 francs, M. Pontmercy. It is honest money. You can be rich without concern. You must have a carriage, from time to time a box at the theaters, beautiful ball dresses, my Cosette, and then give good dinners to your friends; be very happy" (*Les Misérables*, trans. Lascelles Wrax [New York: W. Allison Co., n.d.], last chapter).

lowance for countless failures and abusive actions, what labor unions have done for a fair estimation of human needs is to be admired among the greatest accomplishments of mankind's social genius.

2. Co-operatives tend to establish strict equality between cost of production and sale price by returning profits to their members. It should be remarked that the co-operative movement, in its more recent phases, has often lacked the conquering energy which marked its early progress. Most communities are very far from having exhausted the possibilities of co-operation with regard to equality in exchanges. This failure may be due, in part, to habits of passivity generated by the state management of social problems.

3. Concerning free distribution, the great problem is to make it independent of the arbitrariness of individual whims without delivering it up to the arbitrariness of public powers and their bureaucracy. This twofold freedom is actually achieved, in a considerable measure, by numerous organizations which collect and distribute huge sums for relief, scientific research, art, education, and religion. True, the successful operation of autonomy, here and elsewhere, demands industry, labor, obstinacy, imagination, creativeness. An inquiry into the varieties of institutionally organized free distribution throughout the history of economic life might render great service by stimulating the imagination of planners. The worst thing about state management is that it makes people unimaginative; now, when people lack imagination, all that is left is state management.

4. It is hardly necessary to recall that in countless instances freedom from exploitation was served by diverse measures of state intervention. Such measures were eagerly promoted by those democracies which are historically inclined toward state socialism. In other democratic countries they were envisaged with extreme reluctance, then adopted and main-

tained under the pressure of obvious necessity (minimum salary, social security, subsidies to agriculture, etc.). It happens, not infrequently, that state intervention ought to be accepted in spite of its involving a curtailment of autonomy. But there are cases in which the intervention of the state serves to strengthen autonomic institutions and to increase social guaranties against all threats of imperialism, including those which may come from the democratic state. An example would be supplied by laws designed to protect the farmer's ownership of the land. If such laws are applied successfully, the resulting situation contains a new line of defense against the appetites of financial oligarchies and against those of public powers as well.

Our concluding remarks will be dedicated to the problem of classes. In conservative circles it is commonly held that the division of society into classes is natural and essential. A classless society is described, in these circles, as an equalitarian utopia, a mendacious picture calculated to produce a lust for the kind of equality that human relations do not admit of. Yet the division into classes, if words are used with any propriety, is a new situation, restricted to a short period of history. The first sentences of the *Communist Manifesto* contain a confused interpretation of the problem, together with much oversimplification: "The history of all hitherto existing society is the history of class struggles." Apart from the fact that history includes many events with but a loose relation or no relation at all to the class struggle, this sentence implies that society has always been divided into classes. Plainly, there has been some amount of class organization and class struggle in all times, but Marx and Engels mean more than this, as can be understood from the following sentence: "Freeman and slave, patrician and plebeian, lord and serf, guild master and journeyman, in a word, oppressor and oppressed. . . ." Marx and

Engels are using here a loose notion of class, understanding by this term the *orders* of the old society as well as the classes of modern society. Confusion is increased by the wholesale condemnation aimed at whatever group holds the upper part in the struggle.

In order to clarify the concept of "class" let us consider the most definite case of class organization, viz., the industrial proletariat of modern Europe.[19] The legal condition of the proletarian, unlike that of most workingmen in earlier ages, is one of complete freedom. If he falls into some sort of legal bondage, as may result, for instance, from heavy debt, we understand that his is no longer the common proletarian condition but another condition, involving distinct problems and reminiscent of the slavery or serfdom of old ages. The connection between the proletarian and his employer is merely contractual and essentially dissoluble. When in a small enterprise we notice that the employer has a paternal feeling toward his employees and that the employees recognize and appreciate such a feeling, we are again confronted by a situation distinct, in varying degree, from the proletarian condition. So long as there is a relation of the paternal type between employer and worker or, more generally, between those who occupy the upper rank and their subordinates, struggles are not class struggles, no matter how violent they may be, and the division of society is not a division into classes.

A legal situation which deprives the employer of all paternal status brings about, between him and the employed, the relationship of contract partners. Later, this contractual relationship will be strengthened and stabilized by legal guaranties, in such a way as to give the partners the character of well-disciplined and really civilized members of a community; this

19. The following description is, for the most part, taken from Goetz Briefs, *The Proletariat: A Challenge to Western Civilization*, trans. Ruth A. Eckhart (New York and London: McGraw-Hill Book Co., 1937).

institutionalization of labor relations marks the beginning of an effort to replace the proletarian condition by some condition deemed preferable and to overcome the division of society into classes. This division is sharpest when there obtain, between the groups divided from each other, a situation and a feeling of nonsolidarity. Anything that maintains or restores solidarity (for instance, membership in a guild or vocational community, common patriotism, common religion, attachment to a common way of life) lessens the sharpness of the division into classes and, correspondingly, the sharpness of the class struggle.

The contract of employment is made necessary, in a regime of legal liberty, by the separation between the laboring force and the ownership of the instruments of production. There is no question of such a contract when the laborer owns his part of land and the tools to till it, and there is no ground for such contract, either, when owner and laborer are connected by such a bond as slavery, serfdom, or a relationship of the father-to-son type.

A social class is a thing which does not possess full reality so long as it has not achieved consciousness. Moreover, the consciousness of being a member of a class does not produce the effects typical of the class structure unless membership is enduring and known to be such. Accordingly, the employment contract, even if we suppose a complete lack of solidarity between employer and employed, would not produce a class system if circumstances did not make for permanence on either side of the class division. On the side of the employer, permanence of status is guaranteed by ownership. On the side of the employed, permanence of status is caused by a rate of wages possibly equal and possibly inferior, but not much superior, to the requirements of daily life. The proletarian is a permanent and hereditary wage-earner. He is not necessarily poor; his living standard may be much higher than that of many people who were reputed well off in earlier times; but it is essential that his wages be low enough to make it impossible for him to escape from the wage-earner's condition through the acquisition of an estate.

The rigor of such an ideal-typical definition is necessary to evidence the peculiarities of the class structure. The division into classes, though not unknown to any society, does not seem to have been of dominant significance prior to the dissolution of the predemocratic society. The old orders—clergy, nobility, Third Estate—were not classes. Democracy put an end to the division of society into orders or at least reduced it to a factor of secondary importance, and it is democracy which released the forces that were to cause the division of society into classes and the class struggle. Ever since socialism has become fully class-conscious, the socialist movement has been divided into two currents: one holds that democracy, which proved able to overcome the inequalities of the order system, will also, through gradual or through abrupt change, overcome the inequalities of the class system; another socialist current holds democracy incapable of putting an end to the class structure of society and to the kind of inequality connected with it. These two currents have in common the theory that a *sine qua non* of the classless society is the abolition of private property, so far, at least, as instruments of production are concerned.

It is perfectly obvious that the separation between the labor force and the ownership of the tools is such a necessary condition of the division of society into classes that, if private ownership is abolished, the class system, such as we know it, necessarily disappears and is replaced by another organization which may be better or worse. Prior to, say, the 1920's, the disposition describable as "socialistic optimism" could not be shaken by any experience, for mankind had no experience of what follows the suppression of the class system through the socialization of the instruments of production. In the course of the last generation the history of Russia has made it clear that a new regime ushered in by a very thorough abolition of private property could be an abyss of suffering and crime. Socialistic hope disappeared from a great part of the world. Its disappearance left a destructive vacuum.

Having realized that the abolition of the class system through the suppression of its *sine qua non*, private property, does not necessarily improve the destiny of mankind, we are disposed to envisage different lines of approach in the justified struggle toward a state of affairs in which normal inequalities, both natural and structural, would no longer be associated with the peculiar kind of inequality embodied in the class system. Private ownership is a necessary, but by no means a sufficient, condition of the division of society into classes. Progress toward the classless society can be accomplished through any measure designed to abolish or to weaken any of the several conditions of the class system. Paramount among these conditions are the isolation of the worker and the exploitation of the economically weak through unequal exchanges. The organization of labor and the promotion of equality in exchanges—through a variety of methods which include, of course, changes in property relationships—may not bring about, within the explorable portion of the future, the complete suppression of the class system; but they certainly may cause such a decline of its importance that it should no longer be an insuperable obstacle to the democracy of the common man. What is left of its inconveniences, then, may have to be tolerated as the inevitable counterpart of what property does for liberty.

It should be observed, moreover, that the evils of the class system are greatest when the class system is complicated with ill-adjusted remnants of an order system. Between class relations in Europe and in the United States dissimilarities are striking, though hard to define. Most of these dissimilarities are epitomized by the consideration that, unlike the American upper class, the European bourgeoisie, in many if not in all cases, is a successor to aristocracy. The European bourgeoisie, throughout the nineteenth century, was an aristocracy-aping upper class, with the same materialistic claim to excellent blood and hereditarily transmissible excellence as that of the old aristocracy. The struggle of the proletariat against the bourgeoisie was, in part, the continuation of the old struggle fought by the rising Third Estate against the nobility. What was described under the name of class struggle was a mixed sociological entity made partly of a struggle of classes and partly of a struggle of orders. Much bitterness was traceable to the conflict of orders which was going on together with the conflict of classes. A pure class conflict may be full of hatred, and conflicts of orders have always been known to arouse violent passions. But it seems that distinct bitterness attaches to a certain combination of the two. People do not always resent aristocratic dignity; under many circumstances they even prove exceedingly willing to believe in it and to draw comfort from the picture of the upper society as a sort of blessed island in this world of suffering and degradation. But the modern proletariat never understood and disliked increasingly, as time went on, the notion of the prerogatives of the nobility being assumed by the bourgeoisie. People are not unwilling to tolerate the traditional privileges of the nobility so long as they are, or are believed to be, associated with such distinctions as military bravery, education, skill in politics and diplomacy, refined manners, a life which is itself, if not a thing of virtue, at least a thing of beauty, kinship with spiritual leaders, and, above all, antiquity, the privilege of communication with the past, the privilege of overcoming the brevity of human life through continued communion with men of other times. An aristocracy is supposed to be that part of society in which man fulfils his wish of transcending time and brings down into temporal affairs a picture of eternal communion. One blunder of the bourgeoisie was their failure to understand that they were only a class, only a social stratum distinguished by the possession of enough wealth—more exactly, of enough money—to go to expensive schools, buy costly instruments, hire costly technical help, and wait for the maturation of slow economic processes.

CHAPTER V

DEMOCRACY AND TECHNOLOGY

✲

RURAL democracy, as a component of American history, is engaged in a contrast which sharpens its significance. For centuries the agricultural communities of the South have presented a picture of oligarchy, with owners of huge estates dominating landless toilers of the soil describable, according to circumstances, as slaves, colored people, poor whites, share-croppers, and Mexicans. This undemocratic system, in spite of its enduring power within the southern states, had comparatively little influence on the nation as a whole. In the national conscience it was defeated by another pattern of rural life, viz., the democratic one, famously exemplified by the early New England towns. A democratic polity, deriving its energy from the daily practice of self-government on the independent farm: this American ideal was voiced, with a kind of definitiveness, by a gentleman farmer from the South and a slave-owner, Thomas Jefferson; but at the time of the Revolution there was no obvious ground for believing that the southern society would remain stubbornly oligarchic, and the abolition of slavery was expected to take place in the near future.

The pattern of rural democracy has continued to exercise influence throughout the history of the American people. There is a paradox here, since the United States soon developed large-scale industry and unique phenomena of urban concentration. But to explain the paradox it suffices to remark that the rise of American industrialism was contemporary with a gigantic process of expansion in space. In most respects the settlement of the West was the work of an agricultural society free from aristocratic influences and little affected by government interference. The conquest of the western wilderness maintained, through a series of generations, conditions similar to those which presided over the formation of the first northern colonies. Amid untamed and prehistoric nature, men of the nineteenth and twentieth centuries lived, by the millions, in isolated communities which could afford to ignore much of what was going on in the industrial cities and in the capitals of the world.

The political ideal of the Americans, in so far as it makes democracy dependent upon the ways of rural life, gives verisimilitude to the theory that a technological society does not admit of democratic government. This theory is old. Over a century ago Saint-Simonism set forth, in an atmosphere saturated with romantic kindness, the construct of a society shaped by the power of technology; the undemocratic character of this construct proceeds, in part, from a keen understanding of sociological trends which were to prove profound and lasting. During the Fascist years we had many opportunities to recognize, in the psychology of industrialists and business leaders enthusiastic about broad plans of "organization," the spirit of the Saint-Simonists. But the atmosphere of brotherly love had dried up in the meantime.

As to the reasons for the traditional belief that small communities of landowning farmers constitute the soundest foundation for democracy, it seems that they can be summed up in the following three propositions: (1) Rural life favors an ideal of happiness and thereby discourages lust for power; (2) it gives citizens the best possible chance for training in self-government; (3) it favors community feelings. We propose to examine, in comparative fashion, the merits of rural life and those of technological society with regard to this three-point basic program: the dedication of man to the pursuit of happiness, as opposed to his being driven by the lust for power; the training of citizens in autonomy, as opposed to their being subjected to the mores of servitude; and the establishment of strong community feelings, as opposed to the prevalence of individualistic loneliness.

One of these points calls for preliminary elaboration. The contrast between pursuit of happiness and lust for power expresses familiar experiences. However, its meaning involves one of the deepest mysteries of moral life. The pursuit of happiness comprises every pursuit, whether of power or of anything else. Happiness is the all-embracing and naturally determined object of all acts of will, and in a certain sense it is improper to set in opposition happiness and, say, power, since no one seeks power except inasmuch as he places his happiness in it.

Yet it would be poor psychology to content one's self with the consideration that all seek happiness and diverge only with regard to the thing in which happiness is placed. One day, as Zarathustra sat on a stone before his cave and silently gazed, "his animals went thoughtfully around him and at last stood in front of him. 'O Zarathustra,' they said, 'dost thou peradventure look out for thy happiness?' 'What is happiness worth?' he answered. 'I ceased long ago to strive for my happiness: I strive for my work.' "[1]

Who would question the psychological relevance and the profundity of the contrast set here between dedication to one's happiness and dedication to one's work? True, it can be properly said that Zarathustra places his happiness in his work; but this valid remark does not destroy the significance of the contrast. Maritain wrote that it is the distinction "of our humanistic civilizations to place happiness in happiness, the end of man in human happiness."[2] The expression "placing happi-

1. F. W. Nietzsche, *Thus Spake Zarathustra* (*Werke*, 1. Abt., Vol. VI [Leipzig: C. G. Naumann, 1896], p. 343).

2. Jacques Maritain, *Pour la justice* (New York: Éditions de la Maison de France, 1945), p. 20: "Nous savons que les démocraties se proposent, selon une formule chère à

ness in happiness" is not absurdly redundant. Clearly, there is a sense in which every object of desire falls under happiness and a sense in which some objects of desire set themselves in opposition to happiness. But specifying these senses involves great difficulty.

Let it be said that happiness has the character of a form by the necessitating energy of which we will all that we will. This form admits of a diversity of contents, and, because of the imperfection of human freedom, such diversity extends to the ultimate end; for some men happiness consists in wealth, for others it consists in power, and for others in pleasure, etc. Now some contents are such that the form of happiness applies to them smoothly and harmoniously. Other contents seem to revolt against it, and they bring about the feeling that, when happiness is placed in them, not happiness but something else is striven for. Zarathustra's statement voices a perfect example of such a clash.

Suppose that we are trying to understand the psychology of an artist frantically dedicated to his art. We are struck by the ruthlessness with which, for the sake of the work to be produced or perfected, he gives up leisure, pleasure, sleep, and duties. We shall not be astonished if we learn that his life is haunted by some great misfortune, such as the death or the permanent absence of a beloved person; and we shall be aware of expressing a perfectly intelligible situation by saying that he is seeking in his work a consolation, a compensation for his failure to achieve happiness. One truth would be expressed by the proposition that, having failed to find happiness in love and family life, he is seeking happiness in artistic creation. And another truth is expressed by setting in contrast happi-

l'Amérique, la *poursuite du bonheur*, tandis que les régimes totalitaires se proposent la poursuite de l'empire et d'un pouvoir illimité, en asservissant à ces fins tout ce qui est dans l'homme. À vrai dire l'homme ne peut rien désirer sinon en désirant le bonheur, mais il place son bonheur ici ou là; et c'est le propre de nos civilisations humanistes de placer le bonheur dans le bonheur, la fin de l'homme dans le bonheur humain."

ness, which he no longer seeks, and the work of art for which he dies. The lust for power would lend itself to a similar description. When a person shows an unusually domineering disposition, the first hypothesis to be tried is that he is unhappy and seeks in the manipulation of his fellow-men a substitute for the happiness that he cannot obtain. In some cases a life of pleasure would also suggest a similar description. If a man disregards all the prudent calculations recommended by the Epicureans and delivers himself up to pleasure in reckless fashion, without consideration for society or for his own survival, our first guess is that his striving for pleasure originates in bitterness about frustration of his hope for a happy life.

In these three examples the thing striven for is plainly incapable of procuring happiness. Further, it clashes with the form of happiness in such fashion that sentences contrasting happiness and work, happiness and power, happiness and violent pleasure, are obviously meaningful. The understanding of such contrasts is made easier by the supplementary consideration of cases in which no opposition appears between the form of happiness and the content to which it is applied, even though the thing striven for is no less incapable of procuring happiness. One example would be a life of pleasure moderated by skilful calculation and enjoyed in the company of friends; genuine happiness cannot be found in such a life, which contains much evil and inevitably some crime. But nobody would say that the man who chose this way of living has, like Zarathustra, given up happiness. We merely consider that he erred by placing happiness where it cannot actually reside. The form is applied to the wrong content, and there is no more to be said. A similar description would hold in the case of one who places his happiness in the peaceful satisfaction of his intellectual curiosity and the unloving enjoyment of his culture. Let attention be called, finally, to a most striking example found in Rousseau's *Reveries of a Solitary*. The writer has just shown that happiness cannot be genuine unless it achieves independence from the past and the future by transcending time. Then he goes on to describe an experience that he had often had at Saint-Pierre Island, as he was lying on the bottom of a drifting boat or sitting near the shore of the lake or near a whispering rivulet:

What is it that one enjoys in such a situation? Nothing external to one's self; nothing, except one's self and one's own existence; so long as this state endures, one is, like God, self-sufficient. The feeling of existence, stripped of all other emotion, is by itself a valuable experience of contentment and peace, which would suffice to render this existence dear and sweet to whoever succeeded in freeing himself from all the sensual and earthly impressions which ceaselessly distract us from it and spoil, here below, its sweetness. But most men, agitated as they are with continual passions, are little acquainted with this condition and, having had no more than an imperfect experience of it for a very short time, retain only an obscure and confused idea of it, which conveys no realization of its charm.[3]

Placing happiness in sheer and naked existence is a metaphysical mistake of the first magnitude and of great profundity—of such profundity, indeed, that the metaphysician at once recognizes in it the kind of error from which much can be learned. The plenitude that happiness implies is not found in naked existence but rather in the climax of actuality reached by the rational being in the ultimate exercise of his best activity. In no undistinguished fashion Rousseau misplaces happiness; but the illusion-causing content to which he applies it, far from rebelling against the imposition of such a form—as in the case of the work of art, of power, and of violent pleasure—produces, by uniting with the form of happiness, an inebriating harmony.

From these examples the distinctive features of two types

3. J.-J. Rousseau, *Rêveries du promeneur solitaire*, Cinquième promenade (Paris: Bibliothèque indépendante d'édition, 1905).

can be tentatively disengaged. Among the objects that human desire strives for, some unite smoothly with the form of happiness, and some bear the appearance of being at variance with it. One characteristic of the first category of objects is that they are or seem to be *in line with human nature*. Not everybody is willing to confess that he wants to be happy. Willingness to be happy implies acceptance of nature such as it is and such as we did not make it. Many would find it intolerably humiliating to be suspected of seeking happiness simply and unpretentiously, like children, like uneducated people, like saints. Zarathustra phrased the catchword of many an artist: these gentlemen are too proud to be happy and find it more becoming to strive for their work. A second attribute of the thing in harmony with the form of happiness is that it is necessarily *interior to man*. It may be health, it may be the feeling of being alive, it may be the sentiment of existence, and it may be pleasure—though not of the violent kind—or culture—though not of the perverse description; but it cannot be a thing exterior to man, such as a work of art. Third, the object in congenial relation to the form of happiness is *enjoyable in peace*. Things that cannot be enjoyed except in violent action, in painful tension, in excruciating conflict, or in agonizing privation do not stand very well the form of happiness. Fourth, things in harmony with the form of happiness are *enjoyable in common*.

Nothing is more instructive, in this last connection, than the psychology of solitary life. In solitude the Christian exercises the highest form of sociability; by delivering him from the impediments that lower systems of social relations involve, solitude disposes him to live more intimately in the communion of the Divine Persons and in the communion of the saints. As for the romantic seeker of solitude, he commonly indulges in bitterness and misanthropy. Yet his soul is filled with expectation. His real purpose is not to live in uninhabited wilderness; as he steps out of the society of men, he means to step into another society, whose members would be more reliable than human beings: the reliability of the things of nature is as complete as the natural determination of their operations. But loving fancy endows things of nature with the character of personality; they finally turn out to be regarded as thoroughly reliable persons. The meaning of romantic theism is sometimes uncertain because it is not always possible to decide whether the name of God, in romantic language, refers to the transcendent cause of nature or to a community of natural energies personified by the idealism of the solitary wanderer.

ON TECHNOLOGICAL SOCIETY

The notion of technological society calls for a great deal of preparatory elaboration, the first step of which concerns technique itself and its relation to human use. A technique is a rational discipline designed to assure the mastery of man over physical nature through the application of scientifically determined laws. In a certain way every technique is indifferent to the use made of it. Use is extraneous to technique, superadded to its essence, incidental to it. One may possess a technique and not use it. Actual use of it may be ethically right or wrong, and it may be right or wrong from the point of view of the technique itself. In Aristotle's example a grammarian, by the fact that he masters the rules of grammar, is in a particularly good position to break them. Grammar is a thing which can be used against its own finalities. A chemical engineer is the logical man to sabotage the operation of a chemical plant. If we were allowed to consider technique abstractly, unqualified negation would be final, and there would be nothing to be said over and above the indisputable proposition that the essence of technique comprises no tendency relative to its use. But tendencies relative to use are often embodied in the human and social existence of technique.

Clarification of this subject requires a survey, no matter how brief, of the general theory of use.[4] Use is the act by which man applies a thing to some human purpose; it is the point where the universe of nature and the universe of morality come into contact. The thing which is being used is good or bad, independently of the use made of it, according as it satisfies or not the requirements of its type; the goodness proper to it—whether there is a question of a thing of nature or of a work of art—is physical. Moral good and moral evil reside in the use of things by human freedom. Roughly, matters of use can be divided into (1) external things, (2) the body and its organs, (3) cognitive powers, (4) the will, (5) the sense appetite.

In many cases there is no definite relation between the physical state of a thing and the moral quality of its use. A man owns a car in perfect condition; he may use it for excellent purposes, and he may, just as well, make criminal use of it. He may also make good use or bad use of a poor car. It is clear at once that the physical perfection of a thing does not, under any circumstances, entail its good use. Our engineers are likely to improve indefinitely our means of transportation, but it can be safely predicted that a car privileged with guaranties of ethical use is a thing that no dealer will ever be entitled to advertise. The relevant question is whether it can be said with equal universality that the condition of a car never determines to any degree an inclination toward good or wrong use. Think of a car whose brakes are poor; we feel that we are somewhat unethical in procrastinating about repairing it, as if keeping poor brakes in one's garage was the beginning of murder by imprudence. True, a car may remain unused, whether its condition is good or bad. But fast and restful transportation is for all men, especially in technological societies, the object of an urge felt at frequent intervals. Whoever has a car in his garage, even in bad condition, is inclined to use it often if it is

4. See Thomas Aquinas *Sum. theol.* i–ii. 16.

drivable at all. Now there are many opportunities for perfectly ethical use of a car that has such defects as low speed, high consumption of oil, etc., but cases in which it is ethical to use a car whose brakes are poor are few.

This example suffices to show under what conditions the physical defects of a thing may cause, though never in necessary fashion, an unethical use of it. A first condition is that there be in man, either on natural or on historical grounds, an enduring tendency to prefer use to nonuse; the second is that the defect found in the thing be of such a nature as to make good use improbable.

Over and above such a possible relation between physical defect and defective use, things may contain threats of wrong use because of sheer contrariety between their proper operations and the real good of man. If man is permanently inclined to prefer, with regard to these things, use to abstention, availability entails a tendency toward bad use and a frequency of wrong actions. There is nothing physically bad about opium; but there is in many men an inclination to get quick relief from pain and to secure euphoria at will; on account of side effects, the use of opium is frequently unethical and rarely lawful. In some extreme cases things are so constituted by nature or so perversely designed by human art that the use of them can hardly be ethical, unless it is altogether incidental: instruments of torture, forged coins, poisonous food, would be examples.

What holds for external things holds for the body, the cognitive powers, the will itself. Physical deficiency does not entail bad use, physical integrity does not entail good use, and yet there are cases in which wrong use is made more probable by physical deficiency. One can make either a good or an evil use of a healthy organism, and there are also good and bad uses of diseases; a nearsighted or hard-of-hearing person is not, as a rule, particularly inclined to make bad use of his senses.

It is good to have a strong will, just as it is good to be in good health, but a strong will is not necessarily a morally good will, and a man of good will may be plagued with a naturally weak will. On the other hand, a man plagued with a weak will is particularly exposed to laziness, cowardice, etc., so that, if his will is good, he does his best to make it strong.

In the case of the sense appetite, the problem of the relation between physical integrity and ethically good use presents very particular features. Because it is an appetite, its determinations are related to effectuation in existence. I may possess a science or an art and feel no inclination to put these intellectual dispositions to work, but I cannot have a passion and not be inclined to let it reach actuality. On the other hand, because the sense appetite is, in itself, nonrational, its determinations may, prior to the operation of freedom, determinately incline man toward what is good or what is bad for him; in the former case good use is by no means guaranteed, in the latter case the only possible use is wrong and abstention alone is ethical. The wretchedness of our species is aggravated by the fact that the sense appetite is the most unsteady of our powers. A trifle upsets its balance and produces in it a disposition of which no good use can be made. Because of this peculiar relationship between physical integrity and use, the border line between ethics and psychiatry is uncertain. A perverse disposition of the sense appetite is a physical infirmity, just like nearsightedness; but it is possible, under almost all circumstances, to make good use of poor eyesight, and it is not possible, under any circumstances, to make good use of a perversion. The moralist has no major interest in the healing of nearsightedness, but he is greatly interested in the healing of perverse tendencies. Take, for instance, the case of homosexual inclination. Actual indulgence is not strictly inevitable; apart from complex cases in which the operation of reason and freedom is suspended, the person afflicted with such an inclination is able to hold it in check and may remain free from moral stain. In fact, all but the strongest wills are likely to undergo occasional defeat, with great moral and social harm. Thus it is highly desirable, from the very standpoint of ethics and society, that the perverse tendency be replaced by a normal one. Complete healing does not solve any problem of use: change a homosexual into a sexually normal man, there is not any guaranty that he will make virtuous use of his recovered health. But recovery means that his new inclinations, unlike the old ones, admit of righteous use, which is not inconsiderable. What is absurd in the popular notion of applied psychology and psychiatry—a notion interestedly entertained and promoted by many psychiatrists and psychologists—is the understanding that a problem of use can be solved by the mere application of positive science. Such nonsense would be easily disposed of, were it not that the healthy condition of the sense appetite, though no solution to any problem of use, is a thing that cannot be ignored in the search for solutions to the problem of use. This complex picture can be summed up in the following propositions:

1. Physical integrity does not in any case whatsoever constitute by itself a guaranty of righteous use.

2. Yet, prior to the examination of particular cases, it is never possible to assert that physical integrity is of no relevance for righteous use. There are cases in which physical evil renders bad use probable.

3. Apart from all physical defects, the relation of a thing to man's nature and man's desire may constitute the foundation of a tendency either toward righteous use (wheat) or toward wrong use (opium). In such a case the practical issue concerns the availability of the thing.

4. The situation of the sense appetite is distinguished. Here a unique relation obtains between physical integrity and use, inasmuch as lack of physical integrity may determine an inclination admitting of no good use.

Turning, now, to techniques considered concretely, i.e.,

with the properties that follow upon their existence in society, let us discuss, first, the question of use as opposed to nonuse. The meaning of this question can be evidenced by comparing technique with such a widely different product of civilization as metaphysics. With qualifications due to the peculiar difficulty of the subject and to several historical accidents, it can be said that for centuries the science of metaphysics has been available to men, just as calculus has been available to them ever since the time of Newton and Leibniz. But quite a few can manage calculus, and almost none metaphysics. Indefinite progress of metaphysical knowledge is possible, and our rational nature demands that it be achieved. In fact, the future of metaphysics is entirely uncertain. On the other hand, the disciplines meant to assure the mastery of man over physical nature appeal to such human interests and have aroused such historical forces that, unless a catastrophe destroys to the last man the scientific circles of the world, their falling into disuse or their ceasing to achieve progress and to conquer new fields are extremely unlikely hypotheses. The positive tendency of techniques (considered in their social existence) toward use as opposed to nonuse holds in a threefold sense; it implies (1) that the knowledge of technical subjects will not die out but will be entertained and grow; (2) that it will not remain in a theoretical condition but will be steadily applied to the transformation of nature; and (3) that the products of such a transformation will not be left idle but will go into human use. None of these happenings is strictly necessary, but the character of historical inevitability that all three evidence can easily be accounted for. Under primitive conditions the relation of man to nature involves unspeakable suffering and dire threat to life; increased power is needed for survival, for rest from pain and disease, for leisure, and for culture. A good part of what literary gentlemen call the "materialism of the modern man" boils down to the fact that the pathway to quick progress in the control of physical nature was discovered but recently. This pathway is the so-called "scientific method." In so far as it has become clear that the products of technique are in countless and daily circumstances the only means to survival and freedom from pain and drudgery, interest in life and well-being entails interest in technique.

The positive relation of technique to use can be most relevantly expressed by saying that the first law of a technological society is a tendency to remain technological. True, such a society is in many respects a frightening thing to live in. But, in order that the urge toward simpler ways of life should not lead into antisocial dreams, it must be understood once and for all that our societies will not cease to be technological unless their technical power is destroyed by unprecedented and altogether undesirable catastrophes.

Plainly, domination over physical nature is part of the vocation of man. This is a rational truth reasserted by revelation: "Fill the earth and subdue it; have dominion over the fish of the sea, the birds of the air, the cattle and all the animals that crawl on the earth" (Gen. 1:28).[5] In the fulfilment of his vocation it was normal that man, after having used empirical procedures for many generations, should develop scientific methods and put them to use. This does not mean that the process by which societies became technological was governed by strict necessity. It is said that Greek artisans, who were able to make machines and were aware of such ability, voluntarily restrained their creative genius; apparently, the fear of placing great power in unworthy hands played a part in the situation which prevented Greece from developing a mechanical civilization. Out of a sense of danger, men might have decided to observe moderation in the conquest of nature. As a matter of fact, restraining factors were defeated in the long run, and a

5. The views of a remarkable theologian on *the human value of technique* are found in an unsigned article of *Nova et vetera* (Fribourg, Switzerland), No. 1 (1950).

day came for each nation when survival required the speedy growth of the technological environment. From that day on, all the weight of society was directed toward ever expanding use of technical possibilities.

We now propose to describe some general effects of the technological environment on men and human relations. Ultimately these considerations are regulated by universally human finalities; but, in so far as the problem is engaged in history, successful treatment depends upon the understanding of historical relations. Following as a pattern an expression coined by A. N. Whitehead, let attention be called to the "fallacy of misplaced novelty": it is a very simple accident which consists in interpreting as novel and peculiar to the historical phase in which our existence is comprised a state of affairs or a trend that is really much older and may even be universal. In our time of anxiety and despair the fallacy of misplaced novelty applies almost exclusively to uncongenial aspects of our experience. To confess that a hated state of affairs has been a fact for a long time is unpleasant and calls for great fortitude, since it means that we shall have to put up with such a state of affairs, and give up all hope that it will be corrected within the explorable future. It is much handier to imagine that the ugly features of our environment are things new and unprecedented, inflicted upon our lives by uniquely wicked circumstances. Escape, then, can be found in the future or in the past. The fallacy of misplaced novelty is, in most cases, sheer expression of weakness and frivolity.

Those effects of technology which seem to be of particular relevance for the theory of democratic government will be discussed, or at least indicated, under six headings: time, nature, life, reason, labor, leadership.

1. Technology altered our relation to time, inasmuch as it caused our short existence to be crowded with man-made proc-

esses having the character of wholes. In pre-technological societies men were accustomed to work on projects begun by
prior generations and designed to be completed by unknown
men in the remote future. The circumstances of daily work
were a telling reminder of the meaning of society as a thing
which transcends individual existence in the past and in the
future. Means of extremely quick execution, by fostering a belief that things can be done in the present, weakened our sense
of dependence upon the past and future of society and, together
with it, the experience of immortal life in society through generation and work. Our uncertainty and our isolation increased.
The "dreadful freedom" described by the existentialists comprises, as one of its main components, the loneliness of petty
demiurges deprived, by their very power of speedy execution,
of a dwelling place in social duration.

2. As an effect of technology, the ratio of the man-made to
the natural in the environment of our daily existence has increased enormously. Notice that in the context of human sentiments the notion of the natural is much more narrow and the
notion of the artificial much broader than in the context of
physical laws. For the chemist a sample found in nature and a
sample produced by laboratory synthesis are indistinguishable
if the arrangement of elementary particles is strictly the same;
the latter sample is not considered any more artificial than the
former: all that matters is the deterministic system embodied
in them. But when things are related to the moral activity of
man, any modality traceable to human initiative changes the
picture, decreases the ratio of the natural, increases that of the
artificial. Suppose a swimming pool so designed as to dupli-
cate exactly all the physical and chemical influences to which
lake swimmers are subjected; from the standpoint of moral
psychology there remains a world of difference between a natural lake and such a piece of artificial environment as a swimming pool. Canned food, in terms of biological properties,

may resemble fresh food very closely; but, in terms of moral psychology, enjoying vegetables fresh from the garden is an operation quite distinct from that of enjoying canned vegetables. A sun lamp may produce effects indistinguishable from those of the sun on the skin and glands of human beings, but not on their personalities.

3. In close relation to the preceding point, let us mention the altered ratio of the living to the nonliving in man's environment. In the pre-technological age most human existences were surrounded by overflowing life; but the living environment of the modern city dweller is restricted to pets, trees in straight lines, and a few bushes in public gardens. Just as, through quick execution of human projects, technology tends to impair the integration of individual existence in the transcendent duration of society, so, by increasing the ratio of the artificial and of the nonliving in our environment, technology threatens to impair the communion of man with universal nature.

4. Under primitive circumstances human life is overwhelmingly confronted by casual situations. Every civilization has among its proper effects a greater amount of rationality in the arrangement of things. But prior to the opening of the technological era the rationalization of man's environment was a slow, restricted, and discontinuous process. In technological societies the characteristics of this process are acceleration and pervasiveness. It takes only a short time for a scientific theory to modify some phase of daily life. Within the last generation a qualitatively new state of affairs was reached, inasmuch as rationalization brought about an unprecedented relation of man to *danger* and *security*.

Everybody takes it for granted that a certain probability of fatal accident is inherent in human life; common risks, which cannot be ruled out by any means, are ignored in ordinary calculations. We know that walking in the street involves risk of death; but so does staying at home. Such risks exercise no influence on our decision to stay at home or to take a walk. The issue would be different if our house was threatened by a tornado or if the street was swept by machine-gun fire. Until recently technical feats involved a high ratio of failure and, in many cases, grave dangers. Aviation in its incipient stage aroused enthusiasm, but for a quarter of a century it was taken for granted that whoever intrusted his life to a flying machine was courting death.

Over and above such improvements as the conquests of new domains, increased power, greater speed, and greater precision, techniques acquired, in the last thirty years or so, a new character of rationality. In an ever growing number of technical procedures the ratio of failures has become negligible for most purposes. Technical risks which used to be frightening no longer exceed conspicuously those inherent in human life. Long and extremely fast trips are undertaken without any particular sense of danger, and people worry little about common surgery. Such unprecedented ability to control accidents fosters unlimited confidence in the human planning of physical processes. Between a highly mechanized environment in which machines often get out of order, as they used to do not so long ago, and a mechanical environment possessing a degree of reliability never attained by nature there is a qualitative difference of major importance. The former remains a world of chance, the latter is a world of law and calculation. The psychological and social effects of such greatly increased rationality in the framework of daily life are immeasurable. We are disappointed to realize that the human world is not in harmony with the rationality of our mechanical environment. The pattern supplied by almost infallibly operating techniques exalts the rule of expertness. The mystery characteristic of human affairs becomes more and more bewildering and uncongenial. People can hardly tolerate an extremely high ratio of failure in economic and political processes when they are used to almost uninterrupted success in the operation of their machines and generally in the application of their science. The world of man, i.e., a world in which freedom undergoes frequent defeats, becomes irritatingly unintelligible. The untrustworthiness of man is more and more of a scandal as we come so quietly to trust physical processes controlled by techniques. The problem of evil, more than ever, centers about evil in human will. Not only have techniques brought about regularity in their own operation, they have also procured security in human life, though in highly conditional fashion. Most diseases are conquered. Premature death by so-called "natural" causes has become extremely infrequent. Yet our anxiety is overwhelming, for we know that mischievous wills can use for gigantic destruction those techniques which prove so marvelously able to protect human life and lessen human suffering. What we dread is less and less nature, more and more man. It takes fortitude not to succumb to the temptation of hating the only agent that still opposes victoriously the reign of reason in this world: man is this agent. The new rationalism born of the rationality of our technical environment may be the least reconcilable enemy of democracy and more generally of liberty. If human liberty was independent of every element of weakness and passive indifference, it would still be exceedingly uncongenial to that kind of rationalism. But in its human condition liberty is inevitably associated with such features as ignorance, doubt, hesitancy, trial and error, inconsistency, irresolution, perplexity. The rationalism born of technological pride hates human liberty both on account of its excellence and on account of its wretchedness.

5. The following remarks concern the relation of man to his own labor: (*a*) Division of labor is an old thing. It is too well known that in a technological society it is often extreme. (*b*) Technology has immensely increased the productivity of

unskilled labor. If recompense is proportional to production, unskilled laborers, for the first time in history, enjoy a high economic position. (c) In so far as it is impossible to crowd into an academic program both the humanities and scientific techniques, the decline of humanistic studies in our societies resulted inevitably from the growth of technology. Although we are short of statistics in such domains, it is reasonable to believe that the proportion of men who have recently gained access to technical education and to whatever amount of scientific instruction is necessary for the handling of techniques is much greater than the proportion of men who have recently lost access to the humanities. Putting aside all comparison between technical education and classical education in terms of human worth, it may be said that the substitution of technical for humanistic culture has probably been accompanied by a large increase in the ratio of those who participate in relatively advanced forms of education.

6. In an entirely normal state of affairs, leadership belongs to prudence, not to expertness; rather than the bearer of a technical ability, a leader is supposed to be a man of virtue, a man of human experience, a man who knows men, who loves them and succeeds in persuading them. Perfect order would want experts to be kept in subordinate positions under leaders who should be good men rather than good experts. Occasionally, however, a leader may have to decide issues in which the human and the technical are so closely connected that wise judgment is impossible without some amount of expertness. Such occasions are increasingly frequent in technologically advanced societies. The expert is often placed in a position of authority. Even when he retains the instrumental rank which is his, he is likely to act upon society in more than instrumental fashion. An instrument must be light; as a result of technology, the expert has become an instrument so heavy as often to get out of control.

At the end of this inquiry, conclusions ought to be drawn concerning the good use of techniques. The enlightened man of the eighteenth century indulged in the belief that technical progress infallibly entailed the betterment of man's condition. Coupled with the postulate that nothing could ever stop technique in its march forward, such beliefs made up a great part of the so-called "theory of necessary progress." In our time this myth of the eighteenth century has been to a large extent superseded by the more up-to-date myth of the inevitable destruction of mankind by its technical creations. Faced as we are with these conflicting superstitions, the temptation is great to seek refuge in the consideration that technique is a thing which admits of good and evil use and that the relation of technical progress to human welfare is left indeterminate by the nature of things. This consideration is absolutely true, but preceding inquiries evidenced its incompleteness. We have understood that in their human existence things intrinsically indifferent to whatever use is made of them may involve tendencies having significance in terms of use.

1. It was mentioned above that in certain cases a physical deficiency in the thing used constitutes a special danger of bad use. This remark holds for techniques. Prior to the discoveries of Pasteur, surgery could not be used for the welfare of man except in a small number of desperate cases. Today, the troubles caused by new technical procedures during the early phase of application are watched with confident expectation; experience shows that technique, as it were, takes care of itself and that the bad effects due to its deficiencies do not last long. In so far as bad use of techniques is caused by their imperfection, technical progress makes for good use. This is the only sense in which the eighteenth-century belief in the betterment of man's destiny by technical progress is not devoid of foundation.

2. The problem of evil would be greatly simplified if it were always possible to trace evil to some antecedent deficiency,

either on the side of the agent or on the side of its instruments or on the side of that which is acted upon. But deficiency cannot be primitive; ultimately, the origin of evil lies in the contrariety of the goods. In so far as the damage brought about by technique results from a contrariety of goods, technical improvement, far from procuring a remedy, causes a greater threat. There is incompatibility between the goodness of an explosive in act and the perfections of life within a disquietingly growing radius. Techniques take care of their deficiencies, not of the inhuman use made of their excellence. In the middle of the twentieth century, men have come to consider that the really dreadful effects of techniques are those traceable to their excellence, not those traceable to their deficiencies—a view which to some extent accounts for the fact that the technological optimism of the eighteenth century has been so widely displaced by technological despair.

When a thing is of such nature that its excellence contains a threat of evil use, societies attempt to restrict its availability. Thus poisonous drugs are not supposed to be delivered without control. To the question whether society can protect men against the bad use of technical knowledge by surrounding it with secrecy, the answer is a melancholy one. The restriction of the availability of knowledge is a procedure applicable in an emergency, but unlikely to work satisfactorily for any considerable time. The short history of atomic techniques shows that the protection secured by secrecy may not even last until the end of the most extreme emergency.

3. Many put the blame on a lack of balance in our educational system. It is said that our education is at fault for not giving the student a chance to learn the proper use of techniques. The optimistic implication is that humanity, so badly endangered at the present time by technical monsters, can be saved by educational reforms. The problem would be to define the disciplines from which the good use of techniques can be

learned and to appoint the proper men to teach them. This approach generally leads to plans for a revival of humanistic studies. Interestingly, it is often considered that the so-called "social sciences," inasmuch as they follow the pattern of the physical sciences, would yield some "technique of social processes" (whether this expression be contradictory or not) rather than the knowledge of the righteous use of techniques. Such knowledge is expected to be procured by the humanities or by humanistic methods in social science. The optimistic flavor of the system comes from a never formulated postulate concerning the existential conditions of the knowledge of use.

We saw how techniques behave with regard to use as opposed to nonuse. That they should be actually used rather than allowed to fall into disuse is determined, for all practical purposes, by the weight of history. As long as the means of technical knowledge are not violently destroyed all over the world, it can be safely predicted that techniques will keep being cultivated and keep growing, that they will continue to be applied on an ever increasing scale, and that their products will not remain idle. Our anxiety would disappear if we believed that the knowledge of righteous use behaves in similar fashion and that, once it has taken shape in our universities, it will inevitably be confirmed in existence, grow uninterruptedly, and actually control the acts of man. But such a picture is merely a modernized version of the Socratic error. The proper use of techniques, in so far as it can be taught, remains abstract and devoid of necessary influence upon action; and, in so far as it entertains an infallible relation to action, it cannot be taught. The fully determinate and unmistakably effective knowledge of the right use is not science, but prudence; it is acquired, not principally by reading books and taking courses, but by practicing virtue. Whatever is scientific and teachable in the knowledge of use admits of being ignored at the time of action and of remaining without effect upon action. Moreover, the knowledge of the right use, even in so far as it is scientific and teachable, involves difficulties which render unlikely its uninterrupted maintenance and continuous progress. In this respect the science of the proper use of techniques—one function of ethics—resembles metaphysics rather than positive science. Like metaphysics, the science of ethics possesses, in history, the character of a rare and precarious achievement, more threatened by decadence and oblivion than blessed with promise of maintenance and progress.

This does not mean that curriculums should not be reformed. In order that the surgeon may be good not only as a craftsman but also as a human and social character, what do we want him to learn over and above surgery? With good schooling in surgery he can be expected to live up to the rules of his art; but it would be exceedingly naïve to believe that with good courses in history, literature, the classics, philosophy, art criticism, etc., we can also expect him to live up to his ethical and social obligations. The classics, modern literature, art criticism, philosophy, theology—a surgeon well trained in these disciplines may remain an antisocial character, unwilling to work without fee, ready to advise recourse to surgery whenever there is a nice fee in sight, addicted to the practice of corrupting physicians in order to get more opportunities for operations and fees, etc. On the other hand, if a young surgeon is sincerely anxious to behave in ethical and social fashion, acquaintance with the human world (literature, history, etc.) and the science of morality (philosophy, theology) supplies his good will and his well-directed judgment with helpful material and valuable instruments. The orders of material and instrumental causality define the capacity in which moral and humane education contributes to good use. Indeed, neither the "merely material" nor the "merely instrumental" is unimportant. But there is no short cut to the proper effects of virtue.

4. Although everything technical admits both of good and of bad use, some technical developments are much more likely to help man, others to hurt him. Throughout the technological era, societies have done much to promote those considered beneficial and thereby to divert some energy from the harmful ones. Of all the methods by which society can foster the good use of techniques, this is apparently the most efficacious. Constant attention to novel possibilities for the direction of technical energy toward genuine human good has become a task of major importance. But, in order to determine what technical directions serve man best, a sound knowledge of human finalities is necessary. In many cases such knowledge is obtained easily, and no room is left for disagreement. But the cases which matter most for the future of societies are obscure and controversial. It is clear to everybody that it is better for children not to be crippled by poliomyelitis than to be crippled by it. On the other hand, a diversity of theories on the functions and character of the family entails divergencies concerning home architecture and all the environment of family life. These are questions which do not admit, in fact, of general agreement, and the true answers, whenever available, have to fight their way in the midst of ever recurring opposition. Moralists can make themselves really useful by going into a minute analysis of the relations between the particulars of the technological environment and the behavior of men. These relations are sometimes definite; if they were more systematically studied, men of good will would be in a better position to serve the nobler ways of life through the promotion of particular lines of technical progress.

It is hardly necessary to mention that the predominance of techniques friendly to man requires a state of peace, both at home and in the world. Threats of war cause a frantic development of the most destructive techniques: this fact has assumed an appalling significance in our time.

5. In most cases the *distribution* of technical power contains elements of guaranty against evil use; for one thing, by the very fact that power is divided, it is less destructive in case of misuse; further, the distribution of power entails the establishment of balances and mutual checks of such a nature as to restrain disorderly ambition; lastly and perhaps most importantly, wide distribution has to comply with the interests and tastes of the common man, who may be silly and wasteful in the demands that he makes of technology but who must be given credit for being more interested in the protection than in the destruction of human life. One major reason for the maintenance of private property is that without it technical power would inevitably be centralized. The distribution of technical power, one of the greatest problems confronting democracy in our time, is a task to be carried out against an extraordinary coalition of adverse forces. As a result of its determination to proceed rationally, to be economical, to increase output and speed, and to reduce waste, any technological organization is inclined to favor concentration and centralization; it thus tends to place huge power in a small number of hands. Another element of opposition is modern totalitarianism, and another one is traditional conservatism. A Fascist, a Communist, and a landed aristocrat equally dislike the picture of ordinary people being made independent by the ownership of powerful machinery.

6. Since the sense appetite is a nature possessed with a deterministic pattern, there is not, in principle, any reason why it should not be possible to develop techniques concerned with its control and to make a good use of them; such techniques would be the nearest approximation to the great dream of the "scientific man" from the time of the Renaissance to this day—that of an art having for its subject man himself as agent of social life and cause of history. Such techniques do exist, and, among the great changes which have occurred in the

twentieth century, few, if any, have caused such lasting bewilderment as the gigantic progress accomplished by them in
recent years. They work in two ways, according as the disposition which they generate remains subject to the control of free
choice or attains such intensity as to suspend rational processes. In the first case the power wielded by the operator is
considerable, in the latter case it is absolute.

Techniques concerned with man's appetite involve terrific
danger of bad use. Keeping these techniques under control is a
task of major importance, which may prove as difficult as that
of controlling the deadliest forms of physical energy. The following remarks are meant to have merely indicative significance: (*a*) A technique acting on the appetite of man is likely
to cause damage unless it possesses a high degree of intrinsic
perfection. (*b*) By accident but inescapably, the judgment
about health and disease in the sense appetite is inseparable
from judgments concerning the right and the wrong. Consider, for instance, worrying—a process which easily reaches
pathological intensity. Since the definition of health pertains
to natural science, natural criteria should always, in principle,
suffice to decide whether worrying remains within the limits
of emotional health or transgresses these limits either by abnormal direction or by abnormal intensity. In fact, simple
cases are the only ones in which purely natural criteria work
satisfactorily. Sound knowledge of morality is not indispensable for understanding that there is nothing pathological
about a mother's being slightly upset whenever her children
are late in coming home after a ride, and no knowledge of
morality is needed to recognize a pathological feature in the
person who worries so much about germs that handwashing
becomes for him an exhausting drudgery. Between such extreme cases there are many in which the criteria applied by
natural knowledge are insufficient. If, for instance, a man
worries intensely about his real guilt, the answer to the ques-

tion whether his case is pathological may not be separable from ethical considerations relative to remorse and repentance. It follows that, in order to be acceptable to society, technicians operating on the human appetite ought to satisfy requirements never imposed on other technicians. If the problem is to repair a broken leg, all that society demands of the health-man, over and above his surgical ability, is that he should live up to a very simple contract and obey elementary rules of his profession. If the question is to repair an appetite damaged by anxiety, the health-man may need to possess, over and above his craft, exact notions and righteous dispositions concerning the things that are worth worrying about. (c) As to the methods involving the suppression of deliberation and free choice, the main question is whether society should aim at their complete elimination or tolerate them in restricted cases. In fact, the most redoubtable of these methods, viz., intensive propaganda, is difficult to control because of its resemblance to moderate propaganda, without which there would be no democracy and no civil life.

Of all the suggestions made here in relation to the good use of techniques, none is glamorous in any respect, none carries enough weight to procure reassurance or consolation. To achieve glamour in this domain, it would be necessary to indulge in the illusion that the knowledge of the righteous use enjoys in social existence a behavior patterned after that of technique itself. If such illusions are kept aside, the reality with which we are confronted appears irreducibly tragic. In the light of history it is to be expected that the wrong use of techniques, on a large scale, will never cease to run concomitantly with their good use. The final picture is neither one of inevitable progress nor one of inevitable decadence. It is rather that of a double movement carrying mankind, through the fire of sharp conflict, toward greater good and toward greater evil. Maritain described this twofold movement as a general feature of man's earthly destiny.[6] By increasing the power of man, for better and for worse, technique supplies a major contribution to this antinomic aspect of history. What societies can do for righteous use is not enough to solve the antinomy, but it may be enough to restrain effectually the tendency of techniques to produce extreme evil, and it may be enough to release all the technical forces that are friendly to man.

THE PURSUIT OF HAPPINESS AND THE LUST FOR POWER

Right after the Napoleonic wars nations received with eagerness the prediction that the technological era would be one of peace and brotherly love. The Saint-Simonists voiced the great hope of their time as they announced that domination over physical nature, through science and industry, would supersede the domination of man over man and that the rational exploitation of nature would put an end to the exploitation of man by man.[7] The cause and the ways of these substitutions were explained in the *Exposition of the Doctrine of Saint-Simon*, made by the disciples a few years after the death of their master. Prior to the industrial era, lust for wealth meant lust for power, more particularly for domination over slaves; since war was the main way to procure slaves, the age of slavery was predominantly a military age. Huge conflicts

6. See in particular *True Humanism* (London: G. Bles, 1938), chap. iii.

7. *Doctrine de Saint-Simon. Exposition. Première année* (1829), ed. C. Bouglé and Élie Halévy (Paris: Rivière, 1924), p. 144: "The basis of societies in antiquity was slavery. War was for these peoples the only way of being supplied with slaves, and consequently with the things capable of satisfying the material needs of life; in these peoples the strongest were the wealthiest; their industry consisted merely in knowing how to plunder." P. 162: "Material activity is represented in the past by the twofold action of war and industry, in the future by industry alone, since the exploitation of man by man will be replaced by the harmonious action of men over nature." Pp. 225: "The exploitation of man by man, this is the state of human relations in the past; the exploitation of nature by man associated with man, such is the picture that the future presents."

had just taken place; the Saint-Simonists wanted their listeners to realize that war was an absurd survival of the time when slaves were needed to make a man wealthy. Throughout the nineteenth century the notion that industrial expansion meant the reign of peace enjoyed a high degree of popularity. A long period of peace seemed to confirm the expectations of the early philosophers of industrialism. True, the "great peace" of the nineteenth century was interrupted by a number of wars; but these were limited to rather small areas, and, so far as bloodshed was concerned, most of them did not compare with the great slaughters of the preceding centuries. The American Civil War was very bloody; but it was an accident brought about by a unique set of circumstances and unlikely ever to be duplicated; moreover, it took place at such a distance from the centers of world opinion that it did not have much effect on the destiny of general beliefs. Faith in the peaceful disposition of the industrial world was not seriously shaken until ninety-nine years after Waterloo, when the great peace of the nineteenth century ended in the first World War.

The optimistic outlook proposed by early industrialism implied a definite interpretation of the lust for power. The Saint-Simonists expressed themselves as if predatory practices, war, conquest, enslavement, and, more generally, domination of man over his fellow-men originated in the lust for wealth. We recognize here the deceitfully simple psychology of the *homo oeconomicus* made popular by the economists and later erected into a dogma by the popularizers of Marxism, if not by Marx himself. True, lust for power is sometimes an effect and an instrument of lust for wealth, and, in so far as lust for power is subservient to lust for wealth, technology may cause the decline of lust for power. Not all is wrong in the Saint-Simonists' argument. If the terms under comparison are, on the one hand, a primitive tribe for which warfare is a basic condition of economic improvement and, on the other hand, a modern society equipped with industry, it is clear that technique, through its ability to procure wealth without plunder and without enslavement, possesses some ability to bring about peace. There is no doubt that several aspects of the great peace of the nineteenth century must be traced to this capacity of technique to procure wealth peacefully. Louis Philippe, who in his youth distinguished himself on the battlefield, might not have been such a peaceable monarch if territorial expansion had been the only way to satisfy his money-hungry supporters; but expanding industry was, under the circumstances, the better and safer way to make money.

Yet, even if power is viewed as merely instrumental in the acquiring of wealth, the proposition that technology discourages the lust for power has to be qualified. An abstract comparison between the amount of energy produced by slave labor and that produced by machinery suggests a picture of emancipation through the machine. In fact, machines did not put an end to the exploitation of man by man and did not always make it less severe. Not infrequently mechanical conditions stimulated a desire for absolute power over the men assigned to the service of the machine. Revolutionary socialism was to take advantage of what it described as the great deception of bourgeois industrialism, viz., the promise of an emancipation to be brought about by the sheer power of technology, without any basic change in the ownership of industrial wealth.

But, most of all, it is imprudent to assume that the lust for power dies away as soon as power is no longer needed for wealth. The complete subordination of lust for power to lust for wealth may be observed in cases that need not be considered exceptional. To erect it into a general law admitting of few or no exceptions is shallow psychology. There may be men who do not find any specific enjoyment in the exercise of power but do enjoy the possession and use of wealth; these men are free from all lust for power as soon as they are offered a better way to wealth. But very often it is the lust for wealth which is subordinated to the lust for power. Interest in indefinitely accumulated wealth springs principally from either or both of these passions, the lust for power and the lust for security. In so far as wealth is subservient to power, there is not the slightest reason why a technological state of affairs should weaken the lust for power. Notice, moreover, that, by increasing the amount of goods available, technology gives to many men their first chance to look beyond the satisfaction of elementary needs. Some of them, as they no longer feel hungry, turn toward literature and music, some toward wild pleasures, and some toward the intoxicating experience of power. The ratio of each group is entirely indeterminate.

Attention should be called, further, to the patterns of irresistible power with which technology surrounds human life. As has been recalled, an advanced technological environment implies an increased ratio of the rational, a decreased ratio of the casual. No wonder that modern societies keep being ceaselessly haunted by the dream of rearrangements which would bring about the rational society. The mental habits generated by the technological relation of man to nature are characterized by strict discipline and remarkable clarity. The social engineer is an extremely popular myth; this shows that many are tempted to transfer to the social order mental habits born of our relation to physical nature. In so far as such a transfer is effected, the attitude of submission to nature's laws becomes a longing for the relief that passive obedience produces; control over natural phenomena gives birth to a craving for the arbitrary manipulation of men; the element of mystery in mankind is violently put aside. But mankind cannot become a thing as simple as laboratory material without a great deal of human substance being disposed of. The most significant of modern utopias are engineers' dreams in which the desire for domination over nature is prolonged with a technocratic appetite for the rearrangement of human affairs. Contrary to a romantic hope, no utopia was ever realized through the harmless help of a millionaire and the persuasion born of early success. By the time Lenin reached maturity, social thinkers had understood that the realization of a social theory—of course, these scientific gentlemen would never call it a "utopia"—demanded a totalitarian state, held well in hand by one party, itself subjected to dictatorial discipline. A new lust for domination over men, shaped after the pattern of domination over nature, had developed in technique-minded men. The Saint-Simonists set forth, ultimately, a construct in which men are controlled with a precision reminiscent of the engineer's methods. The highly emotional humanitarianism which pervades the system did not blind everybody to the fact that a new imperialism, a new lust for absolute power, was finding expression.

The case is made more dreadful by the character of the world picture which haunts the minds of nearly all in a technological society. This picture is mechanistic. The universe of mechanism is made of extension and motion. Motion, in this system, is not a change but a state; further, it is understood in terms of relativity. There is nothing irreducible about life and sensation; there are no sense qualities and no species. This universe is not tragic, it does not keep man company in his anxiety. It contains no divine ideas and no ideas whatsoever except those that it pleases man to embody in the arrangement of his thoughts. It offers a picture of parts arranged in a certain fashion and speaks of unlimited possibilities of rearrangement. The key to these possibilities is delivered by formulas whose simplicity increases as our knowledge improves. In such a demiurgical position man is likely to lose his equilibrium and to erect himself into a sort of cosmic engineer strongly inclined to despise the mystery of nature and the greater mystery of human liberty. The history of man, as well as that of the world, is "a tale told by an idiot . . . signifying nothing."

Today's attempt to build a new humanism ought to be considered against a background of mechanistic technology extended to man. This attempt aims at approaching with appropriate instruments the aspects of human reality which cannot be successfully approached through the methods of positive science. It aims at achieving a fresh understanding of man as a voluntary and free agent. This cultural trend is related to the epistemological theory that there is an essential difference of method between the sciences of nature and the sciences of man. Mechanistic principles would hold in the former case, not in the latter.

Thus mechanism is taken for granted so far as physical nature is concerned. Consequently, it is not in nature but in art that an environment suitable to man is sought. As a matter of fact, it is by no means obvious that the universe of mechanism is the true universe of nature. And it is by no means obvious that art can produce an environment worthy of man if nature is held incapable of being such an environment. The crucial problem, with regard to culture and education, concerns the meaning of "mechanism." Referring to Maritain's analysis,[8] let it be said that mechanism can be interpreted either as a method or as a philosophy. The mechanistic method has abundantly demonstrated its power in many fields of knowledge, but the common identification of mechanism as a method with mechanism as a philosophy should be carefully reconsidered; it may be no more than a psychological accident. If the mechanistic philosophy of nature is erroneous, a doctrine of man and of culture which does not explode such an error has little chance to fulfil its humane purposes. A sound philosophy of man without a minimum of soundness in the philosophical interpretation of nature is inconceivable. It can even be said that a better understanding of man makes it more urgent to achieve a correct philosophic interpretation of na-

8. Jacques Maritain, *Les Degrés du savoir* (Paris: Desclée de Brouwer, 1932); *La Philosophie de la nature* (Paris: Téqui, n.d.).

ture. The materialists of the preceding centuries were perhaps able to enjoy some sort of peace in their unified mechanistic vision of man and the cosmos. But nothing is more likely to cause frenzy than a vision in which man, verily understood as a voluntary and free agent, appears surrounded by a universe with no qualities, no ideas, and no ends. Nature and art are so related in culture that reforms calculated to foster the humane merits of art are of little significance so long as the meaning of nature remains falsified by the erection of a sound method into an absurd philosophy.

It is impossible not to be impressed by the fact that in our time reaction against the sort of barbarism favored by positive sciences and technology constantly tends toward an exaltation of the most sophisticated forms of art. The word "sophistication" and related expressions, which used to participate in the derogatory meaning attached to sophistry, have recently become laudatory. It would be easy to show, in the history of the last three or four generations, how the cult of "sophisticated" forms of art grew parallel to increased dissatisfaction with the mechanistic universe substituted by the prevailing philosophies of nature for the garden of inexhaustible wonder, the woods haunted by sacred awe, the springs inhabited by benevolent emotions, in which mankind spent its youth. Turning away from the hopeless gloom of the mechanistic universe, man intrusted to his own fine arts the task of creating for him a world of variety, of fancy, of unpredictability; a world of surprise and bewilderment; a world of sophistication, where boredom, at least, could be overcome. The reformers of culture have not given enough thought to our need for achieving new familiarity with nature; for learning again how to find, in things of nature, a meaning, a language, a company. Cultural refinement all too commonly means the defeat of nature within the artist himself. It is not without a lasting cause that the unnatural plays such a great part not only in the life of the artist but also at the core of his art. Unless the connections between man and nature are restored, art-centered education cannot do much to control the particularly dreadful forms that the lust for power assumes under the influence of the mechanistic world picture.

When the relation of man to nature is considered from a psychological and moral standpoint, men are primarily divided into those for whom nature constitutes the environment of daily life and those for whom it does not. Few country people have daily experience of the wilderness, but the relevant fact is that all of them are much closer to untamed nature than is the big-city dweller; notice, also, that in small-scale farming the environment of daily life is closer to untamed nature than it is in industrial farming.

At this point it becomes possible to attempt an interpretation of the movement of aversion to technology and city life. It would be poor psychology and sociology to interpret it as sheer escapism, although there is some escapism in it. Beyond idle talk about industrial monsters, the monotony of assembly-line work, etc., and beyond the romantic dislike for the rational, our agrarians, with their longing for primitive ways of life, fulfil among us the all-important task of keeping alive the experience of communion between man and nature. Most supporters of humanistic education, in our time, are city children, and their only concern is to save man from disappearing into mechanistic meaninglessness. To suggest that a part has to be played, in the cultural reformation whose need is so acutely felt, by men ignorant of literary cafés and cocktail parties would be an extremely unpopular paradox. Yet a good safeguard against the frantic lust for power that technology can stimulate is found in the sentiments of universal reverence, of mystery, of awe and unity, that result from communion with nature in daily life. Today as well as in the time of Jefferson it is up to the rural people to exalt, in their silent fashion,

the quiet ambition to achieve happiness. A society so indus-
trialized as to leave no room for family-size farming would
be devastated by unchecked lust for power.

THE TRAINING OF FREE MEN

As we are about to discuss the respective merits of rural and
industrial environments with regard to the training of free
men, let it be remarked that the comparison, to be relevant,
must take place between typical forms. Accordingly, industrial life will be represented in this inquiry not by the small
workshop somewhat reminiscent of the good old days but by
the big plant, and rural life will be represented not by so-called
"industrial agriculture" but by the family-size farm.

Ever since the early phases of industrialism it has been said
that big industry treats the laborer as a servant of the machine
and destroys his personality. In our time, they remark, further, that an automatized laborer is an ideal subject for a dictatorship dedicated to the technocratic manipulation of men.
When such views fall into the hands of literary gentlemen—
whose individualistic culture makes it nearly impossible for
them to understand the data of a social problem—they are generally so simplified as to become blinding clichés. It is unwise
to allow one's self to be guided by a cliché, and it is unwise to
reject a proposition which may have some truth about it, for
the mere reason that it has become a cliché. Throughout the
present inquiry the picture of the big-industry worker reduced
to the condition of a piece of machinery will be borne in mind.
Yet we do not take it for granted that it is altogether truthful.

1. Let us consider, first, the effects of *labor processes*. For the
purpose of this inquiry the relevant feature of the industrial
process is the division of labor. We may not trust romantic
descriptions in which the wretchedness of the assembly-line
worker is pathetically contrasted with the bliss of the medie-
val artisan. But one hard fact stands: highly divided labor does

little for the intellectual culture of the laborer. By general assent, many functions of big industry require only a very short apprenticeship, and years of experience add little to the skill acquired in a few weeks. In order to estimate the significance of this fact, consider that the core of all intellectual culture is constituted by intellectual qualities which, on account of their object, imply essential steadiness, necessity, certainty, indefectibility. Science is one of them; others are art and prudence. Art, like science and virtue, is structured by necessity; it is something hard and stiff, certain, reliable, and uncompromising, like a nature. Such dispositions, structured by objective necessity, are called "habitus" in good philosophic language.[9] Intellectual qualities devoid of certainty and necessity are of great human and social worth when their growth centers about habitus and supplements them with an element of flexibility and charm. But if habitus are wanting, the mind can hardly rise above the level of amateurish adornment. The most serious effect of extremely divided and monotonous work is that it deprives men of their chance to acquire intellectual habitus during their working hours. An assembly-line worker,

9. At the time when modern philosophic languages were formed, the concept of "habitus" was ignored by the prevailing philosophies. Accordingly, no modern philosophic language, to our knowledge, has an appropriate expression to convey this very important concept. Under these circumstances the wise thing to do is to take over the Latin word—a practice extremely common in all scientific branches. But, following the line of least resistance, many writers use the words that resemble "habitus" most: "habit" in English, "habitude" in French, etc.—which makes for nonsense, since a habitus is, in a way, exactly the opposite of a habit. Both are steady, but the steadiness of the habitus proceeds from objective necessity, that of a habit is a disposition generated in a *subject* by a repetition of acts or impressions. Such abuse is particularly shocking in English, since the meaning of the word "habit," in the language of Hume, is made unmistakable by the celebrated analyses in which Hume endeavors to show how the factual and subjective steadiness of habit counterfeits objective necessity. In our quotations of Pegis' translation of Thomas Aquinas, we took the liberty of inserting in brackets the word "habitus" whenever the word "habit" was used instead of "habitus" by the translator; we also inserted the word "habitus" when the corresponding Greek word ἕξις was unintelligibly translated by W. D. Ross (*salva reverentia*) as "state of character."

if he makes good use of his considerable leisure and reads wisely chosen books, may become a man of culture in the conventional sense of the term, and his case, ultimately, may be considered satisfactory by professors of culture. Yet, except inasmuch as he may profit by the requirements of a lofty moral life, such a man is unlikely ever to become more than an amateur. Scientific information will not reach the state of science in his mind, and his keen interest in music and painting will not develop into art. Under other circumstances he might have become a man of art, through the constant exercise of skill. But no technical habitus can be acquired without steady participation in the planning of action upon nature, and every planning is concerned with wholes. In Aristotle's philosophy of labor it seems that the only functions endowed with the privilege of generating intellectual culture are the so-called "architectonic" ones; the manual laborer, exemplified by the mason, is described as a mere agent of execution, whose virtue consists mainly in carrying out the orders that he is given. The stain attaching to manual labor, as a result of its being commonly done by slaves, seems to have blinded Aristotle to the large amount of technical thinking and planning required of all skilled workers. The connection established by him between architectonic thinking and the art habitus holds; Aristotle's error consists in his failure to see that every skilled worker performs intellectual operations similar to those which make up the dignity of the architect. In so far as he exercises domination over a plurality of parts and arranges this plurality for the sake of an end, the artisan does, on various levels, what the architect does on a high level, and, like the architect, he normally acquires an intellectual habitus. But, in so far as the object with which a worker is concerned has the character of a part, there is less of an opportunity to exercise domination, to arrange, distribute, subordinate, and co-ordinate—in short, to exercise technical thinking.

As an effect of technical development, engineers have considerably increased in number; moreover, they have been subjected to ever more exacting requirements. By "engineer" we designate, in the present connection, any person specialized in technical planning, who directs the action of others on physical nature but does not exercise such action himself. In so far as quantitative expressions are tolerable in these matters, it can be said that the amount of technical culture has considerably increased in modern societies. The fact which causes difficulty is that this growth of technical culture has taken place in aristocratic fashion. As a result of extreme division of labor, an unprecedented separation has taken place between planning and execution. Architectonic functions have been taken over by a large minority possessed of increasingly distinguished knowledge and ability. But simultaneously a great number of industrial workers were assigned to tasks which, on account of their being concerned with parts rather than with wholes, are altogether devoid of architectonic character. Many industrial workers exercise no self-government in the labor process; government is concerned with wholes.

Lack of autonomy in such an important phase of human life as daily work is by itself a very grave privation. Considering, further, that there is inevitably a certain amount of interdependence between intellectual functions, it is reasonable to fear that a man deprived of a chance to govern himself in the process of labor will have a hard time learning to govern himself in moral and social life. Of course, the connection between the ability to achieve self-government in the labor process and the ability to achieve self-government in human and social life is by no means essential; but it is psychological and likely to be a matter of fact in a majority of cases. It is, accordingly, reasonable to conclude that extreme division of labor tends to produce circumstances unfavorable to the training of men in self-government.

In contrast with industry, agriculture does not admit of extremely divided labor. The biological rhythm of nature and the alternation of seasons make it generally impossible for a man to repeat the same operation throughout the year, as often happens in industry. Most of all, the circumstances of daily work in the family-size farm aiming at self-sufficiency make it necessary for all to be acquainted, though in varying degree, with all the processes of agricultural labor and with all phases of each process. Laborers trained under such circumstances do not need to be directed in all their actions by specialized brains. They commonly possess such ability to govern their own work that the son of a small farmer is generally able, when his turn comes, to run a small farm.

These characteristics of wholeness and integration are due in part to the nature of the living processes with which the agricultural worker is concerned; but they are principally due to the nature of the unit within which these processes take place. Inasmuch as production processes are aimed at satisfying all the needs of the farm, the integrating center of work lies in man. *The essence of humanism is the use of a reference to man as principle of integration.* When labor processes are calculated to satisfy the needs of the human unit within which and by which they are planned and executed, the laborer is given a guaranty of human finality. In order that human labor may be properly related to man, two things are necessary: (*a*) that the product of labor be designed to satisfy some real human need and (*b*) that proportions measuring various products be determined by proportions existing among human needs. In the family farm, futile effort, unrelated to the genuine needs of man, arbitrarily directed toward the satisfaction of fanciful wishes is kept down to a minimum; balance is maintained among the various components of production. It is hardly necessary to point out that industrial production is much more subject to distraction by casually or artificially created demands and to those ruptures of equilibrium which often bring about abundance of the less needed products, together with scarcity of the more needed. In short, the laborer enjoys, under the circumstances of the family farm, the benefit of a man-centered system of integration that industry does not provide. The industrial laborer, working under the circumstances of highly divided labor, is directed by his experts—his "betters"—toward accomplishments which may well not be centered about man but rather about such things as profit (in the so-called "free-enterprise system") or something worse (in the enterprise controlled by a party bureaucracy).

Thus farm work normally has, both in reference to technique itself and in reference to man, a character of wholeness and integration that industrial work cannot, in most cases, be expected to possess. All other things being equal, the farm worker finds in the conditions of his work an opportunity for training in self-government, both in the technical order and in the human order, which industrial conditions do not furnish. If the industrial laborer is to possess, with regard to self-government, a chance equal to that of the farm worker, it will be through the operation of factors capable of compensating for serious deficiencies.

2. Another phase of the inquiry concerns the character of the *working unit* in industry and in rural labor. Relevant questions may be stated under the headings of personality, authority, and justice.

The wide and enduring influence exercised in our century by a variety of personalistic doctrines and movements is plainly due to the common experience of threats made to personality by the circumstances of modern life. Of those threats, the most apparent and perhaps the most central originate in technological organization. The type of organization promoted by technology makes for large and sometimes huge units in which

302 PHILOSOPHY OF DEMOCRATIC GOVERNMENT

the uniqueness of the individual person is, in many cases, unlikely to be remarked, remembered, pondered over, and sympathetically understood. Further, division of labor, in so far as it renders special skill and apprenticeship unnecessary, gives manpower the character of a fungible commodity. There is something depressing about the feeling that one is lost in a multitude, undistinguished, unrecognized, unknown, and that one will never possess ground for recognition—since the function satisfactorily performed by one person is known to admit of equally satisfactory performance by any number of equally unrecognized persons. Such a feeling discourages or perverts the natural urge toward autonomy. The orderly pursuit of self-government requires that I should be aware of the true law of myself, that I should perceive, beyond the confusing whims of pleasure and passion, the real meaning of my uniqueness. I am unlikely to achieve sound understanding of those things if I know that they are inevitably ignored by society. Opposite conditions are found on the farm. Even if the task of the farm laborer is so simple as to admit of being fulfilled by any unskilled worker, the closeness of human relations would still force upon the group the realization of what is unique and irreplaceable in the individual laborer. In so far as the recognition of personality stimulates the urge toward self-government, rural life supplies a framework more favorable to the attainment of autonomy than the technological workshop does. Allowance must be made, however, for various corrections brought about by organizational skill.

With regard to authority, the fact of decisive importance is that the unit of labor in the small farm is centered upon the family and participates in the propensities of the family community. Family life, in the present connection, would be properly described in terms of a twofold system of relations, viz., biological and spiritual. The former are primitive and necessarily implied; the latter have the character of a terminal

attainment and often remain beyond the range of actual accomplishment. Now both these systems of relations tend to
bring about paternalism, i.e., a state of affairs characterized
by the permanence of the paternal function of authority and
its factually indissoluble union with the functions relative to
the good of the community. In the family and in any community patterned after the family, the distinction between the
business of the individual and the business of the community
is uncertain; consequently, authority can hardly discharge its
functions in relation to the common good without taking a
chance to control, by accident, things that really concern the
individual person alone.

Inasmuch as personal freedom implies freedom from interference by authority in the pursuit of personal good, the farm
community is not the framework in which the greatest amount
of personal freedom can be achieved. All other things being
equal, the industrial setup would give personal freedom a
better chance. In many cases the migration of the youth from
the farms to the big cities has been a movement away from
paternal rule, toward conditions of more complete personal
independence. Attention must be called, however, to the particular version of paternalistic government that party bureaucracy or a state bureaucracy, when given a free hand, usually
inflicts upon industrial masses. This variety of paternalism is
characterized by impersonality, rationality, efficiency, and the
finality of its decisions.

Concerning justice, the main point is this: inside the family
and to a lesser degree inside any unit patterned after the
family, unity is too intimate for justice to assert its type in
unqualified fashion. Briefly, justice implies diversity, it consists in an ethical relation between two human terms (which
human terms may be persons or groups or a person and a
group); the distinction between these human terms may be
complete and may be qualified; if it is qualified, the relation of

justice, considered precisely as a relation of justice, is itself qualified. A qualified relation of justice is no less an ethical relation, it is not less binding, than a relation of unqualified justice, but it is less of a relation of justice. Between father and son, unity is too close for justice to obtain in the purity of its distinctive essence. The proposition that the son is something of the father expresses, over and above a biological relation, a state of moral *unity* which prevents justice from realizing the integrity of its essence; for justice implies otherness. The duties of the father toward his son are not in any way less certain than the duties of justice properly so-called; they are, by all means, stricter. But the qualified fashion in which they embody the essence of justice entails consequences which deeply affect human relations. Of these consequences, the most important concerns the enforcement of rules. One property of justice properly so-called is that its rules are normally sanctioned by the power of society. If one partner fails to live up to a contract, courts are supposed to see that justice is done — if necessary, through coercive procedures. When, on the other hand, justice is qualified by excess of unity between the terms of the relation, enforcement of the rule cannot be guaranteed in so strict a fashion; it is, to a large extent, intrusted to the good will of the parties. Whether the obligations of the father toward the son are actually lived up to depends, most of the time, upon the good will of the father. If he does not want to fulfil his obligations, there is not much, in most cases, that society can do. Society uses its coercive power only in extreme cases, as, for instance, when a child is badly mistreated. If relations of qualified justice are not controlled by love, as they normally are in the family community, they are likely to be managed in rather casual fashion.

The relations of qualified justice, which, again, owe their qualification to excessive unity, can foster the goods of unity, under appropriate circumstances, more successfully than can pure justice. Even outside the family community, the advantages of closer unity should never be dispensed with lightly. Recall, for instance, the tragic consequences of the abrupt suppression of family-like relations between management and labor in the early phases of industrial expansion. Between the landlord and the serf there obtained a paternal relation of qualified justice under which a laborer could expect some help in case of disease and in his old age. Many landlords felt greatly relieved when, by order of law, they no longer had to do with serfs but with proletarians who were supposed to take care of themselves in health, in sickness, and in old age as well. Yet, all other things being equal, relations of unqualified justice are more favorable to the training of men in self-government.

Relations of unqualified justice, with no remnant of paternalistic rule, are found in organized industrial labor, a typical product of the technological environment. So long as the labor union remains faithful to its idea and keeps itself free from corruption by economic power, free from monopolistic practices, free from subservience to party ambition or state bureaucracy, it constitutes a unique means to train masses of men in self-government. If labor is not organized, the relation between employer and wage-earner is, at best, paternalistic; a contract is signed between these two men, but, even if no party is dishonest, one condition for the genuineness of the contractual relation is imperfectly satisfied, viz., the equality of the contracting parties. If the employer feels like taking advantage of his privileged position, there will not be any sanction. The only thing which makes the system workable is goodheartedness on the side of the employer and reverence on the side of the laborer. The labor union, through the procedure of collective bargaining, which is its proper instrument, establishes equality between the contracting parties and gives full reality to the contractual character of their relations. The strict discipline required by the labor process in any technological setup has, for the laborer, the character of a self-imposed rule, in so far as he joined the plants by genuine contract and in so far as workshop regulations have to be assented to by the laborers. Over and above resistance to unfair management, labor organizations have accomplished the double feat of helping to establish discipline among masses of men and of giving such discipline the higher meaning of autonomy. What this great product of the technological society —the labor union—has done for autonomy is of such exceptional value that any reform which would jeopardize the operation of labor unions or alter their essential constitution is bound to arouse the suspicion of the democratic mind.

3. Let us now consider in what ways the local forms of public life are affected by rural economy, on the one hand, and by industrial economy, on the other hand. In agricultural districts the unit of public life is small; we call it a village or town. Technology, on the contrary, promotes big cities. It is often said today that gigantic enterprises prove wasteful and that the tendency toward extreme industrial and urban concentration is likely to subside. This anticipation is of no essential concern to the present inquiry, for, if the industrial city of the future is less gigantic than Birmingham or Detroit, it will still contrast significantly with the rural village or town.

With regard to autonomy, the small unit of public life is distinguished by the following features: (a) The uniqueness of the individual person has a better chance of being recognized. In this connection the remarks made above concerning the farm hold for the small community of farmers, and those made concerning the big industrial plants hold for the big city. (b) The small rural community is about the only place, in modern public life, where some sort of rotation in power is practicable. The management of such a community requires no high degree of expertness; it may, consequently, be intrusted to any prudent person. True, violence is done to the nature of public life whenever government is in the hands of an expert rather than in those of a prudent man. In public life government by experts is government by outsiders. But in technological societies the expert often becomes so important that it is hard to keep him in purely instrumental functions. Rule by experts is a frequent accident in modern states and in big cities as well. Against such accident the small rural community asserts the autonomy of public life by intrusting leadership to persons that have no other distinction than their being good and experienced citizens.

A state directly governed by the people is hardly conceivable under modern circumstances, and, anyway, many disadvantages attach to government without distinct governing personnel. Yet direct democracy remains the archetype of all democratic organizations, and, if it were to perish from the earth, representative democracy might soon be transformed into some sort of oligarchic or aristocratic polity. Large cities are not different from states with regard to the need for distinct governing personnel; but in the town and village elected councilors and officers are in such relation to the whole of the people that local government amounts to a close approximation of direct democracy. The modern democratic state draws much of its spirit from the small rural unit of public administration. Democracy on the level of the state depends to a large extent on the intensity of democratic life in the rural community. A democratic polity is hardly possible in a nation in which the countryside is subjected to oligarchic rule, whether by landlords of the old-fashioned type or by companies.

COMMUNITY LIFE VERSUS INDIVIDUALISTIC LONELINESS

As background for this inquiry let us bear in mind the mass surrenders which sanctioned the victory of totalitarian parties in several countries. The vanquished were without resentment, and, when they were not stunned, their defeat resembled a liberation. In fact, they felt that they were being freed from a condition so painful as to leave no sense for the worth of freedom. Such escape was particularly frequent in the proletariat and the middle class of the big cities. It interested young men rather than mature people. Individualistic loneliness was the condition, less tolerable than servitude, from which many were escaping into servitude.

There is nothing paradoxical about feeling lonely in a city. Descartes remarked that a large city gives a very good chance to the seeker of solitude; a place where voluntary solitude is easily found may also inflict solitude upon those who do not seek it. But solitude involuntarily experienced in a thickly populated place is particularly cruel. Every inhabitant of a large city is caught in a closely woven system of obligations; in all phases of daily life he has to choose against his own inclination; allegedly, the life of the city would be impossible without such continual sacrifices. If the individual feels that the returns are not fair, bitterness follows. As a recompense for loyal fulfilment of their duties toward society, men expect food, shelter, physical security, recognition, consideration, love. Notice, further, that the most generous component of man's sociability proves the most troublesome if it is denied satisfaction. According to the law of trans-subjectivity, which is that of rational nature, the frustration of the inclination to give causes more disorder than that of the inclination to grasp. Besides sociability by way of need, there is such a thing as sociability by way of dedication. The peculiarly dreadful frenzy caused by inclinations pertaining to the latter, when they are violently repressed, makes us realize that the act of dedication, which transcends all need, is, in a way, more needed than any object of need.

Thus, during the era of the dictatorships, which opened a short time after the first World War and whose end is not in

sight, the story was gradually accredited that modern industrial life drives men into a state of isolation in the very midst
of the crowded cities; isolation under such circumstances, so
the story goes, causes anguish, frenzy, a sense of urgency, a
craving for violent relief. Totalitarian movements grow out
of this situation. A fitting leader for a totalitarian organization is, first of all and most indispensably, a man who knows
how to give millions an intoxicating experience of integration
in a community and of participation in its great work. The
conclusion of the story is that technological society, by pro-
ducing mass phenomena of individualistic loneliness, calls
into being the totalitarian state and ends the era of democracy.

1. As a factor of loneliness, urban concentration itself must
be mentioned in the first place. Communication with one's
fellow-men is easier among few than among many. In the
highly complex relations of the industrial city, involuntary contacts, which are superficial and leave the person alone and un-
helped in the mystery of his destiny, leave little time and little
energy for more genuine contacts and deeper communications.
It may even be said that these quick and superficial encounters
of daily life cause a real aversion to man. Without our being,
in most cases, aware of it in the least, meeting a man, especially if he is such a familiar character as a companion of work,
always arouses in us some hope and some expectation; our desire for communication and communion is stimulated and left
bruised by disappointment. The prevalence of irony, sarcasm,
skepticism, and cynicism among big-city dwellers may originate in such daily experiences. The cultural products of the
modern cities—novels in particular—often express, together
with misanthropy, a bitter resignation to the futility of relations which stimulate the social appetites of man without
ever bringing about exalting communion or comforting communication.

2. As just recalled, the sentiments which cause the most

painful restlessness when they are frustrated are not the most selfish ones. Generous sentiments, if denied opportunity, grow rebellious. Now there is normally, in the life of labor, a sentiment which, by transcending subjectivity, gives man a chance to enter into communication and communion with his fellowmen: it is the sense of *service*.

Most of the time the worker works not for his own consumption but for that of another person; he is thus rendering a service which is balanced by a recompense (wage, salary, fee, etc.). When everything is in order, the balance of service and recompense brings about marvels of social virtue. Through smooth relations of service and recompense, justice is satisfied in countless daily actions under conditions of faithfulness reminiscent of regularity in the processes of physical nature.

In a primitive economic system service is commonly rendered to known persons with whom the worker has a unique relation. The artisan, the small merchant, the small farmer, know many or all of the beneficiaries of their services. Personal interest in the consumer stimulates good work, and good work, in turn, fosters friendship. It is only natural to have friendly feelings toward a person for whom one works hard and conscientiously. But in modern industry there is almost always such a distance between the worker and the user of his products that the sense of service, deprived of the stimulation of personal acquaintance, is likely to be impaired unless it is subjected to stimulations of an almost sublime character, which are felt by only a few. The difficulty is increased when extreme division of labor deprives the worker of a chance to grasp, in a living and moving intellection, the purposes of the product. An assembly-line worker may, no doubt, entertain a very lofty sense for the service of man as he thinks that the finished product of which he makes a part will, in some unknown place of the world, satisfy human needs. His sense of service has to be refined and lofty; it cannot afford to be just sound and homely. But not many men are sensitive to the welfare of a deeply unknown, remote, impersonal, and even problematical consumer. If such lofty considerations are not effective, the sense of service is impaired and the worker's psychology centers about recompense. From then on, everything is out of order. The product, as it leaves the hands of the worker, disappears into a vacuum, falls into an abyss where men can neither be seen nor heard, although there is abstractive awareness that the product is actually delivered to them, at least in a majority of cases (for sometimes it is wasted or voluntarily destroyed). To be deprived of communication with those for whom one works—this is a tremendous factor of loneliness, commonly felt in the daily life of industrial masses.

3. Distinction is a thing for which man craves; if he cannot obtain it on grounds bearing some appearance of reasonableness, he will be happy to obtain it on grounds built by unrealistic fancy and irrational emotions. Complicity in racial crimes was accepted by millions of persons for whom to be neither a Negro nor a Jew was the most highly valued privilege. Among the sentiments that account for the success of racism, none is more common or enduring than the desire for aristocratic distinction. It would be poor psychology to put all the blame on human pride. As they go looking for distinction with such eagerness as to welcome the most ridiculous grounds, countless men are more concerned with their survival than with their pride; lack of distinction means to them the most unbearable privation. Distinction procures company, and lack of distinction contains a threat of solitude.

The subject of uniformity in technological civilization has been so cheaply exploited by literary-minded amateurs that it calls for special precautions. As always happens with complaints voiced by literary men, the picture is distorted by exaggeration and by the fallacy of misplaced novelty. It remains true, however, that there is incomparably less diversity in the life of the modern industrial worker than in that of the traditional farmer. Notice, most of all, that uniformity, in technological organization, is not an accident; it is through uniformity of products that technology achieves the double purpose of cheap production and high wages. Thus uniformity must be considered a permanent feature of technological society.

It is easy to see how variety helps to satisfy the desire for distinction. When there is great diversity in possessions—to say nothing of personal qualities which, of course, are to some extent shaped by diversity in the environment—each person has a claim to uniqueness, at least within the circle of daily life, and beyond that circle few things are of much significance. I think, for instance, of homes and estates in a farming community of old Europe; one family has the distinction of living in the oldest house of the village; another one, that of owning the spinning wheel used by the last wheel spinner, several generations after the construction of the mule-jenny; another family owns an unusually large tree; one home commands beautiful scenery; another one is situated at the very place of a historic event; etc. Is it silly to draw satisfaction from the fact of being born in the oldest house of the village? None would pay much attention to such titles of distinction if they did not act as *signs* of a far-reaching fact. By granting me special consideration because my house is the oldest, the community expresses its disposition to consider me unique and most excellent in some respect. Whenever uniqueness is socially recognized, a man feels that he is not ignored, that he is not left alone, that he is not treated like a fungible good. What underlies common striving for distinction in society is not so much a desire for superiority as a desire for the recognition of one's uniqueness and of the uniqueness of one's possible excellence. Not to obtain such recogni-

tion is to feel ignored and rejected. Industrial workers are better housed in mass-produced houses than are old-fashioned
farmers in damp and obscure dwellings built in the seventeenth
century; their mass-produced food is wholesome, etc., but
achieving social recognition of each one's uniqueness is for
them a difficult task in which many fail.

4. Bearing in mind as a background the picture of the old
system of orders in which most men were bound or strongly
urged to remain in the social category in which they were
born, let it be said that the first decisive step toward a *fluid
society* was made when the principle of equal opportunity was
posited. Although technical evolution had something to do
with the abandonment of the order system, it is impossible to
see in the principle of equal opportunity a proper effect of
technology. Assuming that this principle was already asserted
when society became technological, we propose to examine
the contribution of the technological environment to social
fluidity.

a) Industrial necessities and expediencies often cause instability with regard to place. In 1850, when the French bourgeoisie decided that the vote of the factory workers should not
be a significant factor, a handy solution was procured by making franchise conditional upon a residence qualification of
three years. This requirement was commonly met in the farming population and in the middle class but rarely in the industrial working class, as a result of which elections would be
overwhelmingly conservative. Recall, also, the quick movements of population occasioned by the discovery of mines in
the North American West and by the early exhaustion of
many of them. Besides such extreme cases, which may be
limited to periods of transition, an important factor of instability in place is the mobilization, at irregular intervals, of
additional labor by industrial centers. The working population of an industrial region comprises a nucleus of families en-

joying stable residence and several layers of temporary residents; as a rule, skilled labor enjoys more stability, and the most unskilled laborers are those who shift most often according to the demand of the labor market.

b) Over and above fluidity with regard to place, a great part of the industrial working class is subject to fluidity with regard to occupation. Among the factors of change in occupation let us mention the progress of technical education and the ability of rationalized industry to make highly productive agents out of unskilled workers.

c) The artificial environment of daily life, which plays a great part in the shaping of personalities, changes fast in a technological society. Through most of recorded history quick changes in this environment were restricted to dress and particulars of minor significance. The dwelling, at least, was a thing designed to last. But an idea which has recently gained much ground is that, in order to enjoy the best housing conditions, we should plan homes of short life, to be replaced as soon as better techniques make better ones. The high cost of construction has, so far, restricted the tendency to include dwellings among the things which should wear out so fast. as never to slow the march of progress.

d) Changes in family mores follow upon the facts just mentioned with an appearance of inevitability. The least that can be said is that, all other things being equal, quickly changing environment causes a tendency toward instability in family relations. Tendencies of this kind are never necessitating, but they may exercise decisive influence merely by increasing the difficulty of certain courses of action. Faithfulness and never ending devotion in marriage and family life are, at all events, difficult and are rarely carried to perfection. If they are made incomparably harder by the instability of the circumstances, the ratio of virtuous accomplishment is bound to decrease. People of distinguished morality can preserve all the goods of absolutely

stable family relations under all circumstances, but the great
number of men, though capable of heroism on the battlefield,
are known not to have the kind of fortitude needed to overcome extreme difficulties in daily life.

5. It seems to be the consensus both of men of common experience and of sociologists that evidences of individualistic
loneliness are few and of minor intensity in societies characterized by the stability of family relations, the pervasiveness
of family influence, the extension of the family circle, and the
recognition given to families by society at large. Using this
common opinion as a regulating postulate, we shall try to describe some effects of the technological environment upon the
family with regard to stability, pervasiveness of influence, and
social recognition.

It would hardly be exaggerating to say that the whole story
is epitomized by the adventures of the word "economy" and
its derivatives. Our concept of economy is so related to the nation and to the world that we always feel somewhat amazed
at remembering that "economy" originally meant nothing
else than the government of a household. The description of
the family found in Aristotle's *Politics* (Book i) is that of an
institution dedicated to the welfare of man in the needs and
acts of daily life; with regard to such needs and acts, the family
aims at self-sufficiency. Except for slavery, the Aristotelian
description remained until recently the pattern followed by
the rural family. It is hardly necessary to stress the advantages
of a system which incloses the whole cycle of wealth, from
ownership of the land to the use of the product, within a small
unit in which strong feelings of friendship make possible an
almost complete community of goods. Such a system rules out
the infuriating disorders, so intensely resented by the men of
the twentieth century, resulting from the nondistribution of
the available product. It was inevitable that the traditional
pattern be challenged when a number of duties previously dis-

charged by the family came to be fulfilled (often in more satisfactory fashion) by other agencies. Technology played, directly or indirectly, a decisive part in the process which deprived the family of such functions as weaving, baking, schooling, nursing, entertaining, etc. Whether a family deprived of these functions still has enough weight, enough life, enough discipline, and enough charm to constitute the basic community in which man finds the safest refuge against loneliness is dubious. There are idealists who believe that the oaths exchanged by the spouses on their wedding day, the natural inclination of parents for children, of children for parents, of brothers and sisters for brothers and sisters, etc., should suffice to keep the family stable, closely knit, indispensable to the individual's happiness, and capable of giving all its members a sense of perfect security. Of course, it is always possible to find excellent personalities who defeat the influence of the environment; such examples are significant in several respects, but they do not invalidate laws expressing the tendency of environmental data to produce definite effects on men. With due allowance for exceptions, it cannot be questioned that the technological society such as we know it has enormously contributed to the weakening of family life. In so far as men deprived of community life and delivered to loneliness are ready material for antidemocratic movements, it must be confessed that technology, by creating circumstances unfavorable to the family community, prepared material for government by the leaders of the mob.

However, the superiority of rural life with regard to community feelings does not hold in all respects and is not unqualified. In old-fashioned rural families, community feelings are generally restricted to a narrow group and are accompanied by isolationist dispositions which may prove acutely antisocial. Intense devotion to the family often combines with readiness to treat the rest of the world as foreign and hostile;

the sense of justice is often uncertain when the partner does not belong to the family circle or to the native community, which is confusedly identified with the family. Besides its general inconveniences, such an attitude of distrust beyond the limits of a small circle is exceedingly harmful to democracy. It makes impossible the normal operation of two essential organs of democratic life—the party and the labor union. In societies where family feelings are so exclusive as to arouse distrust of every outsider, political parties turn to cliques, and exploitation thrives on unorganized labor.

The merits of the family community are at their lowest with regard to international and world relations. The two world wars and a few other recent events have compelled us to realize the necessity of a world consciousness, of a world conscience, and, generally, of the enlargement, to the dimensions of the world, of all social sentiments. This realization often was exceedingly painful. In other times the ratio of crime was high, but people were blessedly ignorant of what was going on beyond the limits of the town or county. We are tempted to regret the happy days when good hearts were protected by limited information and restricted conscience. Were not the sufferings of our village hard enough to bear? Why should I be born in a society which constantly arouses my emotions in relation to remote sufferers, to the atrocious mistreatment of the innocent in a hundred parts of the world? Peace and justice may be undisturbed for a while in our home and in our city, but the world is never free from an awe-inspiring amount of crime. Just as the sun never set on the empire of Charles V, so crime, horror, hatred, and anguish are always at work in the world. If my awareness extends as far as the borders of mankind, there will never be for me any rest or any unmixed joy. This means great suffering, but the dignity and the fertility of such concerns and sufferings are obvious. We are witnessing the incarnation of an old Christian idea, that of the universal republic under God, *respublica sub Deo*. This idea is now descending into a body of moral sentiments and natural emotions. In order to experience these sentiments and emotions, not exceptionally but in daily life, it is no longer necessary to be distinguished by enlightenment, extreme generosity, vibrating sensitiveness, or inappeasable anxiety. None of these distinctions is needed in order to have a conscience as large as the world. No more is needed than willingness to heed the suggestions of the technical environment. For it is technology which, with quick communication, instantaneous information, duplication of sense appearances, and increased range of the means of destruction, has made it possible and easy, though painful, for the ordinary man to have a moral conscience equal to mankind and proportionate to theological charity. Men whose community feelings fall short of complete coincidence with the border line of mankind are still in a primitive and childlike state of moral conscience. In a technological world the common man can develop community feelings equal to the dimensions of the human community.

At the conclusion of this long exposition a fresh effort is needed to overcome the depressing effect of what sounds like a hopeless platitude. The eighteenth-century theorists were not entirely wrong. The rural environment is in many respects the more favorable to the ethic of democracy; yet some phases of democratic life are greatly enhanced by technology. This conclusion is unglamorous; it is not of such a nature as to appease our anxieties; but it is not, either, expressive of despair. Its dualistic character may seem to suggest an attitude of disillusionment and passivity; it is rather meant to express a program of never ending inquiry into difficulties which cannot disappear but can be defined with more and more precision.

The radicalism often observed among our agrarians is barren (so far, at least, as theoretical understanding is concerned, for as a psychological disposition it may lead to worthy achievement). There is no use for this most unreal of all constructs—a general return to primitive conditions with no motor transportation and no heavy machines. On the other hand, the picture of a society in which the farm and the industrial city are related as sources of opposite and supplementary forms of democratic life appeals to creative thought. To recall only one example, we consider it obvious that the goods of family life, though not unattainable in the industrial city, are found more certainly on the farm. Even if endeavors to restore family morals in large cities succeeded beyond hope, it would still be reasonable to consider that the exaltation of family ideals is in a peculiar sense the duty of the rural home. And no matter how broad-minded farmers may be, organized industrial workers will remain those whose special duty it is to extend a sense of brotherhood, with noble readiness, to newcomers, passers-by, unidentified members of the laboring community (from which it follows that a disaster takes place whenever labor indulges in policies of racial discrimination and strict control of immigration).

Concerning communications between the farm and the industrial city the present state of affairs suggests the following remarks:

1. There is a steady migration of the farm youth to the city; this may be deemed regrettable, but little or nothing can be done about it on a broad scale.

2. Many city dwellers seek refreshment, recreation, fun, and, when they are too old to work, a convenient retreat in the countryside; let us call them "tourists."

3. The category of the so-called "rural nonfarm" increases steadily. These are people who work in town and live in the country, draw money from a job in town but grow most of the food needed for family consumption on their small piece of land.

The movement of the rural youth toward the city cannot be considered a link between the farm and the factory; it would be one if many went back to the farm after a few years; but this is not the case. Tourists and rural nonfarm people connect the city with the countryside but in different ways of unequal value. Attention should be given here to the great psychological significance of the division of human activities into those which obey strict rules and those which call for fancy. Let the first be described as the "system of legal fulfilment," the latter as the "system of free expansion." The connection between the city and the farm, in order to be meaningful, ought to be contained within the system of legal fulfilment. The factory worker who becomes acquainted with the farm in the same way as a traveler with a Baedeker city may go back to work with fresh energy and spirits; this fine result does not shorten the distance between the factory and the farm by any means. No relation of far-reaching significance is established by such a division of life as labor in the city and pleasure in the country. Rural nonfarm people, also described as "one-foot-in-the-landers" have a distinct sociological significance, inasmuch as they exercise activities of legal fulfilment both on the land and in the factory. No room is left for amateurism, sentimentalism, histrionic attitudes; both ways of life mean to them life in earnest. The semirural people are many millions. So far as big cities are concerned, their movement is not likely to grow far beyond its present limits. But many signs support the forecast that industry, in the future, will no longer produce gigantic cities but rather favor the scattering of enterprises in cities of moderate size, where heavy concentration will be avoided. Around such cities many more millions of industrial workers will enjoy some of the privileges of rural life.

Let us remark once more that in the general relation between industrial and rural mores the leading role belongs to typical forms, i.e., to highly rational industry, on the one hand, and to comparatively simple farm economy, on the other hand. Fatal rupture of equilibrium would follow from the disappearance or extreme weakening of either. Now it seems that simple methods of farming, anterior to industrial agriculture, are so completely doomed by irreversible developments that people engaged in these methods exist merely as survivors of another age; they are still numerous, but they lack wealth, and, above all, as an effect of their antiquated way of doing things, they seem hardly capable of leadership. Men lose courage unless they feel that their effort concurs with the general movement of history. The romantic primitivism common among our agrarians may be nothing else than a distorted expression of a truthful perception: the maintenance of rural life, with all the virtues attaching to family economy, is a task which demands a special kind of enthusiasm. Over and above the generous emotions without which nothing great is accomplished, this task demands a conscious determination to assert man's freedom against, if need be, historical forces bearing an appearance of inescapable necessity.

Among the objective demands discoverable in a given state of society, some are such that, by general agreement, there is no reason to worry about the possibility of their not being satisfied. We use a variety of metaphorical expressions and of *entia rationis* to voice our certitude that such and such a line of events, firmly drawn in the past and down to the present, will actually extend into the future. Considering, for instance, that modern societies need industrial production organized in such fashion as to attain the triple goal of abundant output, low prices, and high wages, we know that, except in case of unprecedented and unforeseeable catastrophes, the operation of the technological apparatus will not be interrupted and the triple goal will remain within human reach. Between such a trend of events as the enduring operation of scientific industry and human freedom, the relation is such that the suspension of the former by the latter is devoid of probability. In order to keep this trend going, human freedom needs merely to follow, in daily occurrences, the line which spares everyone the cost of rebellion against overwhelming powers.

But it is also easy to recognize, in any given state of society, demands which, though real and all-important and urgent, are so related to human freedom that, in order to satisfy them, man needs to exercise, with a high degree of self-consciousness, his mastery over the nonrational part of his self and the nonrational elements which weigh so heavily on human history. Such profound acts of freedom are decisive in spite of the small number of those who perform them and the secrecy in which they are performed. It is unreasonable to oppose technology; it is not unreasonable to consider that a small number of lofty souls can give the family farm, in our time, a historic and, as it were, transcendent meaning. Things may be eased by the distribution of technical power; but, even if extreme difficulties had to be met in never ending struggle, the enthusiastic few needed to maintain the family farm as a pole of attraction acting upon the whole of society will not be lacking. All that is necessary is awareness of a link between farm life and the preservation and promotion of things that can never become indifferent to men—communion with universal nature, the conquest of time through everlasting faithfulness, temperance, dignity in poverty, holy leisure, contemplation.

INDEX

Acton, J. E., 75 n.

Affective knowledge, 23–30, 219–22

Alienation, 231, 232, 234, 246, 248

Almain, James, 160

Aquinas, 21 n., 22 n., 23 n., 34 n., 35 n., 37 n., 39–41, 59, 60 n., 61 n., 69, 72 n., 74 n., 80 n., 82 n., 107, 108, 109 n., 110 n., 131 n., 158–60, 176, 177, 197, 200 n., 202, 234 n., 239, 240 n., 268, 297

Aristotle, 8 n., 21 n., 22 n., 23 n., 35 n., 52, 53 n., 59, 63 n., 72 n., 73 n., 74, 82 n., 86 n., 107, 109 n., 131, 176, 199, 212, 239, 267, 298, 315

Arnond, Abbé, 169

Attlee, Clement, 104

Autonomy, 15, 55, 71, 75, 129–39, 207, 302

Azeglio, Taparelli d', 33 n.

Balzac, Honoré de, 220, 221 n.

Bellarmine, St. Robert, 161 n., 166–68, 175, 177, 185

Berth, Edouard, 14 n.

Blum, Léon, 224

Bossuet, Jacques Bénigne, 132, 133, 144

Bridgeman, P. W., 209

Briefs, Goetz, 254 n.

Cajetan (Thomas de Vio, surname), 23 n., 35 n., 160–62, 164–66, 175, 179, 182

Campaigns of opinion, 150, 151, 185–90

Capitalization, 245

Catherine the Great, 73

Chang, Sherman H. M., 4 n.

Charles V, 317

Churchill, Winston, 104, 179, 215

Classes, 1, 2, 4 n., 195, 253–59

Cochin, Augustin, 148 n.

Coercion, 7, 68, 69, 108–17, 125–27

Colonial rule, 12, 140

Commerce, 237–41

Common good, 8, 11, 26, 28–30, 36–59, 129

Common man (democracy of the), 215–22

Communism, 1–3

Community versus mere partnership, 48–50, 62–67

Comte, Auguste, 84 n.

Consent of the governed, 174–76, 190–94

Conservatism, 13–18, 196, 207

Courier, Paul-Louis, 147

David, 164

Definition of democracy, 75–76

Demongeot, Marcel, 108 n.

Descartes, René, 308

Desgrippes, Georges, 111 n.

Direct democracy, 76, 119, 149–53, 168, 181, 184, 186

Distribution (free), 245, 252

Durkheim, Émile, 84 n.

Engels, Friedrich, 4 n., 253, 254

Family, 7–10, 17–18, 228, 304, 314–17, 321

Fascism, 1, 5, 261

Feminist movement, 9, 10

Filmer, Robert, 157

Freedom of choice, 31–35

Freedom and servitude, 74, 75, 230, 231

Gerlich, F., 4 n.

Gerson, 160

Gurian, Waldemar, 1 n., 2 n.

Gurvitch, Georges, 84 n., 248 n.

Halévy, Daniel, 3 n.

Hamilton, Alexander, 13, 15, 103 n., 115

Happiness, 261–67

Hegel, G. W. F., 3 n., 84

Hermens, F. A., 99 n.

323

PHOENIX BOOKS

in Political Science and Law